THE PUBLIC IS INVITED TO DANCE

Representation, the Body,
and Dialogue in
Gertrude Stein

■■

THE PUBLIC IS INVITED TO DANCE

Representation, the Body,
and Dialogue in
Gertrude Stein

■■

Harriet Scott Chessman

STANFORD UNIVERSITY PRESS
Stanford, California ■ 1989

Stanford University Press
Stanford, California
© 1989 by the Board of Trustees of the
Leland Stanford Junior University
Printed in the United States of America

CIP data appear at the end of the book

To Bryan

Acknowledgments

Writing, like dancing, can be most pleasurable when one is accompanied by partners—or "twins," as Stein might have it. I have been lucky in the surefootedness and grace of the people who consented to try out a few steps with me, and who often stuck with it the whole evening.

I am especially indebted to those who read and reread the complete manuscript at various stages. Pamela White Hadas has shared her knowledge and keen understanding of Stein with a generosity that has been in itself inspiriting. John Elder has responded even to my most ragged drafts with incomparable intelligence and lucidity. Catharine Stimpson offered a fresh and provocative series of questions at a critical point in my revision, helping me quite literally to re-see the shape of my argument. And without the abundant advice and encouragement of two of my colleagues at Yale, this book could not have achieved its present shape. To Patricia Meyer Spacks I owe deep thanks both for her thoughtful reading of my manuscript and for her original work on literary forms of intimacy in *Gossip*; her influence will be felt in these pages, although I claim all faux pas for myself. Margaret Homans has contributed to the book's unfolding with an acumen and depth of insight I can only begin to repay. Her friendship and rich intellectual presence have been crucial to this work on Stein and to the development of my thought about women and language.

Among the people who have been important to me during the years in which I was writing this book, I owe a special debt to Patricia Yaeger, whose friendship has been a source of strength and intellectual excitement since my first year as a graduate student at Yale. I also wish to thank Wendy Owen for inciting me to work on Stein and for providing me with a model of boldness, engagement, and belief in the transformative power of words. And I find it difficult to express the gratitude I hold toward Sr. Lucia Kuppens, O.S.B., whose belief in me and in this book have continually surprised and motivated me. My understanding of the possibilities inherent in dialogue has been shaped and enlarged by the dialogue I have had the good fortune to engage in with her and with the community of the Abbey of Regina Laudis.

I have been inspired and challenged in my approach to literature by many friends and colleagues. I wish especially to acknowledge my thanks to Marie Borroff, Richard Brodhead, Kathleen Brogan, Robert Byer, Ulla Dydo, Carol Elliott, Charles Feidelson, Jonathan Freedman, Paul Fry, Janet Goodwyn, Amy Kaplan, R. W. B. Lewis, Louis L. Martz, Catherine Nickerson, Robert Pack, Brigitte Peucker, Lawrence Raab, Julie Rivkin, Michele Stepto, Gordon Turnbull, Linda Watts, and Susanne Wofford, in addition to my students, who have entered into Stein's writings with eagerness (only moderately mingled with suspicion) and intelligence. Patricia Klindienst Joplin has brought passionate clarity to our mutual engagement with issues of women and writing. Leslie Ellen Moore has given me precious friendship and the joy of a felt community of spirit. And I have been taught and regaled by Candace Waid, whose knowledge and fruitful imagination have provided me with necessary nourishment.

Stanford University Press has made the completion of this book an unexpected pleasure. I cannot sufficiently acknowledge my gratitude to Helen Tartar, who has changed forever my understanding of what editors do. Her response to this project has been imaginative, rigorous, thought-provoking, and creative. I wish to thank Ellen F. Smith for the care she has taken with the manuscript and for her invaluable presence during the last stages of its preparation.

Yale University supported this project through the award of a Morse Fellowship. I would also like to thank the staff at Beinecke Library for their aid in locating materials about Stein. Finally, I thank New York University Press for permission to reprint as Chapter 3 a modified version of my article, "Representation and the Female: Gertrude Stein's 'Lifting Belly' and *Tender Buttons*," which appeared in *The Book of the Self: Person, Pretext, and Process*, edited by Polly Young-Eisendrath and James Hall (New York, 1986).

The Chessman and Wolf families have given me much love and support during the writing of this book. In particular, my parents, George Wallace Chessman and Eleanor Osgood Chessman, have shown an interest in Stein and in my project that has heartened and sustained me. And I am immensely grateful for the daily dialogue I have had the pleasure of sharing with Bryan Jay Wolf, whose support has run the gamut from the ridiculous to the sublime. His vision has illuminated my understanding of Stein's literary landscape and of the adventure of literary criticism as a whole.

My final thanks go to my children, Marissa and Micah, who have taught me that there is indeed merriment in the midst of writing.

H.S.C.

Contents

Contents

Abbreviations

For a useful bibliography of Stein's publications, including publication dates and places, see Patricia Meyerowitz, ed., *Look at Me Now and Here I Am: Gertrude Stein, Writings and Lectures, 1911–1945* (London: Peter Owen, 1967), 414–17.

A&B   *Alphabets and Birthdays (1915–40)*. Introduction by Donald Gallup. New Haven, Conn.: Yale University Press, 1957.

ABT   *The Autobiography of Alice B. Toklas*. New York: Random House, 1961.

B&W   *Brewsie and Willie*. New York: Random House, 1946.

Blood   *Blood on the Dining-Room Floor*. Edited and with an Afterword by John Herbert Gill. Berkeley, Calif.: Creative Arts Book Company, 1982.

BTV   *Bee Time Vine and Other Pieces (1913–1927)*. Preface and notes by Virgil Thomson. New Haven: Yale University Press, 1953.

CAE   *Composition As Explanation*. London: Hogarth Press, 1926.

EA   *Everybody's Autobiography*. New York: Random House, 1973.

G&P   *Geography and Plays*. Introduction by Sherwood Anderson. Boston: Four Seas Company, 1922.

HTW   *How To Write*. New York: Dover Publications, 1975.

HWIW   *How Writing Is Written. Vol. 2 of the Previously Uncollected Writings of Gertrude Stein*. Ed. Robert Bartlett Haas. Los Angeles: Black Sparrow Press, 1974.

Ida   *Ida, A Novel*. New York: Random House, 1968.

LCA   *Lucy Church Amiably*. Paris: Plain Edition, 1930.

LIA   *Lectures in America*. Introduction by Wendy Steiner. Boston: Beacon Press, 1985.

LO&P	*Last Operas and Plays.* Introduction by Carl Van Vechten. New York: Rinehart, 1949.
MOA	*The Making of Americans: Being a History of a Family's Progress.* London: Peter Owen, 1968.
Narration	*Narration.* Chicago: University of Chicago Press, 1969.
P&P	*Portraits and Prayers.* New York: Random House, 1934.
QED	*Fernhurst, Q.E.D., and Other Early Writings.* Introduction by Leon Katz. London: Peter Owen, 1972.
SW	*Selected Writings of Gertrude Stein.* Edited, with an Introduction and Notes by Carl Van Vechten. New York: Random House, 1962.
TL	*Three Lives.* New York: Random House, 1936.
WIR	Alice Toklas, *What Is Remembered.* London: Michael Joseph, 1963.
YCAL	The Yale Collection of American Literature
YGS	*The Yale Gertrude Stein.* Introduction by Richard Kostelanetz. New Haven, Conn.: Yale University Press, 1980.
WAM	*What Are Masterpieces.* Los Angeles: Conference Press, 1940.

In the midst of writing.
In the midst of writing there is merriment.

(YGS, 54)

Introduction: The Public
Is Invited to Dance

Come pleasantly.
And sing to me.
(G&P, 131)

Gertrude Stein is at once famous and little known. She exists in our imagination as a public figure, a large and eccentric woman who wore sandals and held salons, who knew the most important artists of the twentieth century, lived with Alice B. Toklas, and spoke in riddles like "A rose is a rose is a rose is a rose." Although we know her as the author of *The Autobiography of Alice B. Toklas*, *Three Lives*, and *Four Saints in Three Acts*, her oeuvre as a whole —plays, poems, literary portraits, operas, essays, novels—remains surprisingly invisible in the literary scene. As a writer, Stein has a reputation for being either unreadable or unnecessary. "Gertrude Stein!?" people often say with some uncertainty. "Can you really read her?" Or they might add, even more doubtfully, "Is she really *serious*?" Because of this double reputation for unreadability and triviality, one of the most influential and experimental of all the modernists still waits, by and large, to be read.[1]

Stein's writing, however, is eminently more inviting and readable than her reputation leads us to assume. As the amiable invitation to "Come pleasantly. / And sing to me" suggests, Stein may anticipate a less doubtful and more eager readership. Coming in the midst of one of Stein's voice poems, "The King or Something. (The Public Is Invited to Dance)" (1917), this characteristic Steinian invitation asks its audience to participate in an intimate celebration. Within this piece composed of floating and unnamed voices, the implied "you" and the "me" represent two or more figures engaged in an ongoing dialogue, in which one figure may represent "the public," the body of readers who "come" to the piece and who may

join in its vocal and evocative "dance," as they "turn turn" the pages
(*G&P*, 124).[2]

A second invitation, a few lines later, encourages us to speculate about what form our advent might take: "Come Connect Us"
(*G&P*, 131). The "Us" could be the words or the voices, which
a reader "connects" through the act of reading, just as it could
suggest the conjoining of reader and words: in "coming" to the
words, the reader may connect with them. This potentially erotic
coming together of reading and writing marks a responsiveness on
the reader's part which is both bodily and imaginative; even when
the subject of the dialogue seems uncertain, the reader may still
participate in a valuable connection with the language and with the
sense of an ongoing and constantly shifting dialogue. These invitations ask for the active and intimate presence of a reader. Rather
than taking place from a distanced point outside the play of voices,
a stance which would assume the possibility of mastery over the
writing, reading becomes understood as a lively participation that
does not always or exclusively rely upon referential language to
encompass a response. As the voice poem announces: "Pages of
eating. / Pages of heating" (*G&P*, 127). This playful composition is
good enough to eat, and it warms us as we "turn" with it in bodily
and erotic intimacy.

Stein's invitation allows not only for a connection between the
reader and the writing, but also for a difference. The composition opens with this allowance: "Letting me see. / Come together
when you can" (*G&P*, 122). A reader may wish to "see"—to know
who will be speaking and what they will be speaking about—yet
the composition itself may respond with hesitation ("Let me see").
After all, to come together is not always possible or necessary. Stein
creates a playful dialogic space between the acts of reading and
writing, within which difference may occur. The dialogue incorporates many moments of disagreement, as in "I will not say yes," and
in the brief quarrel (possibly a lovers' quarrel), "We didn't. / Allow
me to differ" (*G&P*, 124). The voices often sound uncertain of the
listener, as in the sudden question, "Were you pleased with this"
(*G&P*, 123) or the more peremptory "Listen to me when I speak"
(*G&P*, 125).

These configurations of voices engaged in dialogue offer a central paradigm for Gertrude Stein's modernist and feminist project.
Stein's feminism (an intricate issue, which I will discuss at further

length later in this Introduction) infuses her modernist form with a concern for the exposure and transformation of all hierarchies, particularly those of gender. Central to this revision of hierarchy is a poetics of dialogue, where dialogue presents an alternative to the possibility of patriarchal authoritarianism implicit in monologue, reliant upon the privileging of one voice, one narrator, or one significance.[3] The equality Stein creates among the different parts of her compositions replaces this model of hierarchy and constitutes the basis for her dialogic form, in which difference may enter without being relegated to a secondary position or subsumed under an authoritarian identity—in Lacanian terms, under the Name of the Father.[4] In Stein's sense of language, new formations of relationship are always possible; gender hierarchy itself, so clearly sustained within language, may be undone within the space of the text by new linguistic uses.

In the most familiar sense, this dialogue occurs between characters, as in some of Stein's narratives (such as *Three Lives* and *Ida*), as well as between the narrator and the characters. In other forms, dialogue takes place not only between the reader and the words, but between the words themselves as they create intimate relationships of sound, sight, and meaning, between the writer and the words, and between words and the objects they "caress" but do not necessarily signify.

Steinian dialogue offers significant points of connection with two bodies of theory: Anglo-American object relations theory, especially as this theory (through the work of Nancy Chodorow and others) has come to include the construction of gender; and French feminist thought with regard to language and sexuality. A few Stein critics, including Lisa Ruddick, Carolyn Burke, Marianne DeKoven, and Catharine Stimpson, have begun to explore the idea that pre-Oedipal and presymbolic modes of intimacy have a bearing on Gertrude Stein's sense of language and form.[5] This approach has opened up a new way of understanding Stein's foregrounding of the sensual and material aspects of language. Julia Kristeva has become an especially important source for these critics, especially in her concern for the pre-Oedipal *as* the presymbolic, or semiotic, which can interrupt the surface of symbolic (and patriarchal) discourse. Burke and DeKoven argue that Kristeva's definition of the semiotic can be applied to Stein's experimental writing. In Burke's formulation: "The semiotic mode, in close relation to the unconscious, expresses the instinctual drives through the resources of rhythm, intonation, gesture, and melody." Following Kristeva, Burke links this mode with "the infant's pre-Oedipal (and presymbolic) attachment to the mother's body," and links Stein's rhythmic writing in the early portrait "Ada" with this insistence on the aural and the bodily.[6]

Although this idea of a return to the mother and to a "presymbolic" maternal body is useful for an understanding of Stein, it is important to acknowledge the mythic elements inherent both in these approaches to Stein and in the theories about language in which they are grounded. Whether the myth finds definition in the utopian pre-Oedipal "life of immediate or raw perception" described by Ruddick[7] or in the pleasurable sensations and rhythms of a nonsignifying mode, this pleasant place—the site of Stein's writing—acquires the status of a myth. Further, the concepts of both the pre-Oedipal and the presymbolic often acquire a dangerous element of essentialism, whereby the "maternal" or the "feminine" represents the utterly nonsignifying and bodily other.[8]

Stein's own writing displays a certain utopian element, especially in its attempt to reimagine gender and to subvert violent hierarchies. Rather than attempting to recover "the mother" through a language of pure sound, however, she transfers the early intimacy between mother and infant to a new field: that of lovers or intimate acquaintances. The sexuality of this new intimacy remains open to question in much of Stein's writing. Although the relationship Stein most often invokes appears to be a lesbian one, the inclusion of a culturally identifiable masculinity suggests Stein's effort both to extend her dialogic intimacy to male as well as female figures and to create a safe space within her writing where the differences between the masculine and the feminine can be addressed. Stein holds out the possibility for a utopian mode of relationship to the world and to language, in which one's difference from an other is as valuable and undestructive as one's similarity or near-mergence. Further, although Stein's dialogic form contains elements of a Kristevan semiotic, including an attachment to the body, Stein's language is never simply nonsignifying or disruptive of signification. Stein's writing mixes the figurative and the literal, the symbolic and the bodily. Stein's model of a lover-to-lover bond incorporates a profound commitment to language as the place in which dialogue becomes audible. Even the "dialogue" between two bodies finds indirect expression through words. In this sense, Stein offers an alternative to theories positing "woman" as the silent "other," outside language, which becomes defined solely as the domain of the patriarchal.

Stein's understanding of language as the major site for transformation bears a resemblance in many ways to contemporary French feminist thought. As Domna C. Stanton has suggested, "the premise underlying the work of many contemporary French women writers" is that "the world is the word; it is experienced phenomenologically as a vast text which encompasses the sum total of human symbolic systems. Throughout the history of Western thought, that text, the Logos, has been founded on the structure of the binary—the dichotomy between such culturally determined oppositions as rationality and emotionality, activity and passivity, presence and absence, in a word, 'male' and 'female'." [9] The various French feminist projects, as Stanton argues, tend to agree that language is the primary cultural agency through which the masculine dominates and represses the feminine. This "phallogocentrism" must be deconstructed before any genuine transformation can occur.

The difficulty with this theory, as many critics have perceived, lies in the acceptance of the first term: that language as it has been constructed is wholly phallogocentric. [10] Language, in this sense, becomes a monolithic domain, owned and inhabited by the equally monolithic patriarchy. "Woman's" position becomes problematic, for as the repressed and silenced other, she cannot enter language except as a "masculine" subject (as Luce Irigaray suggests in her central essay in *Speculum*, "Any Theory of the 'Subject' Has Always Been Appropriated by the 'Masculine'"), a disruptive and negative force (as in Kristeva's concept of the semiotic as "the female modality, represent[ing] an essential *negativity*"), [11] or a speaker of a new and as yet only imagined language that will inscribe woman's difference. As Hélène Cixous and Irigaray, among others, claim, this *écriture féminine* will spring from the woman's body, in its essential difference from the man's. [12]

Stein's writing often resembles the post-modernist writings of *écriture féminine* to such an extent that her influence upon the French feminists has emerged as a subject inviting further exploration. She shares with these writers numerous literary strategies: the disruption of conventional grammar, plot, genre, and modes of representation, together with the exploration of plural voices and of a writing attached to the body.[13] Her erotic writings especially, for example, the love poems, plays, and other works from 1910 to 1920, offer a rich area of comparison. In such compositions, she creates a poetics inscribed with a specifically lesbian sexuality; her undoing of conventional form allies itself with her attempt to bring female-to-female relationships into writing.[14]

Stein differs from the experimenters of *écriture féminine*, however, in a crucial way: her poetics of dialogue is not wholly or essentially "female."[15] The various forms of dialogue she constructs occur neither in interchanges exclusively among biological females nor in a discourse posited as springing solely from the female body or the culturally defined "feminine." Biology is almost comically elusive in Stein, at least after her first decade of writing.[16] She catapults us instead into a "world of words," in William Gass's term, in which gender has been inscribed, even as gender's inscriptions can be mimed, parodied, reinstated, critiqued, loosened, and often erased. Whereas in Luce Irigaray's "When Our Lips Speak Together," the doubled voice of the *je* and *tu* represents a female speech wholly attached to the "two lips" of female sexuality, in Stein's comparable writing (for instance, "Lifting Belly") numerous voices identifiable as masculine enter the dialogue. Yet this identification remains open to question, for Stein often makes it possible to imagine male or female speakers within either masculine or feminine modes of language.[17] Our expectations concerning the masculine and the feminine come into question, as with the figures of Andrew and Ida in Stein's novel *Ida* (published 1941): the figure signified by the gender-marked name Andrew offers an alternate form of masculinity, which in its similarity to the feminine (signified by Ida) makes the distinction of "feminine" and "masculine" fragile and unimportant. It is equally possible to find in much of Stein's work the further strategy of a surprisingly ungendered language— a language that calls attention to its freedom from any gender at all.

In calling Stein's project "feminist," I am entering a lively and ongoing debate about whether Stein *is* feminist. This question is intricate partly because of the different definitions of feminism currently in use. Stein does not help us out directly: in her lectures, essays, and autobiographies, she makes no direct or sustained claim for her writing as addressing or redressing women's position (or repression) within culture. In this sense, Stein differs from a contemporary like Virginia Woolf, whose numerous essays about women, including the major essays *A Room of One's Own* and *Three Guineas*, embraced women (and women writers) as a subject understood as deeply enmeshed in patriarchy. Although in *The Geographical History of America* Stein abruptly states, "and so in this epoch the important literary thinking is done by a woman" (183), she does not analyze the significance of this claim, and her placement of the whole subject of "men and women" on the side of "identity" rather than "entity"—on the side of human nature rather than the superior human mind—suggests her resistance to acknowledging this biological or gender distinction as a real or important one: "I think nothing about men and women because that has nothing to do with anything" (178).[18] Stein's politics seem blithely unfeminist, as her famous remark in *The Autobiography of Alice B. Toklas* appears to confirm: "Not, as Gertrude Stein explained to Marion Walker, that she at all minds the cause of women or any other cause but it does not happen to be her business" (*ABT*, 83).

In interpretations of Stein's life, she often emerges as male-identified, simply reproducing in her relationship with Alice B. Toklas the heterosexual (and heterosexist) norm of a powerful and active professional husband, a less powerful and more submissive wife.[19] Catharine Stimpson, in her essay on "The Mind, the Body, and Gertrude Stein," places this issue of Stein's masculine identity, particularly in her first decade of writing (1900–1910), within a historical context: toward the end of the nineteenth century, a "problematic gap" opened up between the "consciousness" and the "flesh," especially of elite women who had been well-educated—a gap "between what they might do with their minds and what they might do with their bodies."[20] As Stimpson suggests, Stein, "consciously or unconsciously, devised several strategies that might enable one to live as a possibly tainted anomaly," one of these strategies being "to deploy a number of conventional and heterosexual terms to describe her life, as if language might sweepingly both name and legitimize the unconventional and then the homosexual."[21] This linguistic strategy, Stimpson argues, helped Stein to differentiate herself from women and to enter the male world of culture and genius. Marianne DeKoven discovers Stein's shift in the mid-1920's to a greater acceptance of her womanhood and a new ability to identify her "genius" with her femaleness.[22]

The question of Stein's sexual, emotional, and intellectual iden-

tity is intricate enough; to move too quickly or easily from interpretations of her identity to judgments about the "feminist" or
"unfeminist" nature of her writing seems dangerous. According
to Carolyn Burke, "the language of gender should be rethought to
name" Stein's and Toklas's relationship, a project in which, Burke
implies, Stein anticipates us.[23] A growing consensus has arisen
among many critics of Stein that her writing, particularly after
about 1910, reveals a feminist concern with gender hierarchy, a system of domination allied with the dominance of certain narrative
and linguistic forms over others.[24] As deconstructionist methods of
interpretation have become joined to feminist questions in the work
of Marianne DeKoven, Neil Schmitz, and Janice Doane, among
others, the feminism of Stein's writing has emerged even more
clearly and persuasively.[25]

Informing my own approach to Stein's writings is a belief in
the feminism implicit in her "invitation" to a new kind of reading.
William Gass asserts that Stein's work poses a "challenge" requir-
ing "nothing less than a study of the entire basis of our criticism,
and it will not be put off."[26] I interpret this challenge as urging us
toward an open-ended and speculative responsiveness to her writing, resisting traditional critical claims to objectivity and closure,
and allowing ample room for subjectivity. Stein encourages her
"public" to form a certain intimacy with each composition and to
engage in reading as a process filled with starts and stops, moments
of confusion or uncertainty, and pleasure in the configurations of
sound and possible significance as these appear to one's senses and
imagination. Stein makes it difficult to master her writing or to
enter into a relationship with the writing that could even figure
mastery as a possibility. As she writes in *Tender Buttons*, "A white
hunter is nearly crazy," a statement evocative of mad Ahab in pursuit of the white whale: if one comes to her writing as a hunter
to his prey, not only is one nearly crazy, in that such pursuit is
crazed, but one will go crazy through the attempt to straighten
out Stein's crazy-quilt. Stein creates forms of writing that resist the
colonialism of reading's empires and that playfully ask us to question our own desire for dominance.[27] Stein's attempt is to shape us
into readers who come to her writing as equal lovers or intimate acquaintances, separate but always open to the possibility of "coming
together."[28]

Stein's sense of reading as an intimate and dialogic act contrasts markedly with the models created by recent theories of reading, even those of Wolfgang Iser or Roland Barthes, who appear at first to suggest points of agreement with Stein's model. Although Iser, for instance, claims an equal relationship between text and reader in the construction of meaning, his formulation reveals a significant inequality. According to his model, the "text" "offers" the reader "patterns" that seem stable and unchanging; it is the reader ("he") who "sets the work in motion." The text is "raw material," curiously silent, while "the whole process [of reading] represents fulfillment of the potential, unexpressed reality of the text." The gender bias implicit in this schism between the silent, material text and the active, imaginative reader emerges more explicitly in Iser's metaphor of holes or "gaps," left "open" by the text. In this narrative of reading, the (female) text is filled (and "fulfilled") by the (male) reader, who must limit the text's promiscuous "inexhaustibility" to one configuration of significance.[29]

While Iser's text offers holes, Barthes's reader creates them in a curiously violent way. In *The Pleasure of the Text*, Barthes defines the new "anti-hero" as "the reader of the text at the moment he takes his pleasure."[30] It is not surprising that the text, as the recipient of this sexual violence, becomes defined here as female, a "mother tongue." This "tongue" is accessible to the disfiguring acts of her writerly sons: "The writer is someone who plays with his mother's body . . . in order to glorify it, to embellish it, or in order to dismember it, to take it to the limit of what can be known about the body: I would go so far as to take bliss in a disfiguration of the language."[31] For Barthes, this violent masculine pleasure is essentially isolated from "the mother tongue." It may derive from the experience of reading, but it is felt privately, just as most of Barthes's figures for readers, like the voyeur or the audience to a striptease, are in the singular. Dialogue is not an authentic possibility: "The text is never a 'dialogue': no risk of feint, of aggression, of blackmail, no rivalry of ideolects; the text establishes a sort of islet within the human—the common—relation, manifests the asocial nature of pleasure."[32] "Dialogue," for Barthes, in any case would allow only for contest and "aggression," not intimacy. Intimacy finds no place, in this construction, either in dialogue or in the blissful monologue of reading, since Barthes defines "pleasure" as "asocial."[33]

The question of how reading occurs, addressed by both Iser and Barthes, acquires a certain urgency with modernist writing, espe-

cially when this writing presents as baffling and experimental a
surface as Stein's. In most critical approaches to Stein, the further
question of whether reading can occur at all becomes central. Ulla
Dydo describes the way in which Stein's writing compels us to
recognize that "reading is a matter of conventions that imprison us
when they become mere reflexes—what Stein called 'habits of association.' She asks that we give up these habits, go back to reading
school and learn to read and write all over again every day."[34] The
question remains: how *do* we "learn to read and write all over again
every day"?

Most critics of Stein choose one of two positions toward reading
Stein: either the belief in the primacy—even the sole importance
—of the "signifier" or the belief in the presence of a "signified,"
in messages that can be decoded, in however indeterminate a way.
Richard Kostelanetz voices the importance of the signifier in his
description of Stein's words as "autonomous objects, rather than
symbols of something else, rather than windows onto other ter-
rain."[35] William Gass, defending Stein in 1958 against her most
vociferous critic, B. L. Reid, argued against a criticism that looks
only for "significance" rather than experiencing the "word made
flesh, the love of the word as a resonance or a shape in space."[36]
This sense of Stein's insistence on the language's surface acquires
a new dimension in the recent feminist and post-structuralist approach of Marianne DeKoven's *A Different Language*. DeKoven describes Stein's project as disruptive: "The modes Stein disrupts are
linear, orderly, closed, hierarchical, sensible, coherent, referential,
and heavily focussed on the signified. The modes she substitutes
are incoherent, open-ended, anarchic, irreducibly multiple, often
focused on what Roland Barthes calls the 'magic of the signifier.'"
"Conventional writing," according to DeKoven, is "the privileged
language of patriarchy," while experimental writing "liberates the
'different' (*différent*) modes of signification which this privileged
patriarchal language has repressed," modes allied with presymbolic
language.[37]

DeKoven's approach to Stein's emphasis on the signifier makes a
valuable association between the "magic of the signifier" and feminist ideology. Yet to insist that Stein's writing is nonsignifying is
to deny its readability. Her concept of Stein's language as "incoherent" leads DeKoven to assert that experimental writing like Stein's
"obstruct[s] . . . normal reading," "prevent[ing] us from interpret-

ing the writing to form coherent, single, whole, closed, ordered, finite, sensible meanings."[38] Taking this situation one step further, DeKoven states that she does not "believe that Stein's experimental writing asks to be interpreted,"[39] implying that interpretation must necessarily participate in a patriarchal discourse. Since DeKoven argues that Stein's experimental texts "have no themes," and that their form is arbitrary, she comes to a conclusion disturbingly reminiscent of Barthes's violent pleasures: "We needn't plough through [this writing] at all. We need pay attention only as long as the thrill lasts, the tantalizing pleasure of the flood of meaning of which we cannot quite make sense."[40] Stein's writing, however, becomes caught in a double bind, for, as DeKoven also argues, *some* meaning is necessary to make writing "successful" and "readable." Using Chomsky's model of grammatical, semi-grammatical, and ungrammatical utterances, DeKoven claims that Stein's writings are successful only when they are semi-grammatical, offering "irreducibly multiple connections among their lexical meanings," as in the *Tender Buttons* period, whereas "Stein's interest, in the late twenties and early thirties, in unrelated successions of single words" results in "unsuccessful" and "unreadable" writing.[41]

The question of readability finds a different approach in the work of Wendy Steiner, one of the first and most influential critics to address with thoroughness the question of signification in Stein's work. Steiner situates Stein's literary portraiture (which becomes representative of the larger oeuvre) within the fields both of the portrait tradition and of modernism itself, finding that, rather than focusing solely on the "signifier," the portrait "makes the modernist issue of self-reflexiveness versus reference stand out in high relief."[42] Arguing that Stein "attempted an uncompromising mimesis" that frequently involved "a direct equivalence between her words and her own thought in perceiving her subjects," Steiner traces Stein's programmatic and logical journey toward a portraiture of "self-contained movement" that became "a dead end," in which the "disjunction between the subject and the perceiver, and between the perceiver and the reader," presented itself with the force of an irresolvable failure of communication.[43]

Many recent critics of Stein, however, have resisted this conclusion and have approached her writing as readable, as offering a signified, however undecidable this may ultimately be.[44] At one end of the spectrum, a body of criticism deciphering Stein's encodings, especially of lesbian experience, has emerged in the work of Catharine Stimpson, Elizabeth Fifer, and Lisa Ruddick, among others, who build upon and revise Richard Bridgman's earlier decodings in *Gertrude Stein in Pieces*. Other critics, like Jayne Walker and Ulla Dydo, have made excellent use of Stein's manuscripts and unpublished notebooks to trace her theoretical concerns during specific periods. Walker uses this material, as well as the texts from *Three Lives* to *Tender Buttons*, to analyze Stein's "uncompromising efforts to embody her sense of reality in language,"[45] while Dydo engages in a similar project for the later period of 1923 to 1932.[46]

At the other end of the spectrum, a further body of Stein criticism addresses the issue of Stein's readability from a less formalist or New Critical perspective. Marjorie Perloff offers one of the most direct arguments for Stein's "poetics of indeterminacy." Perloff observes that "words, as even Gertrude Stein recognized, have meanings"; Stein's project is "not to pretend that meaning doesn't exist but to take words out of their usual contexts and create new relationships among them."[47] According to Perloff, Stein's "verbal configurations are set up precisely to manifest the arbitrariness of discourse, the impossibility of arriving at 'the meaning' even as countless possible meanings present themselves to our attention."[48] This sense of plenitude in Stein's writing holds up in Perloff's own readings (for example, of the early poem "Susie Asado"), although Perloff tends to be more concerned with the relativism and arbitrariness involved in any one interpretation than with the possibilities offered to our attention.

Stein's best critics have been those who have been willing to commit themselves to the process of interpreting a Stein composition with a playful but thorough engagement, even as they show awareness that the reading upon which they embark is one possible reading out of many. William Gass, Pamela Hadas, and Neil Schmitz, for instance, have consented to this heady plunge into Stein's writing in ways that are openly speculative and participatory.[49] As Hadas suggests: "Of course if one does not give willing attention to the individual words as sound as well as sense, one misses the sound sense of having so many possibilities—the major enchantment of such a chant. If there is too great a difference between the acts of creator and re-creator, no amount of weight and volume, of gravity—or levity either—will sufficiently bring their acts together."[50] To read Stein, as Hadas suggests, is to engage in a "re-creation" that corresponds to Stein's own playfulness in the realms of both "sound" *and* "sense."

In this book, I build on this form of dialogic reading—a reading incorporating both the body's and the imagination's response—by asking how Stein's writing invites us to participate in its various modes of dialogic form. Although the book follows a largely chronological order, its primary purpose is not to present a historical argument about Stein, but to address different aspects and ways of thinking about Stein's poetics of dialogue. Each chapter focuses on the interpretation of a Steinian composition, or a group of compositions, that helps to illuminate one of these approaches.

Part I, "Mothers to Lovers," charts Stein's movement from a traditional narrative allied with the maternal to a poetics of dialogue modeled upon the interchanges of two lovers. Chapter 1 argues that in *Three Lives* (1905–6) Stein questions and ultimately abandons the concept of matriarchal authority as a figure for authorship and narration within the realistic tradition. She creates maternal author-figures who share the social and narrative conventions restricting women's lives and life stories, and who become more damaging to alternate and liberating modes of narrative as each *Life* succeeds another. At the same time, these stories show the beginnings of Stein's concern for a dialogic mode of authorship.

Chapter 2 explores this movement toward dialogic form in the early portrait "Ada" (1910) and in the later double "portrait," *The Autobiography of Alice B. Toklas.* This chapter introduces object relations theory and recent French feminist theory as bodies of thought offering useful, if incomplete, vocabularies for Stein's literary interest in doubling. The dialogue between these theories and Stein's writing leads to important points of similarity as well as difference. Although Stein creates a model of dialogue with resonances of mother-infant intimacy, she does not enact a return to this intimacy; rather, her writing embodies new forms of relatedness, especially, but not exclusively, attached to lesbian relationship. Further, although Stein's sense of intimacy finds illumination in Kristeva's concept of the semiotic and in Irigaray's exploration of female sexuality and a newly imagined female language of doubleness, Stein's forms resist location solely within a "female" or a maternal and presymbolic realm; instead, Stein undermines the linguistic and cultural boundaries separating the masculine and the feminine into easily distinguishable sides of a hierarchy.

Part II addresses two important aspects of Stein's "poetics of intimacy": representation and narrative. Chapter 3 explores Stein's feminist and modernist understanding of representation, both as she presents her concept of nouns and naming in her 1935 essay "Poetry and Grammar" and as this concept finds form in *Tender Buttons* (1912) and "Lifting Belly" (1917). I argue that Stein's concern with the "caressing" of nouns—including nouns' caressing of objects and the writer's caressing of both the objects and the nouns—constitutes a resistance to the appropriation both of words by the writer of words and of objects by the words intended to signify them. I place this resistance in the context of Stein's larger dialogue with Romanticism, especially with Emerson and Keats, in which she participates in the Romantic desire to render nature present, even as she attempts to undercut the traditional association of the male with culture and the female with a silent and absent nature, open to the appropriative vision of the male poet. Stein's revision of representation corresponds to a corollary revision addressed in Chapter 4: the substitution of a dialogic form of creation for the more traditional concept of a single origin and narrative line. Interpreting four compositions from the mid-1920's that challenge the concept of monologic creation in different ways, this chapter examines Stein's experimentation with a variety of forms open to dialogic transformation, including the portrait, the birthday-book, the prose poem, and the novel.

In Part III, "Reading as Conversation," I draw on the discussions of dialogue in the preceding four chapters to engage in closely "dialogic" readings of two later novels, *Blood on the Dining-Room Floor* (1933) and *Ida* (1940). Chapter 5 examines Stein's relation to her audience through an interpretation of *Blood*, where Stein voices through the narrator's addresses to an audience as well as through the substance of her murder mystery her fear of an audience's violent misappropriation of her writing, even as she makes one of her most direct invitations to our presence as "understanding" and loving readers. In Chapter 6 all of the aspects of dialogue addressed in the earlier chapters culminate in an exploration of "twinship" in one of Stein's most profoundly feminist novels, *Ida*.

Stein's invitation to her twentieth-century audience is to understand the processes of writing and reading in a profoundly new way. The issue of Stein's readability becomes a rich one indeed, as her writings make it essential for us to question what constitutes our concept of "readability" itself. To approach her work as transparently and consistently readable through the presence of decipherable codes and themes is to run the risk not only of ignoring the difficulty of her writing, but of translating this writing's unusual forms back into familiar conventions without taking into account the ways in which she challenges and alters these conventions. On the other hand, to conceive of her writing as utterly anticonventional (or antipatriarchal) is to risk missing any significance it has, apart from its destruction of all significance. The utopian dimension of Stein's project lies in her creation of a literary language that invites our imaginative sense-making effort as readers even as it successfully resists our desire either to master this language's meaning or to proclaim the language unreadable.

PART I

Mothers to Lovers

Maternal Authorship
in *Three Lives*

She said if I was married I'd have children and if I had
children then I'd be a mother and if I was a mother I'd
tell them what to do.   *(Ida, 43)*

"Baby! if you don't lie still, I think I kill you."
                                                          (TL, 28)

The famous opening line of "Melanctha," the second story of *Three
Lives*, gives us pause: "Rose Johnson made it very hard to bring her
baby to its birth" (*TL*, 85). Like the mother in the first paragraph
of *Ida*, who "held [the baby] with her hands to keep Ida from being
born" (*Ida*, 7), Rose appears to obstruct the birth of her own baby.[1]
Whereas Ida's mother vanishes within the first two pages of the
book, however, leaving Ida to enjoy an eventful life, Rose Johnson's
resistance to her baby's birth continues after the baby is born. Because Rose is "careless and negligent and selfish," "the baby die[s]"
(*TL*, 85).[2]

   This story of maternal resistance to the birth of a baby, coming
as it does at the opening (the "birth") of "Melanctha," forms a parable about the dangers of maternal creation and authorship borne
out by *Three Lives*. Rose "authors" her baby, yet she also has the authority to end or damage the "Life" she has created—as Ida asks at
one point, in relation to the "twin" she imagines into existence, "If
you make her can you kill her" (*Ida*, 11). In *Three Lives*, Stein's first
"baby" to find publication, Stein explores the nature of such power
in terms of her own "making" of fiction. Through her creation of
characters who act as author-figures, as well as through her intricate construction of narrative voice, Stein addresses the difficulties
inherent in the metaphor of the author as mother, as she begins to
define a less authoritative and more dialogic mode of creation and
authorship.

Stein's focus on female rather than male "authors" revises the cultural mythos of literary creativity as a solely masculine gift. According to Sandra Gilbert and Susan Gubar in *The Madwoman in the Attic*:

But of course the patriarchal notion that the writer "fathers" his text just as God fathered the world is and has been all-pervasive in Western literary civilization, so much so that, as Edward Said has shown, the metaphor is built into the very word, *author*, with which writer, deity, and *pater familias* are identified. . . . Indeed, Said himself later observes that a convention of most literary texts is "that the unity or integrity of the text is maintained by a series of genealogical connections: author-text, beginning-middle-end, text-meaning, reader-interpretation, and so on. *Underneath all these is the imagery of succession, of paternity, or hierarchy.*" [3]

Given this tenacious cultural myth, according to Gilbert and Gubar, nineteenth-century women writers faced an almost insurmountable difficulty. The absence of the phallus represented, within the culture's terms, the absence of the power to write in any significant way. The metaphor of the pen for the penis (or the penis for the pen) compelled writers who happened to be women to consider their acts of writing within these terms. [4]

This metaphor certainly has found a home in the twentieth century as well. The home, however, is less stable. Edward Said argues in *Beginnings: Intentions and Methods* that modernism is precisely about the dissolution of paternal authority. Such dissolution may be interpreted as a loss or a gain, depending upon what one stands to lose or gain. For many male modernists, T. S. Eliot foremost among them, the loss appeared substantial, while for women the undermining of this patriarchal myth proved valuable in the new space it allowed for female creativity. [5]

Gilbert and Gubar describe a possibility imagined by certain nineteenth- and twentieth-century women writers: a new world of wholly female generativity. For these critics as well as for many of the writers they discuss, the Sibyl becomes a symbol of "a goddess's power of maternal creativity, the sexual/artistic strength that is the female equivalent of the male potential for literary paternity." [6] Gilbert and Gubar see *The Madwoman in the Attic* as "an attempt at reconstructing the Sibyl's leaves, leaves which haunt us with the possibility that if we can piece together their fragments the parts will form a whole that tells the story of the career of a single woman artist, a 'mother of us all,' as Gertrude Stein would put it, a woman whom patriarchal poetics dismembered and whom we have tried to remember."[7]

The quotation from Stein comes from the title of her last opera, *The Mother of Us All*, about Susan B. Anthony, a play that certainly concerns itself with the relation between women's authority and women's liberation. Yet this relation, for Stein, is problematic rather than straightforward. She differs from H. D. and other women modernists in her refusal to substitute a myth of purely maternal creativity for the myth of a genesis that is wholly paternal. Although Stein often suggests the creative power of the female, she resists the enclosure of such power in any single "female equivalent" of "the male potential for literary creativity." Goddesses—even "mothers of us all"—find little place in Stein's writing. Instead, Stein searches for alternate forms of creativity, which involve, not "dismemberment," but a scattering and diffusion of authority. Although these alternate forms become primarily attached to female figures, this association is not absolute; male figures too (like Jeff Campbell in "Melanctha") may enter into narrative and social configurations in which hierarchy and authority vanish, to be replaced by an open-ended process of dialogue.

As Said argues, narrative traditionally depends upon metaphors of family hierarchy. The questioning of narrative authority in *Three Lives* involves a challenge to the concept of the author as a parent (whether father or mother) who brings a story up and controls its development and growth along one narrative line, one progression from beginning to middle to end. For Said, the story's sequence involves a similar filiation: either the child (the early part of a story) is father or mother to the adult (the later part of the story), or the parent (the early part, or origin, of the story) creates and nurtures the child (the denouement, the story's conclusion). *Three Lives* appears to depend on such a familial lineage, to the extent that each story follows out a "life," from its beginning to its end. In each story this historical movement forms a metaphor for the narrative's own "life," its linear growth from origin to conclusion.

Stein's *Lives*, however, resist their own tendency toward a traditional establishment of authority, in terms of narrative voice and linear sequence. The exaggerated appearance of traditional forms serves in part to parody authoritative and familial narrative.[8] Alternatives to such familial forms remain embedded in the stories as possibilities. The sharing of narrative voice, together with the movement away from linearity and toward the circling of dialogue, mark Stein's early forms of resistance.

The sequence of three stories in *Three Lives*, "The Good Anna," "Melanctha," and "The Gentle Lena," marks in thematic terms a monitory progression. With each story, the dangerous potential of mother-authors increases, as the close association between mothers and fathers becomes more manifest. In addressing this question of maternal authorship, I shall link Stein's representations of mothers and daughters to the forms of narrative she constructs. My own "narrative" in this chapter will address the thematic progression towards women's silencing by mother- and father-authors. However, I shall place the second story, "Melanctha," last, since it represents alternative narrative forms to a much more radical degree than either of the other two stories, which were written earlier. "Melanctha" stands as Stein's ambiguous farewell to the forms of authority proclaimed by the nineteenth century.

"The Good Anna"

"The Good Anna" opens upon a scene of linguistic conquest: "The tradesmen of Bridgepoint learned to dread the sound of 'Miss Mathilda,' for with that name the good Anna always conquered" (*TL*, 11). Anna "conquers" these men by speaking a name that appears to hold talismanic powers. The name is an unmarried woman's, a first name without a patronym. Although such a name might be expected to hold less authority with tradesmen than a masculine one, Anna brandishes it with confidence, and indeed her confidence appears justified, for the name, we are told, inspires "dread."[9]

Anna's linguistic strength shows an ambiguous alliance both to a masculine form of dominance, whereby others may be "conquered" through one's commands, and to the female world she inhabits. Her responses to violent forms of male authority suggest, however, that her commanding mode of utterance situates itself in opposition to male dominance:

Her voice was a high and piercing one when she called to the teamsters and to the other wicked men, what she wanted that should come to them, when she saw them beat a horse or kick a dog. She did not belong to any society that could stop them and she told them so most frankly, but her strained voice and her glittering eyes, and her queer piercing german english first made them afraid and then ashamed. (*TL*, 13–14)

Anna's power lies less in her actual words than in the unusual sound of her speech. Her language is "queer piercing german english," which is neither "German" nor "English," but a third language, powerful in its very otherness.

From the standpoint of a dominant culture, Anna and her language would be considered marginal. Her marginality would be seen to spring from her ethnicity, her class, and her gender. Yet in locating her story in the heart of a "german english," working-class world of women, Stein gives this "marginal" existence a voice, thereby undercutting the sense of its marginality. The "dominant" culture enters in the form of the "large, helpless women" and the kind male doctor for whom Anna works (the only man for whom she works), yet its dominance, although unquestionably present, does not gain our primary attention, for it is Anna who "dominates" the narrative.

The narrative, in fact, shows a surprising absence of traditionally dominant voices. The only direct discourse is that of women speaking to each other. Although Mr. Drehten, the "surly" husband of one of Anna's friends, "joined in [his wife's and children's Sunday festivities] with his occasional unpleasant word that made a bitter feeling but which they had all learned to pass as if it were not said" (*TL*, 46, 47), the narrative does not reproduce his actual words. Similarly, men may "join in" the story briefly, but it is not their story, and the narrative "passes" male speech "as if it were not said." Male speech in general, with the exception of Dr. Shonjen's, becomes literally ignored.

This presencing of female voices links with the voice of the narrator, who uses a language strikingly similar to Anna's, although, as I shall suggest later in this chapter, this similarity only partially hides a crucial difference in status. This narrative is one of speech, linked to an oral tradition of storytelling in which voice and sound become as important as signification. Such oral discourse always implies a context, both of the speaker as a living being and of the others who listen and respond. It is a discourse of potential intimacy and community, although this potential does not find full realization in "The Good Anna." Further, it is a discourse traditionally used by marginalized groups, including women of different classes and races.

Stein looks to this oral language as a means of beginning to "conquer" established conventions of narrative. She develops a language readable as "english," which gains vitality through its deviations from standard English. As Stein observes in her 1935 essay, "Poetry and Grammar," she admires the "mistakes" language can make.[10] The narrator's grammatical "mistakes" allow for configurations of language new to narration, while the oral nature of the discourse allows for a situation of potential dialogue with the listener. At a few points the narrator seems to turn directly to the audience, as in the line repeated with small variations throughout the story: "Remember, Mrs. Lehntman was the romance in Anna's life" (TL, 34, 52, 54, 55). This form of direct address to an audience becomes more pronounced during Stein's second decade of writing, when she began to write plays. In "The Good Anna," it remains a hint of possibility.

The potential for intimacy appears also in the relation between the narrator and the characters. Edmund Wilson long ago observed this intimacy, describing it as "the closeness with which the author has been able to identify with her characters," catching "the very rhythms and accents of the minds of her heroines."[11] Anna's voice mingles with the narrator's to such an extent that the two voices often cannot be distinguished from each other. When we read, for example, that Anna called to the teamsters "what she wanted that should come to them," we hear Anna's ungrammatical and emphatic speech simultaneously with the narrator's.

Stein's use of free indirect discourse, however, often causes the relation between the voices to be more problematic and difficult to unravel. Here is a representative instance: "Anna was a mother now to Sallie, a good incessant german mother who watched and scolded hard to keep the girl from any evil step" (TL, 19). Anna's voice, mingling with the narrator's, can be heard in the definition of herself as "a mother now to Sallie," even a "good . . . german mother," who "scolded hard to keep the girl from any evil step." A gap opens up, however, between the narrator and Anna with the sudden use of the word "incessant," which seems more likely to come from an educated, written culture. This kind of gap forms an integral part of the narrative voice's irony. It poses two conflicting possibilities, with which Stein seems to have struggled at this point in her writing: in calling attention to the boundary between Anna and the narrator, it makes us suddenly aware of the way in which this boundary has been crossed as Anna's voice has mingled with the narrator's; yet it also argues for a significant difference between Anna and the narrator, which involves the narrator's privilege in a hierarchy of knowledge and linguistic power.

I shall address first the more positive possibility: the general creation of a narrative space in which the narration may be shared.[12] The narration does not proceed from one place, or one voice; it is a double-voiced activity. Anna becomes a second storyteller, whose narrations can coincide with the narration of "The Good Anna" or even take over this narration entirely at moments.

Anna's tendency to tell stories supports this link between Anna and the narrator. For instance, "Her voice was a pleasant one, when she told the histories of bad Peter and of Baby and of little Rags [her three dogs]" (*TL*, 13), and she often tells other "histories" to the doctor and to her mistresses, which seem to be precisely the ones told to us by the narrator. This resemblance of story, together with the further resemblance of the narrator's voice to Anna's, allows us to imagine that Anna is at least one of our narrators throughout the story. This perception often finds verification in the literal repetitions between the narration and Anna's discourse. In one instance, the narrator's definition of one of Anna's many "under servants," Sallie, as "a pretty blonde and smiling german girl, and stupid and a little silly" (*TL*, 18–19) is nearly replicated by Anna two pages later: " 'Sallie is such a pretty girl, Miss Mathilda,' Anna said, 'and she is so dumb and silly' " (*TL*, 20).

Anna's (and the narrator's) sharpness in defining Sallie as "dumb and silly" accords with Anna's general confidence in her narrative place and vision. Indeed, Anna represents one of the most positive author-figures in *Three Lives*, in terms of her loyal alliance with a female world and her general use of language to "conquer" those who threaten this world. A darker side to such conquest exists, however, connected to the second possible explanation for the gaps marking Anna's difference from the narrative voice: narration involves conquest over its subjects as well as its audience.

Contrary to the expectations we may have formed from the sharing of narrative space between the narrator and Anna, Anna's relation to her own linguistic authority is not simply innocent and is rarely open to forms of sharing. Other characters find it difficult to answer back to Anna, since most responses would be interpreted as flung gauntlets. She "conquers" not only "evil men," then, but other women as well, albeit for their own "good." She attempts to shape and order the sometimes quite raw material around her —material that is usually female, from the servants "under" her to her friends and the "mistresses" for whom she works. Her story records the sequence of such relationships with other figures, primarily women: she makes order within the household of Miss Mary Wadsmith, then Dr. Shonjen, and finally Miss Mathilda, just as the first servant, "pretty, cheerful Lizzie," precedes the "melancholy Molly," who precedes "Old Katy," who precedes in turn the silly Sallie. In each relationship, Anna may be loving, yet her love comes in the form of the maternal attempt to keep another figure in line. Even though she shows much generosity, her language is one of command; she "scolds" continually—often affectionately, yet always with an insistence upon her own vision of "the right way."

Anna's powers as a teller of stories link in potentially disturbing ways with her further powers as a creator and shaper of other people's "stories," or Lives. The danger of such authority becomes apparent especially in Anna's relation to younger women, for instance Julia, the daughter of Anna's friend Mrs. Lehntman: Anna "watched and scolded hard these days to make young Julia do the way she should. Not that Julia Lehntman was pleasant in the good Anna's sight, but it must never be that a young girl growing up should have no one to make her learn to do things right" (*TL*, 39). Anna's idea of the "right" is a traditional one in both a moral and a narrative sense. Just as a daughter-figure like Julia or Sallie "must" follow a path of rectitude, so the "lives" that Anna authors must follow in straight lines, with as little deviation as possible. Anna's conventional wisdom demands strongly circumscribed possibilities for character and plot. "Goodness" incorporates obedience, sexual chastity, and a nearly blind commitment to one's female duty with regard to others.

Anna's outburst in the carriage to her much-loved female dog, who constitutes part of her family, and whom she has named Baby, gains a haunting significance in this context: "Baby! if you don't lie still, I think I kill you" (*TL*, 28). She certainly does not wish to "kill" Baby; Baby's actual death, later in Anna's life, "left Anna very empty" (*TL*, 75). Her anger at this moment is directed more toward another, human daughter, Mrs. Mary Wadsmith's daughter Jane, who has ordered Anna about to an intolerable degree. Although Anna's anger is understandable, it invokes the sense in which Anna's authorship involves making others "lie still," even when these others include herself and those dearest to her, her "babies."

Miss Mathilda, Anna's last mistress, feels the dampening effects of this authority on her own freedom:

And then Miss Mathilda loved to go out on joyous, country tramps when, stretching free and far with cheerful comrades, over rolling hills and cornfields, glorious in the setting sun, and dogwood white and shining underneath the moon and clear stars over head, and brilliant air and tingling blood, it was hard to have to think of Anna's anger at the late return, though Miss Mathilda had begged that there might be no hot supper cooked that night. (*TL*, 22)

Such "joyous, country tramps" have a movement that opposes Anna's sense of narrative sequence. Within this unusually lengthy description, which breaks out of the spare and undescriptive prose of "The Good Anna," the various aspects of the "tramps" join together with conjunctions in a profusion suggestive of simultaneity rather than of a carefully ordered sequence. Anna stops the sequence, as she puts an end to the gay spirits of Miss Mathilda's crowd. It is little wonder that, as we are told soon after, "often grievously did Miss Mathilda feel herself a rebel" along with the servants laboring under Anna (*TL*, 23).

Happiness occurs in Anna's world when she can scold and no one answers back. In the house with Miss Mathilda, such periods of happiness exist: "Sallie was a good, obedient german child. She never answered Anna back, no more did Peter, old Baby and little Rags and so though always Anna's voice was sharply raised in strong rebuke and worn expostulation, they were a happy family all there together in the kitchen" (*TL*, 19). The only "voice" heard here is Anna's. Her "children" (the dogs and the servant) remain silent. However, despite the narrator's (or Anna's) assurances about the reigning happiness, we must wonder about the apparently cheerful silence of four-fifths of the kitchen population.

"The Good Anna" shares Anna's narrative fervor even as it resists this narrative impulse. The danger inherent in Anna's control of others' stories finds replication within the more traditional aspects of this Life's narration, even as these conventions undergo scrutiny and revision. If we return to the opening line, we may observe the beginning of this struggle between conflicting possibilities for narrative voice and authority: "The tradesmen of Bridgepoint learned to dread the sound of 'Miss Mathilda,' for with that name the good Anna always conquered" (*TL*, 11). This opening marks a situation of linguistic power, defined as female and allied to a female world. The alliance becomes enriched by the use of free indirect discourse, which confuses the boundary separating the narrator from Anna, thereby allowing Anna to share the narrative space. Yet this sharing is incomplete, for the difference between Anna's point of view and the narrator's asserts itself through a delicate use of irony.[13] It is Anna who most likely believes in the tradesmen's "dread," and in the power of the names with which "the good Anna always conquered," while the juxtaposition between such high-flown heroic terms and the actual situation of "conquest" is clearly comic, at Anna's expense. The narrator sees more than Anna can see, and so, of course, do we, a fact that places us in the awkward position of intimacy with a character to whom we feel superior. Our position is equally awkward in relation to her female world, to which we sense an alliance yet from which we are made to feel distant.

Anna uses the name of a woman to assert power over others. Anna herself, however, is named by another; the epithet "the good Anna," resonating throughout the story, calls attention to this act of naming. Anna becomes a name within a story whose teller resembles her and shares narrative power with her, all the while holding a more privileged position than her own. Power lies both in naming and in the ironic distance such naming makes possible.

What constitutes Anna's "goodness," for instance, is a question that the story compels us to ask from the beginning. The very assurance of the epithet causes us to wonder about the source of the assurance. The word "good," as we sense from this opening, contains potentially different meanings for us than for Anna. It may even contain different meanings for the world around Anna, that enjoys and dreads her "goodness." Anna, as the story bears out, never reaches such questioning. For her, the word means something unchanging and absolute; it represents a moral system composed of traditional ideals of female selflessness, duty, and the "right way." Hearing of Anna's goodness through the ironic mediations of a narrator, we see Anna's moral world from a distance, as a system that is as linguistic as it is moral, possessing an arbitrariness Anna would never perceive.

The narration of "The Good Anna" thus employs traditional devices conflicting with the narration's impulse toward equality and a sharing of narrative power. We may often hear Anna's voice merge with the narrator's, yet this mergence coincides with a larger irony, magnified in the numerous moments when the narrator suddenly portrays a character from the outside, as in this picture of Anna: "And the good Anna full of the coquetry of pleasing would bridle with her angular, thin, spinster body, straining her stories and herself to please" (*TL*, 38). This small portrait reveals with poignant clarity the limits of one storyteller—Anna—through the superior position of another. The poignancy of such descriptions resides in our knowledge of the gap between Anna and ourselves as this knowledge comes into conflict with our attachment to her. Our position of superiority comes to seem like a betrayal.

The authority of such traditional narration depends upon conventions of temporality and realism whereby the narrator may occupy a stance above and beyond the story matter, together with a plot structure that follows out a "life," from some beginning point to an end, often to a death. Conventional nineteenth-century realistic narratives depend upon a narrative stance that has the power of knowledge *about* the novelistic world, a knowledge that comes from a position of futurity; that is, the narrator, according to realistic convention, tells the story from some privileged moment later than the moments in which the story occurs.[14]

Stein's *Three Lives*, in this sense, align themselves with a tradition of realism. Yet in her almost extravagant use of these conventions, she compels us to see them in a new and frightening way. Realistic novels often end with summations of the lives that have continued after the main story has come to an end. Often, they end with a sense of conclusion to each life, as in the famous "Finale" of *Middlemarch*, sometimes with a literalization of conclusion through the death of the main characters. Each of Stein's *Lives* ends, within its last paragraph or two, with the death of the character for whom the story is named. The death, although it may be prepared for in the sense that each character becomes physically "worn out" (a phrase Stein makes much use of) in a gradual decline, happens quite suddenly, with almost no comment by the narrator:

In a few days they had Anna ready. Then they did the operation, and then the good Anna with her strong, strained, worn-out body died. (*TL*, 82)

Melanctha went back to the hospital, and there the Doctor told her she had the consumption, and before long she would surely die. They sent her where she would be taken care of, a home for poor consumptives, and there Melanctha stayed until she died. (*TL*, 236)

When the baby was come out at last, it was like its mother lifeless. While it was coming, Lena had grown very pale and sicker. When it was all over Lena had died, too, and nobody knew just how it had happened to her. (*TL*, 279)

There is something cruel about these endings. We are given here bare bones: the fact of death, summed up in one or two undemonstrative, unexplanatory, dispassionate sentences. The "Lives," we feel, "sentence" the characters; after reading this far, for example, in the good Anna's "Life," we cannot help but want more at the end than the unadorned fact of her "Death." The poignancy of such distance becomes stronger with each successive story.[15]

Our frustration with the narrators marks a larger frustration, embedded within the stories, with this form of narrative itself. Even though the traditional uses of omniscient narration and irony seem to win out, such conventions of realism, in their very exaggeration, become exposed and implicitly critiqued. What ordinarily might be a novel's sense of closure becomes intensified here into an almost overwhelming sense of finality. What ordinarily might be a narrator's control over events becomes here the unimpassioned, anonymous recounting of events, a refusal to allow us any further glimpse or understanding of the characters we have attempted to follow. We feel like forcing the narrator to tell us more, to give us a fuller and more human account. Our dependence on a narrator, in being thus exaggerated, makes us question, in a way that goes beyond the questioning evoked by most nineteenth-century novels, the presence of this narrator as a figure holding the story *too* tightly, obscuring the vision that might have been possible without her or him.

To the epigraph from Jules Laforgue that heads *Three Lives*, "Donc je suis un malheureux et ce n'est ni ma faute ni celle de la vie," we might add: it may be neither the character's fault nor the fault of "life," but it could be the fault of this form of narration. The *je* here may be Stein, standing as she does after a long tradition of realism in the novel. *Three Lives* manifests an unhappiness with the traditional form within which it originated, an unhappiness that is especially evident in the two earlier stories, "The Good Anna" and "The Gentle Lena," which remain more attached than "Melanctha" to the conventions of realism. Perhaps Stein felt herself to be potentially as trapped as poor Anna by the confines of convention; yet, fortunately for us, she had a cognizance both of the trap and of the possibility of escape that is largely inaccessible to a figure like Anna.

Anna, then, reveals an attachment to the realistic tradition both by her placement within this narrative and by her own mimetic and realistic narrative powers. In a way that Anna herself cannot see, she suffers damage by the set of social and narrative conventions in which she herself—at least consciously—believes and which dictate a working woman's "Life." She dies finally as a result of sheer exhaustion, for "there was never any end to Anna's effort" in her working to take care of others (*TL*, 80). As a "good incessant mother," then, and a maternal author, she authors a limited life for herself; or rather, she accepts without question the authority of a larger cultural script that constructs definitions of what is "good" and "bad" in women's lives.

Perhaps Anna senses, however, that it is precisely because her "babies" do *not* always "lie still" that she has a story at all. The deviations from the order she imposes allow for journeyings that would not otherwise be possible. The story moves forward as a result of other characters getting out of line, from the adventures of bad Peter to the carelessness of Anna's romantic friend, Mrs. Lehntman. This "getting out of line" often assumes the form of sexual promiscuity in "The Good Anna," in a way that "Melanctha" will intensify and "The Gentle Lena" will suppress. The first words we hear Anna speak involve a romance between a servant and her male companion: "Sallie! can't I leave you alone a minute but you must run to the door to see the butcher boy come down the street" (*TL*, 12). This scolding anticipates Anna's injunction to Peter to "leave [the female dog] Baby alone." "The good Anna," we are told, "had high ideals for canine chastity and discipline" (*TL*, 12). Until this point, Anna appears to believe completely in the point of view she expresses. Yet the energy and persistence of her voice may intimate an interest in such goings-on that is not purely moral. Anna appears secretly, and perhaps unconsciously, to relish the deviance of her charges, as if she senses that such deviance nourishes her life and "Life." Immediately after her reprimands, a series of stories about the dogs and their wickednesses appears. The narrator, who merges here with Anna, shows evident delight in this recounting.

Anna's fascination with the dogs' eventful lives manifests itself in the experiments she devises to test their "goodness." In a comical rewriting of Genesis, Anna as the God-figure of her household retires from what she has "made" only to return for the inevitable judgment:

Sometimes just to see how good it was that she had made [the dogs], Anna would leave the room a little while and leave them all together, and then she would suddenly come back. Back would slink all the wicked-minded dogs at the sound of her hand upon the knob, and then they would sit desolate in their corners like a lot of disappointed children whose stolen sugar has been taken from them. (TL, 13)

Anna's response to her disobedient charges differs markedly from God's. She manifests the curiosity of a storyteller who desires more story material; it is little surprise that "her voice was a pleasant one" when she tells the dogs' "histories" (TL, 13).

Anna experiences an intimacy with these creatures, as with other characters, that her scolding belies. To the side of her focus upon the "right way to do" may lie Anna's desire for an intimacy that would not necessarily be "right" and that might partake of the lively deviation she appears to scorn. Anna's relation with Mrs. Lehntman suggests the form such intimacy might take, for, as noted, the narrator continually reminds us that "Mrs. Lehntman was the romance in Anna's life."

This implicitly lesbian attachment suggests an alternative to Anna's alliance with convention. A potential equality between the two women marks the difference between this friendship and Anna's other relationships. Anna, at first "entirely subdued by [Mrs. Lehntman's] magnetic, sympathetic charm" (TL, 30), temporarily refrains from ordering her friend's life. Mrs. Lehntman resists placement in a traditional plot; like her companion-spirit Melanctha, she "never could be led, she was so very devious in her ways" (TL, 42). Yet the relationship never realizes its potential for equality; rather, the two women remain in a struggle for power that precludes a deeper mutuality. Anna's gradual accrual of "direction" over many of her friend's actions culminates in her insistence upon Mrs. Lehntman's renunciation of an illegitimate infant boy. This renunciation would be not only of the boy but of an illegitimacy connected with autonomy from social strictures. Yet as Mrs. Lehntman eludes Anna's command, Anna begins to lose control over her friend.

Mrs. Lehntman's resistance to being ordered intimates that a less traditional form of maternal authorship may exist, one that could allow for sexual and narrative "deviation." Although Mrs. Lehntman is a mother, she lets her children do what they please, to Anna's dismay. Instead of teaching her children what is "right," Mrs. Lehntman makes a career out of "wrong," although the words "right" and "wrong" have no place within her vocabulary. As a midwife, she "loved best to deliver young girls who were in trouble" (*TL*, 31), suggesting that she may love the girls' mistakes as much as she loves to "deliver" the girls from the consequences of these mistakes. She takes them into her own house until, after the birth, they can return home "guiltlessly" (*TL*, 31). Within Mrs. Lehntman's house, these girls become a new kind of daughter-figure. As traditional "good" daughters, in the world of convention outside her home, they must keep within the lines prescribed by family life—virginity, marriage, and then proper motherhood. Under Mrs. Lehntman's care, however, they find a place which offers their deviation room and love.

This place is, significantly, a household composed entirely of women, where a woman helps other women to give birth. The female makes possible birth by the female, where "birth" becomes a metaphor for creativity in all forms. This house of women provides a key figure for a family that has issue, but no one mother, no clear lines of authority, no ancestors, and no lineage, just as Anna's various households, always "headed" by one woman, create a similar blurring of lines and a constant interchange of positions.

Mrs. Lehntman, like Mrs. Mary Wadsmith, is a "mother" only nominatively; this is the name attached to her own creativity, yet the name comes burdened with the weight of social and literary meanings that she refuses to bear. Anna certainly bears these, as does Anna's other friend Mrs. Drehten, with her "german husband to obey, and seven solid girls and boys to bear and rear" (*TL*, 46). Mrs. Lehntman's position, however, has a certain fragility. She undergoes a change from her original "ease" after she becomes involved with a doctor who, the narrator hints, performs illegal abortions. In gaining "power over the widow and midwife, Mrs. Lehntman," this "evil" and "mysterious" man draws her away from her midwifery and from her position as attendant and companion to female births. From enabling birth she begins to aid a man in enabling the obstruction of birth.

Yet "The Good Anna" sustains the possibility of female intimacy as a desire that can survive the narrative strictures both of Anna's life and of her death. In the last paragraph of the story, after Anna has died, the narrative breaks into the form of a letter:

> Mrs. Drehten sent word of her death to Miss Mathilda.
> "Dear Miss Mathilda," wrote Mrs. Drehten, "Miss Annie died in the hospital yesterday after a hard operation. She was talking about you and Doctor and Miss Mary Wadsmith all the time. She said she hoped you would take Peter and the little Rags to keep when you came back to America to live. I will keep them for you here Miss Mathilda. Miss Annie died easy, Miss Mathilda, and sent you her love." (TL, 82)

This ending softens the starkness of the narrator's account of Anna's death, and offers an alternate form of narration quietly reminiscent of the epistolary novel, a novelistic form shaped by Richardson (Stein claimed *Clarissa* as her favorite novel) and welcomed by many women writers. The fact that this alternative account assumes the shape of a letter recalls the dimension of narration in "The Good Anna" that allows for a sense of intimacy and a sharing of narrative authority, for a personal letter often implies an equality and intimacy between the writer and the receiver subversive of the writer's privilege and distance. Stein's allusion, through this small, awkward letter, to the epistolary narrative tradition suggests her insight into the revolutionary potential of such a form, especially with regard to female authority and voice.

With this concluding letter, the irony present in much of the narration disappears. The gap between the narrator and Anna suddenly closes, as the "narrator" becomes quite literally and simply Anna's friend. Anna is able to share authentically in the narration, despite (or perhaps because of) her death, as Mrs. Drehten transmits without irony Anna's words to Miss Mathilda: "She said she hoped . . ." The last word, "love," is Anna's, carried across to Miss Mathilda by the letter writer in what amounts to a further act of love.

The possibilities inherent in the letter as a narrative form find more extensive consideration in *Ida*, as I shall suggest in Chapter 6. In "The Good Anna," the letter arrives within the field of narration too late to do her preceding "Life" any good, although it is potent enough to hold out a promise for Stein's later fulfillment.

"The Gentle Lena"

"Why, I do anything you say, Aunt Mathilda."
(TL, 253)

Crossing the distance from the first story of *Three Lives*, "The Good Anna," to the last, "The Gentle Lena," is illuminating and saddening, for the movement is a tragic one. Both stories represent the same working-class, immigrant German-Americans in "Bridgepoint" (a city modeled on Baltimore, Maryland, where Stein had lived as a medical student). "The Gentle Lena," in fact, mirrors "The Good Anna" in many ways, yet from a new angle that makes this immigrant world far less bearable, especially for young and "gentle" women. In terms of narrative, the dangers of traditional narration implicit in "Anna" and associated with maternal authority find a frightening literalization in "The Gentle Lena." The possibility of an alternate mode of narrative and cultural authority, although glimpsed in the beginning of "Lena," becomes quickly obscured and ultimately buried.

Lena's story begins in a household similar to Anna's household with Miss Mathilda. In both situations, ordinary hierarchies have given way to more fluid configurations of relationship: Lena is a servant, yet her mistress, like Miss Mathilda, is "pleasant" and "unexacting" (*TL*, 239). Lena could imaginably live in Anna's house, for an Anna figure reigns in the kitchen, "who scolded Lena a great deal, but Lena's german patience held no suffering and the good incessant woman really only scolded so for Lena's good" (*TL*, 239). As in "The Good Anna," although such scolding holds the possibility of a damaging authority, the "good" intentions of the scolder offset this possibility.

This household of women and children protects Lena from other characters' designs upon her. Her life is one of pure being, composed of daily and regular activity that varies in small ways yet remains essentially the same.

Lena's german voice when she knocked and called the family in the morning was as awakening, as soothing, and as appealing, as a delicate soft
breeze in midday, summer. She stood in the hallway every morning a long
time in her unexpectant and unsuffering german patience calling to the
young ones to get up. She would call and wait a long time and then call
again, always even, gentle, patient. (*TL*, 239)

This is a utopian moment, occurring in an urban *locus amoenus*, a
moment to be relished in its constancy ("always . . . always"). A
"delicate soft breeze in midday, summer" is sensual and pleasurable; it "awakens," yet such awakening does not lead out of the
pleasant place, but remains "soothing." As at the opening of "The
Good Anna," voice is primary here, yet Lena's voice differs remarkably from Anna's. When Anna's voice scolds, it creates responsive action, however temporary, whereas Lena's voice caresses
its hearers into a responsive yet quiet state, in which action seems
unnecessary.

Lena's value, indeed her whole delicate existence, seems to re-
side in this voice. Floating outside of a linear and narrated story,
her voice becomes a figure for Stein's impulse, already visible in
"The Good Anna," toward a writing in which the authority of
traditional narration would be shared by other voices, or even replaced by these voices entirely. Lena's actual words do not need to
be recounted, since the sensual dimension of language has in such
moments more value than the representational.

Lena's association, through simile, with a beneficent nature suggests Stein's embrace of a serenity and sensuality figured as pastoral. "The Gentle Lena," however, does not move Lena and her
utopia of voice far enough away from the "real" world, or the
world of realistic fiction, to allow such gentle "calling" to be sustained. Within this world, Lena and voice itself—especially the
unauthoritative, sensual female voice—are doomed. After the first
few pages, the story makes no room for her expression; quite literally, she speaks less and less, until her caressive voice becomes
completely absent from the narrative.

This vulnerability of Lena's voice, and of a writing centering
around voice, manifests itself early on in Lena's interactions with
the other "girls" in the park, as they all look after their little charges.
These young women "liked very well to tease" Lena because language baffles her so easily: "for she could never learn to know
just what the other quicker girls meant by the queer things they

said" (*TL*, 240). In the instance shown us, representative language, in the form of the other women's words, comes to Lena signifying danger; when Lena "suck[s]" a certain substance from her finger, in a spontaneous and bodily attempt to understand what it is, Mary defines the substance as "green paint," which she asserts to be "awful poison" (*TL*, 241). Lena remains uncertain about the truth of these claims: "She did not know just how much Mary meant by what she said" (*TL*, 241). She becomes silent in response, as she "wonders" about the poison; her response again is a bodily one, as she "rub[s] her finger on her dress a little harder" (*TL*, 242), giving rise to her companions' laughter.

The defining of green paint as "poison" hints at the poisonous nature of a language that represents and defines. Lena's cousins use language to define their relatives in the old country as "ugly and dirty," and their town as "very poor and smelly" (*TL*, 244). Significantly, the language these cousins choose to use is English (not Anna's "german english") as opposed to German, English being the language of the dominant and privileged nation. The prejudice the cousins express toward their poorer relatives already has a habitation within the English (at least the American English) language itself. In saying that their cousin was to them "little better than a nigger" (*TL*, 246), they call upon the damaging hierarchies established deep in a culture's very language. It is even more disturbing that the transmitters of language's damage are women, who have suffered as a group from language's powerful definitions to such a serious degree.

Language, however, is necessary within Lena's world and within a story following and defining a "Life." Lena's inarticulateness and her bodily existence outside language as a signifying system only make her into raw material for others' stories. In being a tabula rasa, not yet written upon, she holds the potential for a new use of language, yet she cannot know this, and in any case the narrative does not allow the fulfillment of such potential. Instead, Lena becomes a character in another woman's story. Hurried along a predetermined narrative path by Mrs. Haydon, married off to a man for whom she has no desire, and made into a vehicle for her husband's reproduction through his children, she lives out a story that is almost at no point her own. Her actual death, and her child's, literalize her death within such narrative linearity and convention.

Mrs. Haydon, the most frightening matriarchal author in *Three*

Lives, resembles Anna in her need to dominate, yet lacks Anna's lovingness or capacity for intimacy. Anna, of course, is not a "real" mother, a fact that certainly appears to be in her favor. Mrs. Haydon's primary power is over daughters: her two actual daughters and Lena, for whom (in Mrs. Haydon's words) she "was just like a mother" (*TL*, 255). For Mrs. Haydon, motherhood involves bringing "up" and binding in, just as the daughters' bodies—those "unkneaded, unformed mounds of flesh" (*TL*, 243)—are bound in by the "stiff" hats and "heavy cloth" their mother enforces as their dress. Such dress forms a metaphor for Mrs. Haydon's art, which acts as a "firm, directing, and repressed" (*TL*, 243) stamp, ready prior to the daughters' existence and able to inscribe that existence, which otherwise would form a blank. Their dresses are "the same" (*TL*, 243), unaccommodating to the daughters' differences from each other, and in a larger sense to the difference that is female.[16]

Mrs. Haydon admires and creates a traditional form of narrative that is "brought up," in a clear linear and moral progression. As a maternal author, she depends upon such linearity. Family lines link with a historical sequence of "past, present and future," implying a plot reliant both on family and on history.

Mrs. Haydon liked it all. It was familiar, and then here she was so wealthy and important. She listened and decided, and advised all of her relations how to do things better. She arranged their present and their future for them, and showed them how in the past they had been wrong in all their methods. (*TL*, 244)

The narrator's use of irony ruthlessly exposes the disturbing aspect of this mode of authorship. As an author-narrator, Mrs. Haydon confidently assumes historical movement, from the (wrong) past to the present and the future (which she can make "better"). She decides, she arranges, she shows. Her "relations," in the sense of family, become erased to make room for her narrative "relations."

Lena, just such a relation in both senses, becomes a character in Mrs. Haydon's story—in fact, she becomes the story itself, "The Gentle Lena"—to be brought up and, in the end, concluded. As Mrs. Haydon works on Lena through time, Lena is both created and read, like a novel in serial form: "it was all coming out just as [Mrs. Haydon] had expected" (*TL*, 250). The author-mother attempts to make Lena readable in a familiar way, through the fulfillment of narrative and parental expectations, and Lena proves to be acquiescent to the claims of language and story: "Lena was good and never wanted her own way, she was learning English, and saving all her wages, and soon Mrs. Haydon would get her a good husband" (*TL*, 250). To be easily readable, Lena must begin to fit into the "way" of the text she inhabits. Her learning of English marks precisely this attempt, and it is no surprise that Lena's entrance into English is accompanied by the promise of "a good husband."

Lena thus becomes readable within her own culture, just as "The Gentle Lena" becomes legible within literary culture through its use of the conventional marriage plot. Jane Austen, foremost among the body of novelists to which Stein indirectly responds, both makes use of and parodies this plot. Mrs. Haydon becomes a Mrs. Bennett figure, treated with irony, although much less comically. Whereas Mrs. Bennett loses control over the marriage plots she devises, Mrs. Haydon never loses an ounce of control; Lena is, tragically, not an Elizabeth. Furthermore, Mrs. Bennett's lack of authority finds more than compensation in the narrator's utter authority, and in the ultimate authority of the cultural marriage plot itself; that is, Mrs. Bennett's plans for her daughters achieve realization in spite of her efforts. Stein imitates Austen's irony toward the marriage-happy mother-figure, yet she also ironizes the final acquiescence to a plot that for Stein is much too dangerous.

"The Gentle Lena" follows the marriage plot, yet instead of Austen's comedy we find Stein's tragedy, the tragedy of an ordinary female life like Lena's, caught within the meshes of a cultural imperative that overwhelms her and for which she has no language. Stein's narrative certainly embodies an ironic stance toward this imperative, but irony alone cannot save Lena from the story within which she finds herself. Further, as in "The Good Anna," irony implies a privileged stance that is itself problematic for Stein. In "The Gentle Lena," Stein compels us to ask how any traditional narrative can avoid the kind of damage to others that Mrs. Haydon enacts.

An even more fundamental question lies behind this one: how can one even speak about another who is silent and who has no access to language? To what extent is such "speaking for" the other an act of further silencing? The narrator appears sympathetic toward Lena, in the attempt to present her point of view, yet we must wonder where Lena herself fits within the narrator's presentation, since the narrator tells us what Lena cannot know: "Lena did not really know that she did not like [the life in Germany]. She did not know that she was always dreamy and not there. She did not think whether it would be different for her away off there in Bridgepoint" (*TL*, 246). Lena has no access to knowledge about herself, a fact that appears to spring from her absence of language. In her dreaminess she is not fully within the waking world of language and story; she is quite fundamentally "not there." Although she has a bodily existence, attached to an unconscious realm of dream, she would never be able to translate this existence into a legible story. The gap between the narrator and Lena, then, is a problematic one, for the narrator always "knows" more than Lena, and in articulating this knowledge the narrator forms an unhappy alliance with the figure of Mrs. Haydon, an alliance that intimates the narrator's dominance over and potential betrayal of Lena.

Although until the last section "The Gentle Lena" wrestles largely with maternal authority, this last Life concludes with a sudden and disturbing turn toward the paternal. In marrying, Lena submits to the orders of husband and mother-in-law (the "law" of the mother is thus literalized); she enters their family, their house, and their sense of what her story should be, of what she, as a text, should look like. The bond between matriarchy and patriarchy, half-buried through much of *Three Lives*, suddenly manifests itself. Herman Kreder's mother and father, a brutal pair, force Herman into marriage with Lena, just as Herman and his mother together impose a "law" upon her. Herman is not genuinely "her" man, meaning Lena's; rather, he is his mother's and father's, and in a larger sense he is the culture's, in that he has been written by the culture.

Even more disturbing is the appropriation of the act of birth by the father. Lena becomes a mother, yet not in the sense that Mrs. Haydon is a mother. This version of motherhood would not be available to her. Instead, she gains only suffering from each birth; after the appearance of each child, she diminishes and becomes more "lifeless," until with the final fourth birth (a stillbirth) this metaphor assumes a terrifying literality. As Lena diminishes, Herman Kreder seems to enlarge in happiness. Lena gives birth, but Herman owns the babies; they are only "his," the pronoun that insistently attaches itself to any mention of them. Gradually, Lena vanishes from the narrative. By the end, she is forgotten, not only by her husband and children, but by the narrative itself, which ends with a highly conclusive portrait of father and children: "Herman Kreder was very well content now and he always lived very regular and peaceful, and with every day just like the next one, always alone now with his three good, gentle children" (*TL*, 279).

This final, succinct portrait is also a portrait of traditional narrative, which for Stein depended so thoroughly on succession and continuity. All is now in line, in place. These children, unnamed, have no story outside their placement in their father's line; they are "good" and "gentle," as well as being, one assumes, unquestioning of this familial arrangement. Their sexuality is left significantly out of the portrait; even their sex is unmentioned, except for the first child who is, to Herman Kreder's satisfaction, a boy. The female has essentially been erased.

Herman Kreder's (Her man / credo's—I believe [in] her man) form of narrative (or his mother's—a difficult distinction) has the last word. He takes over the authorship of "The Gentle Lena," even of *Three Lives*. These "three children" may, in fact, be the *Three Lives* themselves. "Good" and "gentle," which are among the last three words of the last story, and which define "his children," are also Stein's epithets for "The Good Anna" and "The Gentle Lena." Herman Kreder's accession to fatherhood over three lives is precisely what brings these *Lives* to an end. His fictive position as their only parent marks their silencing and closure. This conclusive move into patriarchy identifies with a final lucidity the larger cultural structures behind apparently matriarchal authority. Stein's anti-utopian women's worlds, such as Mrs. Haydon's household, reveal a bondage to a dominant patriarchal culture antagonistic to the lyric female impulse associated with freedom from narrative command.

"Melanctha: Each One As She May"

"A nice way she is going for a decent daughter. Why don't you see to that girl better you, ain't you her mother!"   (*TL, 94*)

Stein wrote in *The Autobiography of Alice B. Toklas* that "Melanctha" was "the first definite step away from the nineteenth century and into the twentieth century in literature" (*ABT*, 54). This claim to being "first" may be disputed; in 1905–6, the years during which Stein wrote "Melanctha," Henry James was immersed in his late and highly modernist experiments with subjectivity. Yet Stein certainly joins James as one of the most radically innovative writers in the early years of the twentieth century. For Stein, as for James, this step is preeminently one of form. However, the new formal elements of "Melanctha" show strong associations with the story's representation of family life. The innovations of the story "Melanctha" link with the escape of the character Melanctha from family, especially from mothers and fathers, and her attempt to go "as she may."

Significantly, Melanctha is the only heroine in *Three Lives* whose parents find representation within the narrative. Anna's mother appears and dies within two brief paragraphs (*TL*, 24), and Lena's mother remains unmentioned. Anna becomes an orphan, and Lena is an orphan in effect, since she leaves her home in Germany, happy to cut all ties with her immediate family. Orphanhood, however, which in the later novel *Ida* will liberate Ida from familial and narrative lines, seems in these early stories only to open the space for new families to form: Anna with her mistresses and servants, and Lena with her series of families, each more constricting than the last. The presence of Melanctha's parents, especially at the beginning of the story, provokes a more serious antagonism on Melanctha's part than would be possible for Anna or Lena. Without parents, these "good" and "gentle" women agree to the new configurations of family, whether as mother-figures or as daughters. Melanctha, as an actual daughter, is neither good nor gentle, a fact allowing a place for her resistance to her parents. As the narrator bluntly states: "Melanctha had not loved her father and her mother and they had found it very troublesome to have her" (*TL*, 91). Her troublesomeness is precisely her saving grace, for this family life deserves resistance. Melanctha's major opponent in the first part of her story is her father, who is "brutal and rough" to Melanctha in his attempts to "manage" her (*TL*, 91). This managing occurs primarily in a sexual arena. As a "virile" man (*TL*, 90), he recognizes Melanctha's new sexuality and attempts to prevent its expression or growth, at least outside the family. Anna's outburst to her restless dog Baby recurs in a more serious context when James Herbert says to Melanctha's mother: "Where's that Melanctha of yours? . . .

If she is to the Bishops' stables now with that yellow John, *I swear I kill her*" (*TL*, 94, emphasis added).

The phrasing of this question—"Where's that Melanctha *of yours?*"—suggests that James Herbert links his daughter's waywardness with his wife's in a way that bears significant implications for female power and identity. According to his vision, his wife is the primary figure in charge of Melanctha, although both Melanctha and her mother remain under his overseeing eye; therefore, she becomes immediately responsible for her daughter's deviance, as James's repeated question, "Why don't you see to that girl better you, you're her mother" (*TL*, 91, 94, 103), attests.

Mothers, as he believes, should keep daughters in line. In their very femaleness, however, mothers manifest a suspicious kinship with daughters; indeed, Melanctha's mother "had always been a little wandering and mysterious and uncertain in her ways" (*TL*, 90), a description resembling what we are told of Melanctha herself. Although the mother "never cared much for this daughter who was always a hard child to manage" (*TL*, 110), she manifests a similar unmanageability. She may attempt to "manage" Melanctha, but the narrative does not record the attempt more than to say that Melanctha's "wanderings after wisdom" had to occur "in secret and by snatches, for her mother was then still living and 'Mis' Herbert always did some watching" (*TL*, 97). Even here, the mother's "watching" leads only to "telling" the father. "Mis" Herbert acts as a stooge, but never punishes Melanctha herself.

This relationship between the father and mother evinces a strong hierarchy. The mother is considered secondary within the family. Devalued by the father, she acquiesces to his repressive power, at least on the surface. Like Rose and Sam Johnson, the "family" to which Melanctha will turn at the end of the story, the Herberts "had been regularly married." The repeated use of the word "regularly" in connection with the Herberts' marriage, especially given the brutality involved, compels us to question its meaning. Such regularity revises the good Anna's concept of "the right way," which for Anna included chastity but never the allowance of violence or brutality. "Regularity," then, becomes more seriously undercut than Anna's more innocent authoritative system. Associated with a traditional marriage structure, such "regularity" appears highly problematic.

These configurations of family life embody clear paradigms for narrative. The father urges the mother to attempt to keep Melanctha within a "regular" narrative, dependent upon the repression of her sexuality and autonomy, and upon the presence of a hierarchic narrative structure in which male power dominates. Melanctha feels dissatisfaction with the "Life" of both her parents and herself, yet she desires a story that would accord with her parents' demands upon her. As if she wishes to find herself within "The Good Melanctha" or "The Gentle Melanctha," she consciously longs for a narrative of "peace and *gentleness* and *goodness*" (*TL*, 93, emphasis added).

The two earlier stories, however, have taught us to understand the cost of such goodness and gentleness within traditional narrative. We begin to wonder, then, whether Melanctha's inability to find a narrative of "peace and gentleness and goodness" may not be a *felix culpa*. The narrator, who appears to use Melanctha's own language, voices this inability as a failure: "and all her life for herself poor Melanctha could only find new ways to be in trouble" (*TL*, 93). The narrator expresses pity here for Melanctha's inability to gain her wish for a "good" life. What is tragic in this sense is Melanctha's painful and doomed sense of the division between what she "loved and wanted" and what she actually "found." [17] The phrase "poor Melanctha," however, may encompass a further sorrow: the narrator may pity Melanctha for accepting the definition of her "new ways" as "be[ing] in trouble." The story reveals that Melanctha's "new ways" have value in their creation of an existence and a story able to escape, however temporarily, from the bonds of traditional literary womanhood.

Melanctha's story, then, may look like a series of "new ways to be in trouble," yet the word "trouble," like the words "good" and "gentle," is at least partly ironic. The definition of Melanctha's sexuality as inherently troublesome springs from a repressive cultural attitude toward female identity and sexuality exposed and challenged by the story as a whole. This cultural attitude finds numerous proponents in the story, from James Herbert to Melanctha's lover Jeff Campbell and Melanctha's friend Rose Johnson. Yet through her dialogues with Jeff Campbell and through her redefinition of her sexuality, Melanctha asserts her own innovative power. The narrative itself, after the opening biographical section, moves toward an embodiment of such a power.

The term "sexuality," as I am using it here, suggests much more than Melanctha's specific, physical, and "desiring" being (*TL*, 87). Her sexuality, in this ordinary sense, forms only one aspect of a larger power that I have been defining as sexual, her "power as a woman" (*TL*, 95). This power is not simply bodily, although the body's instinctual life is crucial for Melanctha; rather, her instinctual desire and attraction attach to her whole identity as a "complex, desiring" woman. Melanctha's large and undefined desire, in her "beginning as a woman" (*TL*, 95), compels her "to search" for something more than her "life" (and her Life) has yet offered; this desired value finds articulation as "wisdom."[18] Although the "wisdom" Melanctha seeks depends upon knowledge about the body, it also incorporates the acquisition of a language and a narrative that could leap beyond the constrictions of social and literary convention.

Melanctha desires a "tongue" literally and metaphorically. The literal, in fact, allies itself with the metaphoric, for her new tongue, or language, is one of the tongue, or body. The narrator repeats the perspective of Melanctha's author-parents in the statement that Melanctha had "a tongue that could be very nasty" (*TL*, 91). This tongue defeats the brutal father, for "he feared her tongue, and her school learning, and the way she had of saying things that were very nasty to a brutal black man who knew nothing" (*TL*, 103). Furthermore, her tongue begins to occupy the narrative space during the long and experimental middle section, when Melanctha enters into dialogue with Jeff Campbell.

The narrator, like the narrators of "The Good Anna" and "The Gentle Lena," tends to stay within the boundaries of language imaginable within the world of the story: the criticism of Melanctha's tongue as "nasty" comes from her parents, but in a larger sense from the whole world in which Melanctha finds herself. To the extent that the narrator appears to accept such language without question, s/he is "obtuse," as Marianne DeKoven has argued.[19] Yet as in the earlier two stories, the narrator's use of the characters' visions and language does not preclude an ironic understanding of the limits of such language. This irony works in two directions: it undercuts the limited views of the characters, yet in another sense it sets up the ironic narrator as a privileged spectator, capable of "knowing" the characters better than they do themselves. As I shall argue later in this chapter, Stein begins in "Melanctha" to redefine narrative voice in such a way that the second of these possibilities becomes undermined to a fuller degree than in either "The Good Anna" or "The Gentle Lena."

Once Melanctha begins to recognize her power, both she and "Melanctha" make a new beginning, separate from the old beginning within either Rose Johnson's or Melanctha's home. The Life literally begins again. Because the old "life was too quiet and accustomed and no longer stirred her to any interest or excitement," the story determines a new starting point: "Melanctha now really was beginning *as a woman*" (*TL*, 95, emphasis added). The woman's life (and Life) is to be one of "excitement."

Significantly, it is through another woman that Melanctha "learned to really understand" her "power" (*TL*, 97). At first, she attempts to learn only from men, in both a bodily and a narrative sense; she comes close to them physically through talking with them and listening to their "stories." Yet the "power" that seems most authentic and most accessible to Melanctha is a woman's, even as it becomes a power that must be escaped. Jane Harden represents a female authorial power that must be challenged and left behind, even though she brings possibilities of female identity and sexuality to light.

Jane's relation to Melanctha, like Anna's "romance" with Mrs. Lehntman, suggests the potential for a narrative form based on dialogue, in which one figure does not dominate. As with Anna's romance, however, this potential remains unfulfilled. "Melanctha would spend long hours with Jane . . . sitting at her feet and listening to her stories, and feeling her strength and the power of her affection" (*TL*, 105). The physical intimacy ("sitting at her feet") exists on a continuum with the storytelling ("listening to her stories"), which occurs within the context of a bond of "feeling." Further, Jane's "stories" contain a content and perhaps a form new to narrative: "There was nothing good or bad in doing, feeling, thinking or in talking, that Jane spared her" (*TL*, 106).

This continuum between physical intimacy and storytelling suggests a lesbianism that offers a potential model for a poetics of dialogue. This anticipated model, however, remains tenuous and unfulfilled, for the situation of teaching and learning as Jane and Melanctha experience it is not one of equality. Jane clearly occupies a dominant position, while Melanctha receives what Jane gives, often in a masochistic sense: "here with Jane Harden she was longing and she bent and pleaded with her suffering" (*TL*, 106).[20]

As a female author-figure, Jane Harden presents female "power" in a problematic light, intimating the dangers of a narrative voice claiming certainty and knowledge. If such power assumes the form of power over another, and especially over another woman, how different can this force be from the brutal use of coercion displayed by Melanctha's father? Although Jane Harden, like the narrator of "Melanctha," shows Melanctha a realm of emotion and expression impossible within her father's house, Melanctha "sits at Jane's feet." It is Jane, not Melanctha, who speaks, making use of her speech in a way that sounds curiously aggressive—"In every way [Melanctha] got it from Jane Harden" (*TL*, 106). Although Jane is Melanctha's lover, her loving becomes simply a new version of matriarchal and authorial control linked with the narrator's potential control of "Melanctha." Both Melanctha and "Melanctha" move past Jane Harden on a search for a less dominating narrative form. Melanctha inherits Jane's power, although this power gradually assumes a new form, in which the potential intimacy of this early relationship can be achieved within the telling of the story itself. As the narrator remarks, "Melanctha Herbert never really lost her sense that it was Jane Harden who had taught her, but Jane did many things that Melanctha now no longer needed" (*TL*, 107).

As an author-figure, Jane attempts to act as the source and guide of Melanctha's new life, yet Melanctha refuses to keep within the bounds of Jane's story. Similarly, the "excitement" of the female Life of "Melanctha" springs from its resistance to its own narrative arc of beginning, middle, and end. This "beginning as a woman" for Melanctha (and "Melanctha") sparks a continual act of beginning, causing the past to vanish as the narrative moves from present to present, in a continuous and indefinite series of moments.[21] In "sometimes . . . really forg[etting] how much she owed to Jane Harden's teaching" (*TL*, 107), Melanctha represents a narrative forgetful of its past. The present moment, within this form of narrative, "escapes" from the potentially limiting control of its own origins. The concept of origin manifests not only irrelevance but danger.

The story's movement away from Jane Harden evinces this form of escape:

and so slowly, but always with increasing strength and feeling, Melanctha began to really understand.

Then slowly, between them, it began to be all different. Slowly now between them, it was Melanctha Herbert, who was stronger. Slowly now they began to drift apart from one another. (*TL*, 106–7)

Each sentence makes a new present that is itself in process, towards a newer present. The repeated "slowly now" marks this gradual and sequential movement into a present (a "now") different from the past. Just as these women "drift apart" as time goes on, so the narrative may drift apart from Jane Harden and all that she represents, without having to "remember" her.[22]

Stein addresses this form of the "continuous present" in her 1926 lecture, "Composition as Explanation": "In beginning writing . . . I wrote a negro story called *Melanctha*. In that there was a constant recurring and beginning there was a marked direction in the direction of being in the present although naturally I had been accustomed to past present and future" (*CAE*, 16). Stein clearly links her own "beginning writing" to the "constant recurring and beginning" in "Melanctha." Like Melanctha, Stein turns from the "accustomed" sense of life and story, in her own search for the new as it attaches to a specifically female (but not maternal) creativity.[23]

Melanctha herself becomes a figure for Stein's new concept of authorship. Melanctha's own acts of storytelling bear a significant resemblance to Stein's in "Melanctha," just as they differ from the more traditional narrations of the good Anna. Toward the beginning of Melanctha's "beginning as a woman," the narrator presents Melanctha as an inaccurate teller of stories:

Some man would learn a good deal about her in the talk, never altogether truly, for Melanctha all her life did not know how to tell a story wholly. She always, and yet not with intention, managed to leave out big pieces which make a story very different, for when it came to what had happened and what she had said and what it was that she had really done, Melanctha never could remember right. (*TL*, 100)

The context in which Melanctha tells stories reveals a reason for her omissions important to the narrative of "Melanctha" as well. The men's desire to "learn a good deal" about her suggests her position as a subject for their knowledge and an object of their sexual satisfaction. In leaving out or distorting early parts of her stories, she eludes possession in both an intellectual and a (hetero)sexual sense: as the man would come closer, "Melanctha would always make herself escape" (*TL*, 100), just as a narrative in the continuous present "escapes" at each moment from the moment before.

Melanctha later acknowledges a further reason for her omissions. In response to Jeff's accusation that Melanctha "ain't ever got any way to remember right what [she's] been doing," in terms of her earlier succession of relationships, she replies: "I certainly do call it remembering right Jeff Campbell, to remember right just when it happens to you, so you have a right kind of feeling . . . its real feeling every moment when its needed, that certainly does seem to me like real remembering. . . . It's always me that certainly has had to suffer, while you go home to remember" (*TL*, 181). Jeff's anger comes from his desire to be sure of Melanctha, in a way that connects for him with a reliable narrative memory.[24] Melanctha, in this sense, eludes his confident possession of her, even as she offers him an alternate form of relationship to her, involving a spontaneous responsiveness—"real feeling every moment when its needed"—that does not become ordered into a narrative line.

Both the narrator and Jeff Campbell perceive Melanctha as an inaccurate and unreliable teller of her own history. Melanctha clearly presents a problem to any narrator or lover who hopes to present her life as a coherent development from a beginning to a conclusion. Jeff Campbell replaces Jane Harden as an "author" who desires to write Melanctha's life. In his attempt and in its bafflement "Melanctha" locates a figure for its own narrative attempt to define and account for the life of its subject.

Like Mrs. Haydon, Jeff possesses a conservative habit of narration: "he believed you ought to love your father and your mother and to be regular *in all your life*, and not to be always wanting new things and excitements, and to always know where you were, and what you wanted, and *to always tell everything just as you meant it. That's the only kind of life* he knew or believed in, Jeff Campbell repeated" (*TL*, 116–17, emphasis added). Jeff's credo is familial. He accepts the filial bond to parents rejected by Melanctha, a bond marking (in its echo of the Ten Commandments) a further acceptance of a traditional morality together with the literary "parent" of this tradition, the Bible. He inherits a sense of deep cultural propriety from his own father and mother, who had "been regularly married." His mother's acquiescence to her secondary status marks her position as a culture mother, in opposition to Melanctha: his mother "was a sweet, little, pale brown, *gentle* woman who reverenced and obeyed her good husband" (*TL*, 111, emphasis added).

Within this traditional "life," Jeff feels centered and secure, confident of "where" he is and "what [he] want[s]." Jeff brings this habit of certainty to Melanctha, only to be baffled by the difference of her life. He desires to understand her, to make her legible, a project continually throwing him back upon uncertainty:

These months had been an uncertain time for Jeff Campbell. He never knew how much he really knew about Melanctha. He saw her now for long times and very often. He was beginning always more and more to like her. But he did not seem to himself to know very much about her. He was beginning to feel he could almost trust the goodness in her. But then, always, really, he was not very sure about her. Melanctha always had ways that made him feel uncertain with her, and yet he was so near, in his feeling for her. He now never thought about all this in real words any more. (*TL*, 135–36)

Although Jeff attempts to make his understanding of Melanctha an intellectual one, this attempt meets with failure at every turn. Melanctha cannot be grasped in such terms. Jeff moves closer toward another form of understanding when he puts aside the question of knowledge and begins to "feel," yet "feeling" represents, as Jeff senses with trepidation, a more uncharted and certainly less articulable domain.

Melanctha challenges Jeff's certainties just as "Melanctha" baffles our own desire for certainty. Although she often submits to his obsessive need to define her, she attempts to make him see the cruelty of his definitions. Significantly, Jeff's uncertainty about Melanctha leads him to rely upon the traditional language by which women have historically been defined: she is to him both the "good" (gentle) and the "bad" (sexual) woman (*TL*, 188). In place of Jeff's reliance upon language and the intellect, Melanctha invites him to substitute a narrative without language, in which the body and "feeling" would be primary and in which language would not become an obstacle to understanding. As she says to Jeff at one point, "It ain't much use to talk about what a woman is really feeling in her" (*TL*, 135).

Melanctha's invitation to a more bodily and emotional intimacy poses a problem, however, not only for Jeff Campbell, but for the narrator of "Melanctha" as well. Jeff's perplexity about knowing and feeling culminates in a puzzling statement: "[Jeff] now never thought about all this in real words any more." Although Jeff may not always put such thoughts into "real words," the narrator has already attempted precisely such a linguistic act. As in "The Gentle Lena," writing becomes a fundamentally questionable act of translation.

The impulse toward "omniscience" on the part of the narrator, ironized in all three stories of *Three Lives*, becomes most seriously challenged in "Melanctha." Here the narrator both tells Melanctha's story and offers increasing resistance to such telling, on a linguistic as well as a narrative level.[25] The use of undefined and abstract words like "wisdom," "feeling," and "knowing," for instance, suggests in one sense the narrator's remoteness and possible "wisdom." In a further sense, however, these words act not to define but to keep an entity open to continuous and changing definition.[26] The narrator does not occupy a fully stable vantage point from which to tell the story; Stein's use of the continuous present causes the narrator to remain attached to the processes of the characters from moment to moment, rather than to establish a clear narrative distance.

Further, the narrator often gives up the narrative realm entirely for long stretches, as Melanctha and Jeff enter into the narrative through their long and intricate speeches or letters to each other. Although Jeff professes to possess a language of "knowing," rather than of "feeling," his actual language resembles both the narrator's and Melanctha's not only in its choice of repeating words, but in its rhythms and sound, and in the importance of sound itself, which forms a "feeling" and moving current—and often a countercurrent —beneath the act of signification. The opening of Jeff's letter to Melanctha offers a representative example of this powerful current of sound:

"Dear Melanctha," Jeff wrote to her. "I certainly don't think you got it all just right in the letter, I just been reading, that you just wrote me. I certainly don't think you are just fair or very understanding to all I have to suffer to keep straight on to really always to believe in you and trust you. I certainly don't think you always are fair to remember right how hard it is for a man, who thinks like I was always thinking, not to think you do things very bad very often. I certainly don't think, Melanctha, I ain't right when I was so angry when I got your letter to me. (*TL*, 146)

Jeff's repeated "I certainly don't think," in its very insistence and repetition, gradually causes us to hear this line literally, for in a sense "thinking" is *not* the most important aspect of Jeff's response to Melanctha. The words build and accumulate to form subtly overlapping waves of sound expressive of less articulate emotion.

It is difficult to grasp such a narrative, just as it is difficult, if not impossible, for Jeff to "grasp" Melanctha. Just as the narrator follows with thoroughness and subtlety each fine turn of mood, we find ourselves immersed in each sentence, so caught up in the chanting sound that we begin to give over the usual authority of our interpretation, as we acknowledge the equal value of our more bodily response. As Marianne DeKoven observes, "We feel as if we are living through an experience rather than reading about it; we come away with a feeling of deep familiarity with or rootedness in the dimensions of the situation unextended to a coherent intellectual grasp of them."[27] Such a response comes from the narrator's resistance to her or his own defining tendency. In the midst of the ongoing attempt to translate feelings into language, the narrator makes use of a language charged with feeling, which draws our attention away from the very content the narrator works to articulate. Our response to this feeling marks an intimacy, a bodily "dialogue," with the narration, as "telling" and "listening" come together in a similar movement of sound.

The double narrative impulse in "Melanctha"—to "know" and to "feel," to tell and to resist direct telling—finds an oblique figuration in the situation of Melanctha and her dying mother. When Melanctha first attempts to question Jeff Campbell's certainties, her mother is lying on her deathbed upstairs. As a doctor, Jeff has come to keep the mother alive or to ease her death; in one sense, she represents the tradition of narrative in which he himself believes so firmly. Her "life" is in the balance, and insofar as her life represents the traditional recording of a Life, this "balance" is precisely the subject of Melanctha's and Jeff's argument. The mother has helped to keep Melanctha in line, and with her death Melanctha (and "Melanctha") may be free to wander from traditional narrative. Further, the mother exists on a continuum with Melanctha. "Wandering and uncertain in her ways," the mother dies only as a mother, while her wandering, so similar to Melanctha's, becomes incorporated into the narrative.

If this figure of the mother's "life" as a traditional narrative holds, however, the conclusion of "Melanctha" severely undercuts the concept of such narrative's death, for Melanctha returns in the end to her last author-figure, also a mother, Rose Johnson: "Rose always was telling Melanctha Herbert the right way she should do, so that she would not always be in trouble" (*TL*, 207). In one sense, the traditional narrative wins out. Melanctha desires with increasing intensity a life of peace and stability. Rose, whom Melanctha "wanted . . . more than she had ever wanted all the others" (*TL*, 233), represents this "regular" and correct form of narrative. Rose, however, casts Melanctha out of her house and her story as a result of Melanctha's inability to "act right." The death of Rose's baby, with which "Melanctha" opens, foreshadows Melanctha's later death, as a "baby" who would not "sit still." In another sense, Melanctha helps to cause her own death by her accession to Rose's sense of a "Life," which has clearly involved death for its wandering female characters.

Melanctha sustains, in her very desire for Rose, the possibility of another form of narrative, one that will be fulfilled in Stein's later and more experimental writings, as I shall suggest in the following chapters. The attachment and the love she bears Rose, however, find no corresponding responses, just as her speaking voice and the moving and dialogic narrative form she represents become nearly erased in the story's last pages.

Steinian Dialogue and the Two-Body Relationship

*now you are going to have two, I am going to have a
twin yes I am Love, I am tired of being just one.*
                                                    (Ida, 10)

*I double you, of course you do. You double me, very
likely to be. You double I double I double you double.
I double you double me I double you you double me.*
                        ("Patriarchal Poetry," YGS, 115)

At one moment in "Melanctha," the insistent and lively dialogue
between Melanctha and Jeff comes to a halt, as a new form of communication begins to occur:

Melanctha began to lean a little more toward Dr. Campbell, where he was
sitting, and then she took his hand between her two and pressed it hard,
but she said nothing to him. She let it go then and leaned a little nearer
to him. Jefferson moved a little but did not do anything in answer. At
last, "Well," said Melanctha sharply to him. "I was just thinking" began
Dr. Campbell slowly, "I was just wondering," he was beginning to get
ready to go on with his talking. "Don't you ever stop with your thinking
long enough ever to have any feeling Jeff Campbell," said Melanctha a little
sadly. (*TL*, 131–32)[1]

Although Melanctha at first "said nothing" in words, she speaks
with her body. By her gestures, she suggests her desire for an increasing intimacy, one of "feeling," with little need of words. Jeff's
resistance to this bodily speech and his return to language as a rep-
representation of "thinking" obstruct the development of a dialogue
of the body. These oppositions between thinking and feeling, language and silence, however, begin to dissolve as Stein creates a sensual and rhythmic language incorporating the body. In Stein's later
writings, the "silent" realm of intimacy becomes even more volu-

ble. Each of Stein's styles marks a new attempt to bring a bodily intimacy into language.

Stein's concern for such intimacy bears significant connections with the school of post-Freudian psychoanalysis called object relations theory. Focusing upon the earliest, prelinguistic attachment of the infant and small child to the mother, this theory opens a window onto a realm of intimacy that becomes the ground for later formulations of relationship. Stein's forms of intimacy differ in important ways from those of object relations theory: she does not conceive of intimacy in mother-infant terms, just as she chooses to transform the "prelinguistic" into a linguistic realm approximating and even embodying a state outside of language. Yet object relations theory offers a vocabulary and a set of concepts valuable for articulating this Steinian transformation.

One of Stein's major connections with object relations theory lies in a shared emphasis on relatedness. As Nancy Chodorow points out in *The Reproduction of Mothering,* this theory in general argues against the Freudian model of primary narcissism, where the infant's earliest experience occurs in almost total isolation from another being. Chodorow presents Freud and later ego psychologists as claiming that

the infant originally has no cathexis of its environment or of others, but concentrates all its libido on its self (or on its predifferentiated psyche). The infant is generally libidinally narcissistic; hence, the hypothesis of primary narcissism. . . . This Freudian position also holds that the infant seeks only the release of tension from physiologically based drives—operates according to the "pleasure principle." The source of this gratification . . . is irrelevant to the infant. Accordingly, the child is first drawn from its primary libidinally narcissistic stage because of its need for food.[2]

The child, in this model, is forced into relationship only as a means to an end (for instance, food), where the "end" is still attached to the child's libidinal need. In these early stages, relationship is secondary.

By contrast, object relations theorists like Michael Balint and Alice Balint argue for an infant's connection to its environment beginning even before birth. Paradoxically, even though the infant does not differentiate itself from what surrounds and holds it (originally the womb), it powerfully cathects this very bodily presence. Soon after birth, Chodorow writes, this "generalized cathexis

... becomes focused on those primary people, or that person, who have been particularly salient in providing gratification and a holding relationship." In contradistinction to Freud's theory of primary narcissism, these theorists suggest the hypothesis of "primary love," which "holds that infants have a primary need for human contact itself."[3]

From the first, then, one experiences being in the world (or in the womb) not as "one" alone, but as two, even when one cannot differentiate between oneself and the other.[4] In D. W. Winnicott's terms: "I once said: 'There is no such thing as an infant,' meaning, of course, that whenever one finds an infant one finds maternal care, and without maternal care there would be no infant."[5] As I shall argue in my interpretation of *The Autobiography of Alice B. Toklas* and the early portrait "Ada," this formulation of a doubleness inherent in and essential to identity has a strong bearing on Stein's literary form.[6] The chiasmus of Winnicott's language here even resembles Steinian crossings-over, as in the quote heading this chapter: "You double I double I double you double." Stein's characteristic use of an unidentified or floating "you" and "I" may resemble this mother-infant bonding. However, Stein avoids fastening the identities of these pronouns to this original dyad, for reasons that will become clearer later in this chapter.

Object relations theory holds as one of its key tenets that "the development of the self is relational." As Chodorow suggests (following Winnicott), the inner "core" of the self depends upon a simultaneous "provision of a continuity of experience," just as the sense of "self," in terms of a unity with ego and bodily boundaries, develops through the gradual demarcation from the m/other.[7] As Chodorow adds, this definition through relation is sustained primarily with daughters. Her intricate analysis leads to this concept: "Because of their mothering by women, girls come to experience themselves as less separate than boys, as having more permeable ego boundaries. Girls come to define themselves more in relation to others." Whereas boys move fairly quickly from the dyad with the mother to the triangular relationship of desire between son, mother, and father, involving the son's rivalry with the father, for girls the matter differs: "A girl, by contrast, remains preoccupied for a long time with her mother alone. She experiences a continuation of the two-person relationship of infancy."[8]

For Stein, although the origin of this "two-person" relationship may lie in infancy, this temporal anchorage holds much less importance or even presence in her writing than the transformation of such a relationship into new forms. The mother disappears from the picture, to be replaced by a more equal figure. Yet the equality of the two subjects in Stein's writing resembles the relation between mother and infant in Chodorow's theory. As Carol Gilligan suggests, Chodorow's great contribution has been to substitute the word and concept of "mother" for the more reified "object." Chodorow challenges the way in which the mother as a responsive and human figure in the relationship has been reduced in object relations theory to an "object" that is either constant (and lifeless) or a monster.[9] Chodorow understands the relation between mother and child as always two-sided, involving two subjects. Accordingly, she emphasizes not only the infant's perspective, but the mother's as well.

The mother's experience, as Chodorow argues, tends to create daughters who will be like their mothers, in a long line of "the reproduction of mothering." This situation between mothers and daughters, daughters who become mothers to more daughters, could be looked at from many angles. Certainly, within the context of a patriarchal culture, where gender differences mark a crucial difference in power, this reproduction of mothering perpetuates an inequality that is socially, politically, and economically visible.[10] This asymmetrical development of males and females is constituted in a further important sense by a culturally defined linguistic difference. As Margaret Homans has shown, when we consider the Lacanian structuring of language acquisition in relation to Chodorow's account of asymmetrical gender development, a fuller picture of our gendered cultural mythos emerges.[11] In Lacan's narrative, which assumes the point of view of the son, the maternal represents the silent, the repressed, and the literal, upon whose absence patriarchal culture and symbolic language depend. The boy's severance from the mother at the onset of the Oedipal crisis marks a disturbingly fortunate fall, for her absence enables the son to enter the Symbolic, constituted by figures of substitution for the now lost maternal presence. The daughter's case manifests a critical difference, however: "because of various consequences of the daughter's likeness to her mother, she does not enter the symbolic order as wholeheartedly or exclusively as does the son."[12] The daughter's prolonged pre-Oedipal attachment to the mother, notes Homans, in being thus allied to the uncertainty of her status within the symbolic order, appears from a Freudian and Lacanian perspective as the "daughter's tragedy."

As Homans points out, however, through her interpretation of Chodorow, another "story" is possible. This alternate account, read from "the daughter's point of view," springs from the potential value inhering in the daughter's different relation to the mother:

Although in this new story, the daughter does enter the symbolic order, she does not do so exclusively. Because she does not perceive the mother as lost or renounced, she does not need the compensation the father's law offers as much as does the son. Furthermore, she has the positive experience of never having given up entirely the presymbolic communication that carries over, with the bond to the mother, beyond the preoedipal period. The daughter therefore speaks two languages at once. Along with symbolic language, she retains the literal or presymbolic language that the son represses at the time of his renunciation of his mother. . . . Unlike the son, the daughter does not, in Chodorow's view, give up this belief in communication that takes place in presence rather than in absence, in the dyadic relation with the mother, and prior to figuration.[13]

This access to a presymbolic language continued from infancy holds potential for a poetics created by women writers, as Homans suggests. Yet "speaking two languages at once," when the languages have been valued so unequally within culture, has been no easy matter. The nineteenth-century women writers Homans considers responded to this linguistic situation with an ambivalence that becomes lessened, although it hardly disappears, in the twentieth century. Virginia Woolf "intermittently" expresses "pleasure in a nonsymbolic language," just as H. D. attempts to imagine it.[14] A larger acknowledgment of the cultural devaluation of women's language, however, in Homans's view, tempers such pleasure.

Gertrude Stein's writing is unusual even in the twentieth century for its embrace of language's nonsymbolic dimensions. Homans states, "To write 'literature' is to write within the symbolic order."[15] If this is the case, however, Stein redefines "literature" in powerful and delightful ways. A major aspect of Stein's achievement is precisely to recover the "literal" and to return it to the "letter," even as she makes the letter as literal as possible. Stein gives language to a whole realm of experience culturally perceived as extra-linguistic or extra-literary, yet the language she offers, especially after her first decade of writing when she had to confront and put to rest her own Victorian heritage, is a sensual, aural, and visual one playing always on the borders of the symbolic and the unsymbolic, just as it plays on the borders of identity and mergence with an other. She does, indeed, "speak two languages at once," in forms affording not ambivalence but comedic mischievousness, for the Symbolic order appears in Stein's writing not as an irrefutable Law, but as a structure open to transformation. The value of such play lies, for Stein, in the margin of freedom it grants to make use of symbolic forms in order to create a voice for the unsymbolic, thereby "reproducing" an earlier intimacy based on a dialogue of sound and of the body.

Stein's resistance to actual mother-figures in *Three Lives* continues in her long career of writing, even to the creation of the late opera, *The Mother of Us All*, where Susan B. Anthony questions the authenticity of her own authority and achievement as a "mother" of the U.S.A. (Us All). This resistance would seem to suggest Stein's own burial of the maternal, and in a sense it does. For Stein, the literal mother was dangerous for her suppression of the daughter's story, especially the story of the daughter's sexuality, as in the portrait "Ada." Yet Stein's voluble and intimate poetics of dialogue, foregrounding the sensual and bodily dimensions of language, reworks the pre-Oedipal bond between mother and infant. This early bond may be buried, yet a similar bond most compellingly exists, redefined as an attachment between "others" or lovers.[16]

Stein's rejection of the mother-daughter relation in favor of the relation possible between two subjects—often, but not exclusively, female subjects—resembles Luce Irigaray's account in "And the One Doesn't Stir Without the Other" of a daughter's silencing by the mother and of her attempt to transform the mother into another woman. From the perspective of Irigaray's daughter-figure then, the mergence and identification that hold a positive value in most object relations theory appear claustrophobic and destructive of autonomy for both the daughter and the mother. The reproduction of mothering prevents the formation of identity outside the role of "a mother's daughter," "a daughter's mother." Between these two images, an authentic self cannot emerge. Each daughter becomes merely a mirror (*glace*), frozen into a "reflection" of her mother, who has no identity of her own, stilled as she is within the world of the father, for whom she, and subsequently the daughter, must serve as mirror: "Immobilized in the reflection he expects of me. Reduced to the face he fashions for me in which to look at himself."[17] Irigaray suggests that women may only escape this labyrinth of empty mirrors through a recognition of the otherness both of daughter and mother. This acceptance and enjoyment of difference, voiced also in Irigaray's earlier essay "When Our Lips Speak Together," marks the possibility of a relationship strikingly similar to Stein's vision: "I would like both of us to be present. So that the one doesn't disappear in the other, or the other in the one. So that we can taste each other, feel each other, listen to each other, see each other—together. . . . *I would like us to play together at being the same and different. You/I exchanging selves endlessly and each staying herself. Living mirrors*" (emphasis added).[18] Such "play" between figures similar and yet different also forms the heart of Stein's poetics of dialogue, although Stein's tone is lighter, her forms more experimental, than Irigaray's.

Through the form of these highly lyric pieces, Irigaray self-consciously transforms the nature of her relation to existing disciplines of psychoanalysis and philosophy.[19] The disciplines' own limitations compel her, along with other contemporary French feminists, to begin to write in new and experimental forms. Unlike Irigaray, Stein does not primarily consider herself to be in the realms of philosophy and psychoanalysis, although her writing offers some of the most brilliant revisions of philosophical and psychoanalytical thinking to be found in the first half of the twentieth century, revisions often anticipating recent feminist and deconstructive thought, as Neil Schmitz and Marianne DeKoven, among others, have argued. She was certainly educated in philosophy and in "psychology," considered a new dimension of philosophy in the late nineteenth century, when she studied at Radcliffe with William James, George Santayana, and Josiah Royce. Her serious and imaginative effort to raise questions about language, representation, the mind's processes, and the formation of identity and relationship continued throughout her writing life. She always works intellectual thought, however, into the playful and difficult forms of her literary creativity.[20]

It is within literary form that Stein addresses structures of relatedness described by psychoanalytic and object relations theories in other terms. She also differs from most of these models, as I have suggested, in her transformation of the mother into a loving "other," her dehistoricized rendering of this dyadic relation, and her emphasis upon language as the utopian place where such intimacy can occur in continuous and infinitely nuanced forms. In the rest of this chapter, I wish to twine Stein's literary language with the language of object relations and feminist theory, in order to gain insight into the significant difference Stein makes. The Steinian dialogue I shall explore both in this chapter and in the rest of the book will be both actual and metaphoric. It occurs in myriad forms, yet it is arguably ceaseless, as the primary structure out of which her writing is generated.

"Ada," Alice, Gertrude

In the first edition of *The Autobiography of Alice B. Toklas* (1933), a double portrait of Alice Toklas and Gertrude Stein faces the title page. This photograph by Man Ray presents the two figures in an eery and uncanny aspect. Alice Toklas appears in the doorway of Stein's atelier, an unsmiling and quietly ghost-like figure, looking apparently, not at Gertrude Stein, but into the general dusk of the room, while Stein remains at her desk, pen in hand and head bent downward. Two candles rest on the table between the two figures, as if to mark the space between them. The "story" of this picture is uncertain, even mysterious. What seems most uncertain, and most interesting, is the relation between these two women within the moment created by the photograph, which focuses our attention upon the intricately filled space between the figures. Placed at the opening of this "autobiography" of one woman, written by another, the photograph suggests the mystery involved in such a doubling.

At least two interpretations of this mystery may be seen to bear significantly upon Stein's book. In one interpretation, based on the more overt content of the photograph, Stein is clearly the writer.[21] Solid and still, she sits at a kind of altar, replete with votive candles and, on the shelf above, religious icons, including a heavy cross. Alice is a lesser figure in the temple, although a significant one. Hovering on the margin of the sacred writing space, she is perhaps an intrusive spirit, but one that must be acknowledged. In a sense, she appears as a figment of Stein's imagination. Stein does not need to look up because she is in the process of creating Alice on the page. This interpretation suggests a doubleness involving one primary figure with a secondary, shadowy doppelgänger to the side. The act of writing bears in this sense a sinister edge linked to Stein's possible appropriation of Toklas's voice in *The Autobiography*.

The ambiguity of Man Ray's image, however, evokes a second and contrasting possibility. The placement of the two identical candles symmetrically between the two figures intimates the possibility of another form of doubleness, one of exchange rather than of static dissimilarity. The image offers a visual chiasmus, suggestive of the way in which Alice may take Gertrude's "place," and Gertrude Alice's. The cross on the wall, linking the two similar windows, lends support to such a crossing-over of identity. Literally, Alice may be about to cross the room to Gertrude, just as Gertrude may in a moment pause in her writing to come to the door. In another sense, the two women may hover on the brink of a dialogue, whether of language or of the body.

This photograph forms an ambiguous threshold to this ambiguous "autobiography," for the conflicting possibilities contained within the photograph appear in the book as well. The tension informing the book marks Stein's attempt to convert the concept of single voice and authorship into a richly doubled authorial identity, to prevent "one" from subverting the more utopian possibilities of "two." The narrative voice of *The Autobiography* manifests this tension. On the one hand, Stein performs a sleight of hand, a feat of disguise by which she, as the author and the "real" narrator, speaks through the transparent device named "Alice B. Toklas." On the other hand, the ambiguity inherent in an "autobiography" of Toklas written by Stein challenges the concept of a single narrator or author. A radical doubling may occur, marking a playful and elusive interchange. Stein makes it difficult for us to be certain that the voice we hear is only Stein's, especially since the voice differs in its dry, civilized, and muted tones from Stein's narrative voices until this point. It is difficult to know where Stein's voice ends and Toklas's begins.[22]

The Autobiography compels us to wonder, from the beginning, about the nature of the "auto," the self. We begin to ask, in addition to the question of what the relation is between Stein's and Toklas's voices, the further questions of what is the nature of the writing self and whether a work, even an "autobiography," is ever

genuinely written by one figure alone. Stein attempts to convert
the solitary act of writing into an act shared by at least two figures
who engage in some kind of relationship. The definition of a writing "self" depends upon the often baffling and ambiguous presence
of another. The two figures enact a dialogue, insofar as both voices
may be present. Irony itself—which may be defined as the possibility of one voice speaking "behind" another—takes on the nature
of a dialogue; because we cannot tell which speaker/writer is the
"real" narrator, we cannot be certain of the irony's location.

To explore this doubleness of narrative voice further, we may
consider one of the many instances of actual dialogue in this autobiography so preoccupied with the possibility of dialogue. As brief
and unobtrusive as most of the "remarks" making up this "literature" (following the famous Steinian remark, "Hemingway, remarks are not literature"), this anecdote offers a glimpse into a
world of two figures in intimate dialogue:

> One Sunday evening I was very busy preparing one of these [American
> dishes] and then I called Gertrude Stein to come in from the atelier for
> supper. She came in much excited and would not sit down. Here I want
> to show you something, she said. No I said it has to be eaten hot. No,
> she said, you have to see this first. Gertrude Stein never likes her food
> hot and I do like mine hot, we never agree about this. She admits that
> one can wait to cool it but one cannot heat it once it is on a plate so it is
> agreed that I have it served as hot as I like. In spite of my protests and the
> food cooling I had to read. I can still see the little tiny pages of the note-
> book written forward and back. It was the portrait called Ada, the first in
> Geography and Plays. I began it and I thought she was making fun of me
> and I protested, she says I protest now about my autobiography. Finally I
> read it all and was terribly pleased with it. And then we ate our supper.
> (*ABT*, 139–40)

Alice's concern that Stein is "making fun of [her]" in the portrait
"Ada" could carry over to Alice's protestations about her "autobiography." In one sense, Toklas's "I" is vulnerable to Stein's manipu-
lations. Toklas appears here as a cook, concerned with the tempera-
ture of food rather than with writing. Stein clearly is the writer,
Toklas the (at first reluctant) reader.

This interpretation, however, does not take into account the perspective from which the passage is written. Literally, the account
of Stein's writing of "Ada" becomes inseparable from an account

of how Alice Toklas receives "Ada." Stein's writing has apparently occurred in the atelier, yet the "I" stands in the kitchen, a place to which Stein ("she") repairs as well, as if the atelier—the place where writing occurs in isolation—becomes marginal to the kitchen and dining room, where the writing may be shared through reading what has been written. Reading occurs on a continuum with eating, as an act of subtle and nourishing communion.

The playfulness of tone accords with the playfulness of this exchange in a way that resembles Irigaray's vision of a paradoxical "exchanging [of] selves endlessly and each staying herself." As a domestic quarrel, this dialogue marks a difference between the two figures; they have a "difference," and they differ from each other. The difference is playful in its simplicity: one likes it hot; the other likes it cold. Through language, each asserts a position defined in opposition to the other.

Yet this difference does not cover the whole picture. In the midst of this establishment of difference, a curious event takes place: the two figures seem to merge, their boundaries becoming less distinct ("exchanging selves endlessly"). The absence of quotation marks adds to the confusion; for example, after we hear that "She came in," we come to an "I" in the following sentence appearing at first to be Alice's, yet revealed to be part of a statement made by "She" (Gertrude).[23] We enact a double-take; for an important moment, we believe that this "I" is both Alice's *and* Gertrude's, for the visual marks by which one woman's discourse differs from another's have disappeared. The insistent repetition and dance of the pronouns confuse us as well. The pattern in the first five sentences looks like this:

> I   I
> She
> I   you   she
> I
> she   you

The confusion springs largely from the fact that the speaker/writer Alice B. Toklas (the "I") continually quotes the speaker Gertrude Stein. The quotation, one assumes, was first Stein's, but by its new presence in Toklas's written text, it becomes Toklas's also, inasmuch as she repeats it. Further, as we must remind ourselves, this Toklas is not Toklas at all, but Gertrude Stein, who names herself Toklas. The figure Gertrude Stein assumes the voice of Alice B. Toklas, who quotes Gertrude Stein. To add to the general ambiguity, although Stein writes the portrait under discussion, this portrait forms a representation of Alice.[24]

This brilliant confusion is richly humorous and clever, but it is not merely clever. Stein is suggesting something important about dialogue itself, specifically about the forms that may emerge out of a dialogue between two figures who are similar but different. Such dialogue becomes a metaphor for a certain form of relationship, where two "ones" may be distinguished, yet where the boundaries may also become confused and even disappear. Although difference exists, marked by the "I" and the "she," this difference comes to seem less like an end in itself than the necessary starting point for merging and identification, just as (in this puzzling circle) identification becomes the starting point for difference. Neither "difference" nor "identification" may be defined without the other term, just as this "I" comes into definition through the countering of this "she." What is at stake here is not only the content of the dialogue, or its progression toward a resolution (although such a resolution is often there: "And then we ate our supper"), but the dialogue's metaphoric enactment of a *relationship between* two figures, in a continually shifting exchange that is also an interchange—not only of words spoken, but of the position from which these words are spoken, so that the apparent speaking subject may also become the object spoken about, just as the object may become the subject.[25]

The implications of this form of dialogue unfold further if we turn to the "portrait" generating the dialogue recorded between these two women in *The Autobiography*. Although this three-page portrait, as Stein/Toklas says, is called "Ada," not "Alice," in the original form read by Alice it was still overtly her own portrait. On one level, Alice becomes the object of observation and vision, while Gertrude Stein is the observing, "painting" subject. Yet, as the portrait itself makes clear, Stein's use of dialogue works toward the blurring of such boundaries between the subject and object of representation.

In its last paragraph, "Ada" bursts lyrically into an erotic and dialogic exchange. Yet before this ecstatic dialogue can take place, a more familiar story must be retold and superseded, a narrative about a family in which Ada enters at first only as "a sister" and "a daughter," not as an equal and autonomous speaking subject.

The narrator does not even name her until halfway through her own portrait. "Ada" begins in a literary world close to the stories in *Three Lives*; the excitement "Gertrude Stein" feels in showing Alice Toklas this new piece may have sprung from the knowledge that the portrait shows a clear way to defeat this earlier form of family narrative.

The piece begins, in fact, not with "Ada," but with "A *da*," a father, named Abram Colhard, who is clearly a patriarchal figure in relation to his children. His patronym contains punning implications: "collared" (he collared his son and his daughter); "call-hard" (he makes use of language as a commanding and authoritative force); and "cold-hard," which suggests his cold-heart-edness as well as his male power.[26] The narrative in this early section involves a struggle between father and son, where the son does not wish to do what the father "wanted him to be doing" (*G&P*, 14). Although the "it"—"Barnes Colhard did not say he would not do it but he did not do it" (*G&P*, 14)—remains unnamed, we gather that it represents the career urged upon the son by the father. The father attempts to author his son's story, to make him do one "thing." Yet the son resists the father's narrative by his own digressions and oscillations: "He did it and then he did not do it" (*G&P*, 14). The father, like the matriarchal and patriarchal figures of *Three Lives*, shows a link to sequential and historical narrative embodied in the history that "Ada" rehearses at the beginning.

As one of a long line of Steinian dictators or "officers," Abram Colhard founds his narrative form upon monologue. The son may agree or disagree with the father, listen or not listen; but the son himself cannot initiate his own "tellings." When Ada's relationship with her father finally enters the narrative (after the mother's death), again dialogue does not take place. She tells her father of her unhappiness, for example, yet "he never said anything" (*G&P*, 15). Not responding to her stories with stories of his own, he remains simply silent. Any saying on either of their parts leads to the silence of the other, for even when the father finally "said something" about the daughter's declaration that she will leave him, his saying of something results only in her saying of "nothing": "then they both said nothing and then it was that she went away from them" (*G&P*, 16).

Ada's participation in the story actually begins, not with her father, but with her mother:

She had been a very good daughter to her mother. She and her mother had always told very pretty stories to each other. Many old men loved to hear her tell these stories to her mother. . . . She did sometimes think her mother would be pleased with a story that did not please her mother, when her mother later was sicker the daughter knew that there were some stories she could tell her that would not please her mother. Her mother died and really mostly altogether the mother and the daughter had told each other stories very happily together. (*G&P*, 15)

Language assumes a different role within this mother-daughter relationship: whereas the father uses language to give directions, to tell what he wants, here words become the medium for "very pretty stories." At least some mutuality of relation exists here. Each figure, mother and daughter, tells stories to the other, instead of one telling and the other listening in silence, as Barnes Colhard must listen, or as Ada must listen to her father. The "relation" of mother to daughter is such that the mutual "relation" of stories can occur.

Yet the dialogue, the mutual telling, has flaws, hinted at by Ada's description as "a very good daughter to her mother." Ada may tell stories, but, as a daughter, she may not tell all. What she is not allowed to articulate, one guesses, is her own desire; in the light of the subsequent loving relationship, she specifically desires a woman. Such an expression of her desire, from her mother's viewpoint and in her mother's language, is not "pretty." The unspeakable must be silenced, finding no place in this prettier round of fictions. Significantly, these stories are not private. They do not form figures for an intimacy that makes the circle of telling and listening an inviolable continuum. The stories seem, instead, to be for public (and masculine) consumption: "Many old men loved to hear her tell these stories to her mother." The interest these "old men" take in the stories between a mother and a daughter marks the potentially disturbing attachment of this particular female world to the world of the father and of men. For, although Ada now has a voice, she still remains silent in another sense: her desire, which stands outside the bounds of the familial and the heterosexual, must remain unarticulated just as it must within her father's patriarchal discourse. The old men's "liking" of the mother and sometimes of the daughter suggests that the stories act merely as counters in a game of heterosexual attraction engaged in by the mother, a game that, because they are "old" men, may involve the mother's desire to please those in power. The stories may be about a similar realm of heterosexual "liking." Ada is not named within the text until after her mother has died, as if she herself is the thing that could not be named in her mother's presence, just as she is not named within the narrative about her father.

This situation resembles the knot of family relationships that Luce Irigaray's "When Our Lips Speak Together" attempts to escape: "I love you who are neither mother (pardon me, mother, for I prefer a woman) nor sister, neither daughter nor son. I love you —and there, where I love you, I don't care about the lineage of our fathers and their desire for imitation men."[27] For Irigaray, the mother is merely one member of a larger family structure in which the father dominates. As a mother, she participates in the "imitation" of men, both in the sense that she produces imitations of the father in her sons, and in the sense that she serves as a mirror for him, denying her autonomous female identity. An equal love between an "I" and a "you" can come into existence only after the "woman" substitutes for the "mother" and family lineage vanishes from the picture entirely.[28]

In "Ada" too, only after patriarchal familial obstructions to genuine dialogue have disappeared may the rich doubling of two figures occur. The final lyrical paragraph enacts the engendering of dialogue:

She came to be happier than anybody else who was living then. It is easy to believe this thing. She was telling some one, who was loving every story that was charming. Some one who was living was almost always listening. Some one who was loving was almost always listening. That one who was loving was almost always listening. That one who was loving was telling about being one then listening. That one being loving was then telling stories having a beginning and a middle and an ending. That one was then one always completely listening. Ada was then one and all her living then one completely telling stories that were charming, completely listening to stories having a beginning and a middle and an ending. Trembling was all living, living was all loving, some one was then the other one. Certainly this one was loving this Ada then. And certainly Ada all her living then was happier in living than any one else who ever could, who was, who is, who ever will be living. (G&P, 16)

As this paragraph reveals, "Ada" moves from the nondialogic to dialogue, from narrative to a circling nonnarrative.[29] In the leap outside the traditional lines from father to son or from mother to daughter, the portrait "Ada" leaps both thematically and formally out of historical time and narrative. Time, marked by a series of "thens," becomes uncertain and immeasurable, just as the participles ("living," "loving," "telling") suggest the continuous and uninterrupted flow of such movements rather than precise, sequential action. Although movement occurs within the language's rhythmic and repetitive waves, this motion cannot be fastened to historical progression.[30]

This concern with moving outside of history links Stein with the larger American tradition of narrative. As Richard Brodhead has shown in *Hawthorne, Melville, and the Novel*, the narratives of Hawthorne and Melville manifest a conflict between linear forms of narrative and lyrical moments of epiphany, which tend to disrupt historical lines. His account in turn echoes that of Sacvan Bercovitch and John Lynen, who link the tension between temporal and atemporal modes in American art to an older Puritan habit of thought.[31] From Stein's twentieth-century perspective, the issue is no longer a religious one, where competing narrative styles reflect tension within an older religious ideology, but a secular one, marking a struggle between linear modes of narrative identified with public and patriarchal forms of discourse, and narrative possibilities grounded in alternative social and erotic relations. In "Ada," Stein attaches the leap out of history and story to a specifically female-to-female mode of relationship able to escape from the father's and mother's story at least within the utopian constructs of language. In other compositions, although the female specificity may disappear or become obscured, the structure of dialogue among variously gendered (or ungendered) subjects remains a challenge to this story.

The beauty of this passage in "Ada" lies partly in its mystery: who is this "some one"? Is the "some one" also "that one"? The absence of a name apart from Ada's suggests the manifold possibilities of identity. This subject can, at any point, be double, as in "When Our Lips Speak Together," where Irigaray often uses a double subject, distinguished only by a slash ("je/tu").[32] The English word "one," in its openness, can encompass either figure, or both, in shifting patterns. Some distinction is apparent; if there were no difference at all between these two figures, there could be no "telling" and no "listening." Yet the difference, although we know it must be there, becomes highly uncertain through the refusal, in this passage, to name the difference through naming two different names. The impossibility of distinguishing with any certainty which side is which—the impossibility, even, of finding two "sides"—articulates itself directly toward the conclusion: "some one was then the other one." Which other one? Which is the "some" (the "sum"?)?

In this passionate and ongoing dialogue, as in Irigaray's dialogue between "two lips," *what* is told holds less importance than the process of telling and listening. Stein urges us to hear not the substance of two figures' dialogue, but the rhythm of the dialogue's form, which becomes an almost palpable embodiment of the relationship. Although stories act as the bridge, the connector, between the one telling and the one listening, whichever these ones are, it is the bodily and linguistic bond itself which remains primary.[33] "Listening," "living," and "telling," the participles continually repeating, partake also of "loving," just as "loving," with the change of one letter, becomes "living," and "living" metamorphoses into "listening." All of these movements, in all of their intricate, dance-like exchanges, culminate in a "trembling" attached somehow to the final confused merging of "someone was then the other one." Although the sex of the "some one" is not articulated, the fluidity of identity between the "she" and the "one" suggests an identical sexuality. A kind of mirroring occurs here, where the two figures reflect each other and appear often to be identical, yet where enough asymmetry remains to reveal the fact of doubleness (Irigaray's "*living mirrors*"). The title, "Ada," offers an image of this half-symmetry, where the two "a"s represent the same letter, yet where one letter at any point is capital, the other small.

The representation in "Ada" of this linguistic, erotic, and almost continually epiphanic relationship allows us a partial glimpse into the lifelong dialogue between Stein and her companion and lover, Alice Toklas. This dialogue occurred outside the page, yet finds a significant place on the page as well. Although it is important not to reduce Stein's literary forms to biography, it is equally important to remember that, for Stein, relationships of mutual dialogue such as the one in "Ada" bore a resemblance to an actual relationship that surrounded, nurtured, and in a sense continued her writing. The fluctuating boundary between self and other recorded in "Ada" finds a corollary in Stein's playful mingling of art and life. As Neil Schmitz has suggested, Alice found her way into Stein's writing not only as a listening presence, but as a telling one as well, whose daily words appear to have been received by Stein and interwoven with her own. In this sense, Stein's writing partakes of dialogue in its very creation.[34]

"We to": The Play of the Two-Body Relationship

Recent critics have noted the ways in which Stein's experimentation with a language of the body, foregrounding the erotic and emotional aspects of relationship, resonates with Kristeva's theory of the semiotic as a mode of signification present in "the first echolalias of infants as rhythms and intonations anterior to the first phonemes, morphemes, lexemes, and sentences."[35] This presymbolic mode, according to Kristeva, springs from a double disposition: synchronically, from libidinal drives, and diachronically, from a "continuous relation to the mother, which is a bodily relation."[36] For Kristeva, this archaic language finds new form in "poetic language," where signification remains always uncertain and indeterminate, nonsense replaces sense, and rhythm and intonation replace meaning. Language itself undergoes a metamorphosis through the reinsertion of "desire," as in the writings of Céline (one of Kristeva's heroic writers of the semiotic), where, "within the interstices of predication, the rhythm of a drive" emerges and makes itself felt. As Kristeva then urges:

We must also listen to Céline, Artaud, or Joyce, and read their texts in order to understand that the aim of this practice, which reaches us as a language, is, through the signification of the nevertheless transmitted message, not only to impose a music, a rhythm—that is, a polyphony—but also to wipe out sense through nonsense and laughter. This is a difficult operation that obliges the reader not so much to combine significations as to shatter his own judging consciousness in order to grant passage through it to this rhythmic drive constituted by repression and, once filtered through language and its meaning, experienced as jouissance. Could the resistance against modern literature be evidence of an obsession with meaning, of an unfitness for such jouissance?[37]

Kristeva's dialectic between the symbolic and presymbolic modes, however, is a profoundly gendered one. It is no accident that the modernist and post-modernist writers she most often cites are male. Kristeva locates the disruptive semiotic activity in the male infant, who in returning to the mother becomes again continuous with her body. This concept of a return on the part of a questing infant-author allows Kristeva to talk about the semiotic as a transgression of incest taboos. The mother constitutes "the forbidden"; but for whom is she the forbidden? Such "incest" presupposes a male subject. Kristeva draws here on Lacan's concept of the incest prohibition, which occurs at the same time as the ascendancy of the paternal Symbolic, the Law of the Father. As Kristeva argues, it is the "son" who is "permanently at war with the father," if the "father" represents the Symbolic, signifying system of language. The son attempts "to signify what is untenable in the symbolic, nominal, paternal function."[38]

In an important sense, then, in Kristeva's system the "maternal" (signifying the female itself) does not have much say. Although the mother's body is continuous with the body of the infant, and the memory of her body inspires a rearticulation of the (male) infant's presymbolic language, the mother herself has little access to language of any sort. The language she has emerges only through the "echolalias" of the infant and the rhythms and intonations of the writer of "poetic language."

Stein's concern for a dialogue among "others," not between mother and infant, allows a significantly different dynamic to occur, for no longer is there a silent female body to which one male figure illicitly returns. Instead, both "some ones" participate in a shared and spontaneous play of dialogue that involves not a return but, to use a Steinian word, a "recreation." Whereas in Kristeva's theory the female remains absent and silent, Stein asserts the vital presence of the bodily and emotional realm by bringing it powerfully into language, even as she unties the gendered associations of the female with silence, the male with symbolic language. Although this playful dialogic often involves a thwarting of traditional "sense," its purpose is not simply to "wipe out sense," but to suggest other ways of making sense, inclusive of the body's "senses" and sensuality. The element of play in Stein's writing is crucial, for Stein's more free-floating dialogic writing does not accord with a Kristevan agon between the presymbolic and the symbolic, the feminine and the masculine, the antipatriarchal and the patriarchal, the nonlinguistic and the linguistic. The presence in Stein's language of linguistic elements resembling Kristeva's "presymbolic" discourse does not lead primarily to the agonistic and violent acts of language Kristeva celebrates in Céline.

Stein's writing differs from French feminist theories about language, including Kristeva's and Irigaray's, in its intimation that language is an open field, marked by previous usage but not owned or structured wholly by a patriarchy. Because of the belief in language as patriarchal, French feminists must discover alternative modes of discourse in order to disrupt or to escape from this language. Whereas Kristeva finds such an alternative in the "nonsense" of the libidinal drive, attached to the maternal, Irigaray attempts to imagine a new language springing from the double-subject(s) of "two lips," attached to the specifically female body. Although in Irigaray's writing this language can achieve a valuable dialogic form, the agon is never forgotten. Irigaray's two lips speak together with one primary goal: to defeat patriarchal language's reduction of the female to a silent and acquiescent mirror of itself. Stein's purpose is larger, for instead of focusing on the monolith of the Symbolic, she recreates language as a field of immense possibility for the articulation of intimacy as well as difference.

A useful vocabulary for Stein's sense of play may be found in a place at first glance far removed from these feminist theories of language: D. W. Winnicott's theory of transitional objects. Although Winnicott's focus on the mother-infant relation differs from Stein's concern with more free-floating configurations, his identification of a transitional or "potential" space between two "bodies" or two figures resembles Stein's creation of a similar playful space in her dialogic form.[39] Whereas for Winnicott, however, the "play" occurs largely on the part of the child, in Stein's conception the "other" participates equally in the field of imagination. The mother-"object" of object relations theory suddenly comes alive, ready not merely to provide a stable and essentially mute "holding environment" (Winnicott's term), but to enter into the transitional realm herself. Such a movement marks both her leave-taking of the position of "mother" and her entry into language. The Wordsworthian "mute dialogues with [the] Mother's heart" become, in Stein, genuine dialogues, and not with the "heart" only, but with the tongue. What is considered preverbal in object relations theory, as in the Kristevan theory of a nonlinguistic "semiotic," has been relocated by Stein within language itself.

This playful linguistic dialogue occurs in different forms throughout Stein's writing. To explore one of these forms, in which at least two voices appear to be speaking together, I turn to a moving and significant passage from "Patriarchal Poetry." [40] This difficult composition, mingling poetry, essay, and narrative, creates a language playing upon the boundary of the symbolic and the unsymbolic—playing, that is, in the transitional space "between" these simultaneous modes of discourse.

To be we to be to be we to be to be to be we to be we to be to be to be to be to be to be to be we we to be to be to be we to be. Once. To be we to be to be to be we to be. Once. To be to be to be to be to be we to be. Once. To be we to be to be to be. (*YGS*, 114)

This piece of writing—these pieces of writing—or perhaps we should say, this sequence of cries—speaks plurally: "to be we" is a statement, nonsyntactical as it is, of the existence of more than one. Of "t[w]o"? "To be t[w]o"? ("We t[w]o"?) Around the "be," "to" and "we" often cluster, as if they mirror each other: "t[w]o are we and we are t[w]o," or perhaps "we (are) *to be* t[w]o," a possibility for the future.

This "we-ness," on a "symbolic" level, holds an indeterminate significance. This form of discourse, while it suggests different meanings, does not point to meaning directly. No sentence emerges. Signification in a traditional sense has vanished, although another form of "pointing" may occur. We seem to be at one of the farthest reaches of language as we know it. We recognize certain words—"we," "to," "be," "once"—and certain phrases—"to be" resonating back at least as far as Shakespeare's most uncertain character Hamlet[41]—or do we? For, as soon as we think to have hold of the beginnings of recognition, as soon as we begin to bring these recognized words back within the world of signification, the words themselves start to shift beneath (above?) our glance (our touch?), in ways that have a bearing on the possibility of doubleness and mutuality, of shared speech/writing.

In retyping such passages (which Alice B. ["be"?] *T*oklas did), or in rewriting them, in bringing them even closer to one's own hand, one senses their aspect of sensuality more fully: the slightly irregular and varied but continuous rhythm, the rhymes of "we" and "be," the relief of pauses between phrases or surrounding the "once," come out even more palpably. Pauses become breaths. Words become sounds, intonations, uttered in privacy, to the point of excess ("to" is also "too"). These "words"—designs on paper that we have recognized as words—present themselves to us in visual and aural forms. We hear a near babble, a rejoicing in sound. "We" is also "whee!"—a sound, half voice, half breath, of delight, spoken in the affirmative ("oui"). We begin, through the insistence of the visual patterns of letters on the page, to see these words almost as pieces with which to play. We note that most of these "words" hold two letters together; each grouping is double, with each letter almost touching, and positioned next to, another. Where there are not two letters, there are four ("once"), as if the two have attached themselves to another two, or have multiplied.[42]

Stein returns us here to the graphic dimension of writing in a form that allies itself with modernist painting's effort to explore the materiality of its medium and to break through its own signifying conditions. For modernist painters, the use of abstract and simplified forms, the achievement of an effect of spontaneity, and the emphasis upon the canvas's surface and the medium of paint, often signaled a conscious return to the primitive or the primal. Picasso's and Braque's early cubist experimentations, for instance, gained inspiration in part from the abstracted forms of African art.[43] Stein, however, posits the primal, not as a biological or a historical source, but as a linguistic one. Language itself, in both its signifying and nonsignifying dimensions, becomes the new source, offering an illimitable matrix of sound, form, and meaning with which "we" may create ("to be").

This matrix, unlike Kristeva's silent and absent mother, is full and voluble.[44] As "we" play with language, language speaks with us. Our writing is always double, as Stein suggests in another passage in "Patriarchal Poetry":

I double you, of course you do. You double me, very likely to be. You double I double I double you double. I double you double me I double you you double me. (*YGS*, 115)

The beauty of this formal balancing, this calm and happy interweaving of "I" with "you," suggests again the utopian dimension of Stein's project. For while mothers may suppress the daughters' stories through their domination and alliance with fathers, language allows the possibility for a democratic, nonhierarchic mutuality in which the I and the you can participate in an unlimited exchange. Stein's use of the gender-neutral pronouns, "I," "you," and "we," suggests the way in which this leap beyond hierarchy is also a leap beyond gender. She creates couples that could contain any combinations of gender, in a pleasurably polymorphous field of dialogue.

PART II
The Poetics of Intimacy

: 3 :

The Caressing of Nouns: Representation and the Female Body

I caressed completely caressed and addressed a noun.
(LIA, 231)

It does not need that a poem should be long. Every word was once a poem. Every new relation is a new word.
(Emerson, "The Poet")

Stein grounds her poetics of dialogue in a concept of representation implicit in her compositions and her essays. Although her mode of representation rarely acts directly, through referential language, she often insists on the reality of a world expressed within her words.[1] This reality tends to enter the writing obliquely, allowing itself to be sensed rather than known or seen. In place of "a system to point-ing," as Stein puts it in *Tender Buttons*, an intricate configuration of relationship emerges: not only between words and "objects," but between the writer and the words, and between the writer and the "objects" sensed through the words.

In her attempt to render the world present within language, Stein, like most other modernists, enters into a dialogue with Romanticism. This assertion may at first sound surprising, in that Stein so rarely mentions the Romantics and makes no claim for her project as a Romantic one. To the contrary, she usually presents herself within her essays wholly as a modernist, "creating the modern composition" (*CAE*, 8), a composition preeminently of form.[2] A study of Stein's poetics, however, both in her important 1935 essay "Poetry and Grammar" and in her poetic experimentation from 1910 to 1920, suggests that her modernist project engages Romantic issues in a boldly revisionary way. Central to her concern with Romanticism is its structuring of representation in terms of gender: the ascription of masculinity to the individual poetic voice and of femininity to a sacral and essentially silent nature.[3]

In this chapter, I shall focus on Stein's dialogue with two Romantics: Emerson and Keats. *Tender Buttons* (1912), as one of Stein's earliest and most important experiments in the transformation of the visionary "eye" and the objects it can(not) see, represents both her alliance with and her difference from Emerson. Although Stein shares Emerson's sense of a sacral nature, within which the daily fact appears miraculous, and although she too attaches this natural landscape to the female, she questions and transforms his visionary project, with its impulse to absorb the "not-me" into the "me," and specifically into the transformative "I"/"eye." Stein substitutes for Emerson's appropriative and finally isolated vision a profoundly dialogic modality of touch and sound. She attempts, as with much of her writing of the period 1910–20, to bring the female body into writing in a way that unsettles the binary opposition of masculine and feminine. As a further comparison of Stein's love poem/play "Lifting Belly" (1915–17) with Keats's poetry will suggest, Stein's movement from vision to the other senses resembles Keats's "negative capability," his sense of openness to the realm of nature. Whereas for Keats, however, a female nature becomes ultimately dangerous to the singular masculine poetic voice, Stein reimagines the act of poetry as a dialogic embrace in which writing exists on a continuum with the body, and in which poetic voice is always at least double. The female body, in this sense, can engage in the act of writing, just as writing becomes a domain open to the masculine or the feminine, categories which again shift and become unstable.[4]

Roses and Roses

A valuable entrance into this intricate Steinian dialogue with Romanticism may be found in one of Stein's shortest and best-known meditations on representation: the simple, riddling, and lyrical "Rose is a rose is a rose is a rose." The line became a kind of signature for Stein and Toklas: in *The Autobiography of Alice B. Toklas*, Toklas claims (via Stein) to have "found" it as she retyped one of Stein's love poems, "Sacred Emily," after which she "insisted upon putting it as a device on the letter paper, on the table linen and anywhere that [Stein] would permit that I would put it" (*ABT*,

169). Inscribed around two overlapping circles, the words form a double wedding ring. The women touched the words, the words touched the women, both literally and metaphorically.[5]

This ring of roses plunges us immediately into the question of representation, for the movement from the word "rose" to an actual rose, or even to a metaphoric rose (a woman, a love) is not as simple as the line may suggest. In "Poetry and Grammar" Stein offers an interpretation of her riddle about roses:

> When I said.
> A rose is a rose is a rose.
> And then later made that into a ring I made poetry and what did I do I caressed completely caressed and addressed a noun. (*LIA*, 231)[6]

What is important in this formulation is not the capacity of "rose" to represent, but the relationship between the author and the word. The noun becomes a palpable entity, inviting and participating in a relationship of love. As she suggests in the same essay:

> But and that is a thing to be remembered you can love a name and if you love a name then saying that name any number of times only makes you love it more, more violently more persistently more tormentedly. Anybody knows how anybody calls out the name of anybody one loves. And so that is poetry really loving the name of anything and that is not prose. Yes any of you can know that. (*LIA*, 231–32)

For Stein, the author becomes "anybody," for she is suggesting a form of poetry that is potential to everybody; as she observes, revising Emerson, "So as everybody has to be a poet, what was there to do" (*LIA*, 237).[7] This "anybody" and "everybody" attempt to enter into a relation with language in a sense incorporating both consciousness and the body: as she observes, poetry is "a state of *knowing and feeling* a name" (*LIA*, 233, emphasis added). Words become palpable entities, with weight, volume, and value, capable of being "caressed," even as they come so close to what "anybody" knows and feels that they seem almost to be a part of the one(s) who caress(es) them.[8]

"Rose is a rose is a rose is a rose," then, renders a situation of love. The noun "rose" is precisely, in this instance, what Stein —and anybody else—"loves," "tormentedly," "persistently," and "violently." By calling out to it again and again, she calls out its full weight and value as a word. She offers in this ring an example of "insistence": as she defines this concept in another 1935 essay, "Portraits and Repetition," "Then we have insistence insistence that in its emphasis can never be repeating, because insistence is always alive and if it is alive it is never saying anything in the same way because emphasis can never be the same not even when it is most the same that is when it has been taught" (*LIA*, 171). Each instance of the word "rose," as Stein would claim, is a new one. The word, in appearing not once but many times, draws attention away from its status as a referential sign, which is so familiar to us that we can no longer experience the word's freshness. The word, as a word, renews its immediacy and liveliness, its openness to our caresses, by its insistent and multiple appearances.

"Poetry and Grammar," as a twentieth-century response to Emerson's "The Poet," argues in this sense for a new poetic ground. For Emerson, the poet is the rare being so finely tuned as to receive nature's impressions to "the quick," so that the impressions "compel the reproduction of themselves in speech." The poet must translate the poetry already inherent within nature's symbols and signs: "For poetry was all written before time was, and whenever we are so finely organized that we can penetrate into that region where the air is music, we hear those primal warblings and attempt to write them down, but we lose ever and anon a word or a verse and substitute something of our own, and thus miswrite the poem."[9] Emerson conceives of divine truths already present within the "primal warblings" of nature, to be heard correctly and translated into words by the poet. Words form correspondences with universal and divine truths. For Stein, this concept of correspondences becomes irrelevant. She shifts the focus from the poet's relation to divine nature to the poet's relation to language itself, in which a form of divinity resides, not wholly beyond words, but within them. The "violent," "persistent," "tormented," and unquenchable "love" toward words held by the-poet-as-anyone marks Stein's transposition of a mysterious and compelling divine aura to language.

This Steinian love of the word, however, links with a second and less fully articulated love of something outside the word. Stein's emphasis on the word's palpable presence apart from representation is contradicted by a further concern with the reality "behind" the rose, a concern more closely resembling Emerson's poetic project. To return to the earlier quote: "Anybody knows how anybody calls out the name *of anybody one loves. And so that is poetry* really loving the name of anything" (*LIA*, 232, emphasis added). One may love a name, Stein implies, because one loves the figure it names. The name represents the loved object, who is brought into language indirectly via the name. In this sense, Stein allies herself with the "early poetry" of Greek, Hebrew, and Middle English: "Think of all that early poetry, think of Homer, think of Chaucer, think of the Bible and you will see what I mean you will really realize that they were drunk with nouns, to name to know how to name earth sea and sky and all that was in them was enough to make them live and love in names, and that is what poetry is it is a state of knowing and feeling a name" (*LIA*, 233). Although to be "drunk with nouns" suggests an emphasis on the words as loved entities, the drunkenness connects with "*to know how to name* earth sea and sky and all that was in them.*" This is also, as Stein observes, "what Adam and Eve did and if you like it is what anybody does" (*LIA*, 229).

However, the addition of "Eve" here, and then of "anybody," suggests that Stein's concept of representation is not a traditional one. Stein diverges emphatically from an Adamic tradition of representation, in which a one-to-one correspondence is discovered and then fixed between each signifier and the object it signifies. For Stein, what is poetic about these early namings is the liveliness of the word and of the thing, the freshness of the bond discovered. Yet she argues against an acceptance of earlier namings; just because they seemed lively once does not mean that they remain alive. Stein articulates a familiar modernist predicament, understood preeminently by Whitman (and, although Stein does not mention him, Emerson), yet shared by "any human being living" in the twentieth century:

Naturally, and one may say that is what made Walt Whitman naturally that made the change in the form of poetry, that we who had known the names so long did not get a thrill from just knowing them. We that is any human being living has inevitably to feel the thing anything being existing, but the name of that thing of that anything is no longer anything to thrill any one except children. So as everybody has to be a poet, what was there to do. (*LIA*, 237)[10]

As she articulates it here, the object of poetry is "to feel the thing anything being existing": to achieve an intimacy with the process and movement, the very liveliness, of the world, now described not in an Emersonian language of divine truths, but in terms of a highly democratic and unessentialist "anything." She is concerned primarily with the presence of "things," any things: she wishes "to see that I could find out how to know *that [things] were there* by their names or by replacing their names" (*LIA*, 235, emphasis added).

Stein's concern for a lively language resembles Emerson's. As he observes in "The Poet," "Every word was once a poem," and further:

The poets made all the words, and therefore language is the archives of history, and, if we must say it, a sort of tomb of the muses. For though the origin of most of our words is forgotten, each word was at first a stroke of genius, and obtained currency because for the moment it symbolized the world to the first speaker and to the hearer. The etymologist finds the deadest word to have been once a brilliant picture.[11]

Although this original "brilliance" rests within words as a potential, the poet must create a new luster with "dead" words through discovering, if not new words, then new relationships among words: "every new relation is a new word." In forming these "new words," the poet becomes "the only teller of news": "The poet has a new thought; he has a whole new experience to unfold."[12]

Stein appears to make precisely this bold claim to originality through her assertion that she "discovered [in writing *Tender Buttons*] everything . . . and its name . . . I had always known it and its name but all the same I did discover it" (*LIA*, 235). Her act of naming, however, is more complicated, for her own "discovery" is not of absolute or divine correspondences, fixed in a new system of reference; to the contrary, her discovery is of the moment, particular to the instances of her own seeing. "Anybody" may make such "discoveries" about things, not just "The [one] Poet."

Further, as Stein suggests in an even more radical revision of Emerson, the presence of the object may be communicated not necessarily through the "real" name—the conventional name—at all, but rather through "replacing" the too-familiar name with a new one. Whereas Emerson expands the act of naming things to include either "their appearance" or "their essence," he asserts that the poet as "the Namer or Language-maker" must "giv[e] to every one its own name and not another's."[13] In her *Tender Buttons* period (around 1912) Stein attempts a form of "naming things that would not invent names, but mean names without naming them," just as Shakespeare "in the forest of Arden had created a forest without mentioning the things that make a forest. You feel it all but he does not name its names" (*LIA*, 236). When she attributes names to things, she attempts to "see that I could find out how to know that they were there by their names or by replacing their names" (*LIA*, 235) with new ones. Emerson's concern for each entity's "own name" gives way in Stein to a concern for a new name that cannot be "owned."

Stein's dialogue with an Emersonian tradition may be illuminated by the relation between her "Rose is a rose is a rose is a rose" and Emerson's famous passage about the rose in "Self-Reliance," a passage in all likelihood familiar to Stein:

Man is timid and apologetic; he is no longer upright; he dares not say "I think," "I am," but quotes some saint or sage. He is ashamed before the blade of grass or the blowing rose. These roses under my window make no reference to former roses or to better ones; they are for what they are; they exist with God today. There is no time to them. There is simply the rose; it is perfect in every moment of its existence.[14]

Emerson suggests here the sheer presence, immediacy, and uniqueness of the actual "roses under my window." "The rose" assumes a sacral quality, as Emerson's language describing the rose evokes a theological tradition in which God is timeless, "perfect," and completely and wholly present: "they are for what they are" suggests the movement of God's "I am that I am" into the sphere of nature. In this romantic theophany, nature *is* God, just as God is in the landscape. Stein substitutes for Emerson's emphasis on the rose's reality a new emphasis on the word "rose," yet in this movement from the real to language she attempts to salvage the sacral qualities from a romantic vision of nature for which, at least on the surface, she makes no ontological claims. Language itself—the word "rose" —becomes the locus of timelessness and perfection; as she might restate Emerson: "words are for what they are."

This new emphasis on language finds a certain correspondence in Emerson's belief that consciousness is a place in which nature becomes transformed. As he states in "Nature":

[The poet] unfixes the land and the sea, makes them revolve around the axis of his primary thought, and disposes them anew. Possessed himself by a heroic passion, he uses matter as symbols of it. The sensual man conforms thoughts to things; the poet conforms things to his thoughts. The one esteems nature as rooted and fast; the other, as fluid, and impresses his being thereon.[15]

Yet the imperialism implicit in this vision of the male poet as he who "conforms things to his thoughts" and "impresses his being" upon nature is what Stein hopes to avoid by her partial emphasis on words as unreferential entities. She emphasizes, in this sense, not an author's imposition of language upon the world, but language's completeness in and of itself. She imagines, not Emerson's "transfiguration which all material objects undergo through the passion of the poet,"[16] but the passion of "anybody," who loves words *as* material objects: "poetry is essentially the discovery, the love, *the passion for the name* of anything" (*LIA*, 235, emphasis added).

Emerson's sense of the ultimate subordination of nature to the mind in his essay "Nature" reflects a deep cultural bias that Stein attempts to redress. The association of nature with the female, in opposition to culture (including language) and the male, marks the devaluation and even the burial of nature as "mother." As Margaret Homans argues in *Bearing the Word* about this central nineteenth-century configuration of tropes, "language and culture depend on the death or absence of the mother and on the quest of substitutes for her," the primary substitute being language's figurations.[17] Emerson reveals an extreme ambivalence about Nature as his "beautiful mother" that suggests his acceptance of this hierarchy. After stating, as a summation of his argument about idealism, that "It appears that motion, poetry, physical and intellectual science, and religion, all tend to affect our convictions of the reality of the external world," he makes a guilty turn back to this world:

But I own there is something ungrateful in expanding too curiously the particulars of the general proposition, that all culture tends to imbue us with idealism. I have no hostility to nature, but a child's love to it. I expand and live in the warm day like corn and melons. Let us speak her fair. I do not wish to fling stones at my beautiful mother, nor soil my gentle nest. I only wish to indicate the true position of nature in regard to man, wherein to establish man all right education tends; as the ground which to attain is the object of human life, that is, of man's connection with nature. Culture inverts the vulgar views of nature, and brings the mind to call that apparent which it uses to call real, and that real which it uses to call visionary. Children, it is true, believe in the external world. The belief that it appears only, is an afterthought, but with culture this faith will as surely arise on the mind as did the first.[18]

Emerson's sense of the sacral "rose" recurs here in only a partial sense, for he places the elements of nature in a context that makes nature's presence completely secondary to (patriarchal) culture. His protestation of "a child's love to [Nature]" becomes seriously undercut by his assertion that the man's own consciousness becomes the locus of the real and thus supersedes the child's sense of belief in nature. As a "corn" or a "melon," one notes, given this dichotomizing effort, Emerson could not write "Nature." His vivid protestation that he does not "wish to fling stones at my beautiful mother, nor soil my gentle nest" suggests, in fact, the opposite; for by putting Nature in her "true position," he is able to transcend her mute vulgarity and enter the realm of the ideal.

Stein's foregrounding of nouns as caressed objects in their own right, without any necessary reference to objects, marks her effort to avoid a rigidity of distinction between the "me" and the "not-me," consciousness and nature, or language and its objects, since the words do not attempt to impose upon or to subordinate the world but to "let it alone to be," as she puts it in "Patriarchal Poetry" (*YGS*, 113). Stein, however, like Emerson in his most positive mode, retains a love of the actual rose beyond her expressed love of "rose" as a word. Her difference from Emerson lies in her awareness of the ideology implicit in naming this "rose" directly, in describing the rose and thereby translating the rose's immediate and visible presence into language. Like Emerson and other Romantics, she associates reality with the female; the landscape glimpsed in much of her writing is that of an obscure but potent female body. To represent this landscape, however, is to reenter Romantic poetics, wherein nature holds a secondary and object status as the great and mute Mother who may be "soiled" and upon whose absence poetry depends. Stein's attempt to bring together her two impulses —toward the word as entity, and the world as made present in the word—represents an attempt to bring the female world into her writing without having to ensure its absence through figuration. Only an unreferential language can call her "Arden" into existence.

Tender Buttons: The Slanting Light
of Representation

bend more slender accents than have ever been necessary,
shine in the darkness necessarily.
                                    (Tender Buttons, SW, 468)

In her essay "Portraits and Repetition" (1935), Stein describes *Tender Buttons* as a form of painting with words. In making portraits "of rooms and food and everything," she attempted to add a concern with the visual to her earlier preoccupations with "listening and talking," demonstrated in the portraits of Matisse and Picasso (*LIA*, 188, 189). Through this entrance into the arena of the visual, Stein focuses her dialogue with Emerson upon the intersection of representation and the visible world, carefully distinguishing her mode of vision from the activities of an Emersonian "eye."

Stein's desire to avoid a form of representation binding her subjects to their familiar and conventional descriptions culminates in the attempt to move beyond description entirely, to a more immediate rendering of the objects as they appear in the present instant of her perception. She thought of this problem of representation as one shared by modern painters:

This is the great difficulty that bothered anybody creating anything in this generation. The painters naturally were looking, that was their occupation and they had too to be certain that looking was not confusing itself with remembering. Remembering with them takes the form of suggesting in their painting in place of having actually created the thing in itself that they are painting. (*LIA*, 188–89)

In her interview with Robert Bartlett Haas, Stein completes this explanation of her method as a painterly one:

I used to take objects on a table, like a tumbler or any kind of object and try to get the picture of it clear and separate in my mind and create a word relationship between the word and the thing seen.[19]

In this sense, Stein claims a project of mimesis, although, as Wendy Steiner suggests, this is a mimesis that insists upon the independence of its subjects from any familiar categories: Stein gives us, in Steiner's terms, "a program for a text-object—a piece of writing that is to have the very degree and intensity of movement that its subject has, that becomes independent and unique in order to render with immediacy the independence and uniqueness, the essence, of its subject."[20]

The most cursory reading of *Tender Buttons*, however, causes us to reconsider Stein's claims about making "still lives" of actual "tumblers" and other objects. Although at certain points, especially in the first section, entitled "Objects," the subjects of Stein's perceptions seem relatively sure, partly through her use of titles, the writing appears less concerned either with "looking" or with the mimesis of actual objects than with the attempt to discover relationships, both among words as loved objects, passionately called upon, and between these words and the world. *Tender Buttons*, as Stein observes in "Poetry and Grammar," is "poetry" in Stein's sense of the word. Furthermore, the "world" goes beyond the actual "Objects," "Food," and "Rooms" (the three sections of *Tender Buttons*) upon which Stein claims to have concentrated. This world encompasses the larger, more shadowy, and more mysterious realm of a female landscape, to be glimpsed in fragments and partially rendered, yet never completely "seen" or directly represented.[21]

As Pamela Hadas has suggested, the circumlocutions of *Tender Buttons* may actually lead to a half-submerged narrative. The piece may be interpreted in part as an exploration of differences, between words as between people. Specifically, Hadas uncovers an autobiographical "story" underlying *Tender Buttons*: "a story of what we may surmise was Gertrude Stein's inner and outer experience of the period 1910–13, when *Tender Buttons* was incipient or actually being written."[22] The most crucial change in Stein's life during that period ("The change has come") was Alice's entrance into the ménage at 27, rue de Fleurus, and Leo Stein's gradual disaffection and eventual departure. As Hadas observes, "the permanent relationship with Alice could be seen as restitution for the loss of Leo," a loss that was considerable and painful for Gertrude Stein, just as "the writing of *Tender Buttons* itself seems intended to fill a real or at least potential vacancy."[23] Hadas makes a persuasive case for the presence of this theme of loss and restitution, and of the corollary theme of the difficulties of separation. In this light, both Leo and Alice form presences inhabiting the private spaces of these "Rooms," and coming together amid these "Objects" (with different "objects," or purposes, in mind, and different "objections" to each other) and around the table presenting all these "Foods." The places and things of daily life appear in *Tender Buttons*, then, refracted through the lens of Stein's emotions of loss and happiness, confusion and (at moments) clarity.

As Hadas observes, however, this work is "at least as naturally 'overdetermined' as most dreams."[24] I shall focus less on the auto-biographical dimension of this "dream" than on the way in which *Tender Buttons* represents a highly imaginative attempt to call a certain presence into existence within the very writing: a presence "dreamed" about differently by different readers. This presence, as I interpret it, is a female one; it may be grounded in the actual figure of Alice Toklas, as Neil Schmitz suggests, yet it also expresses a yearning, in a larger sense, for a loved female presence that goes beyond any one figure.[25] If there is no "centre"—"Act so that there is no use in a centre" ("Rooms," *SW*, 498)—there may still be "an occupation"—"There was an occupation" ("Rooms," *SW*, 498)—a word signifying both the writing itself and the way in which the writing may come to be "occupied" by a mythic and scattered female presence, may in fact make "room" for this presence, and prepare her way: "A preparation is given to the ones preparing. They do not eat who mention silver and sweet" ("Rooms," *SW*, 498).

The "buttons" of *Tender Buttons*, in one sense, are the words creating the composition. Stein thought about language in *Tender Buttons* as a medium closely akin to paint; her method, according to this metaphor, was to apply different textures, amounts, and colors of paint with different strokes onto the canvas of the page.[26] It is this dimension of words that she describes in her interview with Haas: "I took individual words and thought about them until I got their weight and volume complete and put them next to another word."[27] One of the major influences in this painterly method, as Stein suggests, is Cézanne, and it is his use of paint that finds a similar spirit and motivation, even ideology, in Stein. She notes especially his "evenness," the even strokes across the canvas, the even value given to different blocks of color and shape. Each corner is allowed equal weight, equal importance. There is no hierarchy, for our eye travels everywhere. There is no one center, but a whole geography where the notion of a center is irrelevant. For Stein, this approach had in it the essence of what she calls "democracy"; and, as Donald Sutherland and Jayne Walker have argued, this radically unhierarchical sense of things is crucial to her literary project, in form and content.[28]

As "buttons" Stein's words manifest an equality with each other; separated from the original places to which they were sewn, and appearing within new and unusual contexts, these buttons call our attention to the value they hold outside of their capacity to represent: their sound, their shape, their rhythm and length, their appearance in relation to the buttons on either side of them. Buttons are important for Stein by virtue of their simplicity, smallness, and ordinariness; these are objects to be held by "anybody," on any day, yet in their different shapes, colors, and designs they present a figure for a continually changing surface. Stein seems to proffer them to us, to "tender" them. They become units of exchange, small gifts offered "tenderly," and to be handled with tenderness by the receiver.

In a further sense, the "tenderness" of these "buttons" is a human and bodily one. Children may be called "buttons," as a term of endearment, just like other loved creatures, or parts of their bodies, as in "button-nose" or "belly-button." The smallness of such an entity suggests its capacity to be held and handled; the familiarity of the name suggests closeness and relationship. In a more specific sense, "button" may call up images or parts of the female body. In all of these senses, *Tender Buttons*, as a body of words, offers its buttons for our handling—"It certainly showed no obligation and perhaps if borrowing is not natural there is some use in giving" ("Glazed Glitter," *SW*, 461).

Tenderness occurs between the author-lover and the words, then; yet the words evoke a further tenderness toward a loved object (or objects), just as in "Poetry and Grammar" the calling out of the names one loves intimates a further love of something "real." In her interview with Haas, Stein acknowledged that her painterly approach to words as the focus and medium of her art could not resist "sense" entirely: "I found out very soon that there is no such thing as putting [words] together without sense. It is impossible to put them together without sense. I made innumerable efforts to make words write without sense and found it impossible. Any human being putting down words had to make sense out of them."[29] The "sense" made by the surprising relationships and choices of words in *Tender Buttons* at many points begins to approach more conventional meaning, yet this "sense" of a meaning just on the other side of the words speaks more to the intuition than to rational certitude. The language nudges us toward meaning, but deflects our efforts to comprehend any meaning fully or in a sustained way: "The teasing is tender and trying and thoughtful" ("Sugar," *SW*, 486).

The opening of *Tender Buttons* addresses our "sense" in a "tender" "teasing" that is "trying": it "tries" us in its difficulty and thoughtfulness, as it tries to rethink poetic language and representation. The first "object" is titled "a carafe."[30]

A CARAFE, THAT IS A BLIND GLASS

A kind in glass and a cousin, a spectacle and nothing strange a single hurt color and an arrangement in a system to pointing. All this and not ordinary, not unordered in not resembling. The difference is spreading. (*SW*, 461)

If, for a moment, we take Stein's "still life" literally, a fairly "ordinary" object may be glimpsed here, one made of a "glass" that is not transparent ("blind"), filled with a liquid (perhaps a wine, *vin "ordinaire"*) that looks deep purple ("a single hurt color") and that somehow "points" (upward?). As with most of the objects and foods in *Tender Buttons*, certain recognizable elements emerge, although in a fragmented form.

As in a cubist painting, however, the emphasis on "pointing" (on representation) to something seen ("a spectacle") gives way to a stronger emphasis on the canvas's surface, on its own "system," for there is "order" in such a canvas: although the representation is "not ordinary," and makes its object appear extraordinary, the portrait is "not unordered in not resembling." The word-painting may be "a cousin" to the actual "carafe" (if, indeed, there is an actual carafe), yet "the difference" is more evident than the "kinship" ("kin/d"), and "the difference is spreading," as the gap between object and words increases. The "glass," in being "blind," does not open onto a familiar reality or "spectacle," as a window might; and it does not attempt to hold the mirror up to nature.[31] It draws our attention, rather, to the "arrangement" of the words upon the page, a new creation.

Yet Stein also hints here, as she does throughout *Tender Buttons*, at a further and largely unaccountable presence somehow incorporated into this "still life." This is "A kind in glass and a cousin, a spectacle and nothing strange": a kind of glass, a relation to the glass we usually think of, and a "kind" one, a tender one (like a/glass,

Alice); a glass which may, like spectacles, readjust and clarify our vision; a strange nothing, or noting, which may also be "kin" to us, if we can learn to speculate differently. The "difference" that "is spreading" here, in a larger sense, may be femaleness itself; perhaps this moment of "spreading" is one of parturition, a new birth of the female. Even in this opaque opening, this "arrangement in a system" of nouns called out in love, in persistence, and perhaps in torment, we can sense the presence of a powerful and obscure femaleness. Otherness ("difference") is now celebrated; the hole, or lacuna, which in a Freudian "system" "points" to such difference can now be sensed to be, not a locus of absence at all, but a rich and indefinable presence.[32]

The "difference" is now not just the gap between object and words, but between old forms of perception and new ones. Stein appears to approach a highly Emersonian stance here. For Emerson, as for Stein, to see the world newly requires, not a new world, but new perception. The new perception Stein offers in *Tender Buttons*, however, differs from Emerson's by its very resistance to vision. For Emerson "the eye is the best of artists," "the best composer," half-creating (and sometimes fully creating) what it sees.

The poet, by an ulterior intellectual perception, gives [natural symbols in the world] a power which makes their old use forgotten, and puts eyes and a tongue into every dumb and inanimate object. . . . *The poet turns the world to glass*, and shows us all things in their right series and procession. . . . All the facts of the animal economy, sex, nutriment, gestation, birth, growth, are symbols of the passage of the world into the soul of man, to *suffer there a change* and reappear a new and higher fact. (emphasis added)[33]

In one sense, to "turn the world to glass" suggests a vision so fine that nature's often opaque symbols become lucid and easily read. In a more disturbing sense, however, the poet's act is both transformative and quietly destructive. The world's "dumb and inanimate object[s]" appear to "turn," with a turn of Emerson's phrase, "to glass," a transparency cleared of mediate (visible) things and dedicated wholly to the poet's less visible vision. Unwieldy and hard physical "facts" like "gestation" and "birth" vanish (although not without "suffer[ing]"), replaced by a similar transparency, "a new and higher fact."

The gendered nature of Emerson's language here is significant. The poet, as Emerson describes him, is always masculine, whereas the material facts and emblems surrounding him participate in a nature that is clearly associated with the female. The citation of "birth" and "gestation" as facts to "suffer . . . a change" reveals an implicit ideology in which a female natural creation (both in the sense of birth and in the sense of nature) must submit to a "higher" fact of a male poet's language. With a turn of his own image in the later essay "Experience," however, Emerson confronts the dangers inherent in this implicitly appropriative vision. As Emerson suggests, the "rapaciousness" of vision "threatens to absorb all things." The image of a glass world changes into an image of "many-colored lenses which paint the world their own hue, and each shows only what lies in its focus." The earlier claim to unmediated vision gives way to an acknowledgment that "we do not see directly, but mediately."[34] Emerson's sense of this subjective and mediate vision is one of utter loss. Since vision is for him (and his poet) the crucial receptive and creative power, loss of "true" vision thrusts us into an unbearable imprisonment. From being the Sayer and the Namer, the god-like figure at the center of the universe, seeing through all forms to the divine forms beyond, the poet becomes aware of his own essential blindness.

Stein transforms Emerson's "colored lenses," and his cause for "hurt" or sorrow, into "a blind glass," a "cousin" perhaps to the colored lenses in its "single hurt color." Blindness, however, for Stein, forms the crucial point of departure. She accepts this modernist dilemma, anticipated by Emerson, and even embraces it through her own feminist "lenses." If a glass is blind, it will not turn the world, with all its lovely and delicious "Objects," "Food," and "Rooms," its interior female spaces, into "glass."

Luce Irigaray's sense of the *glace* of representation as an ice-mirror, in which images become frozen, resembles Stein's making of a "blind" glass. Although Irigaray is more directly critical of a patriarchal form of mirroring (by which, she argues, every object is reduced to an image of "the same"), her poetic imagining of an alternate figure for the mirror sheds light on Stein's project. As Irigaray suggests in *Speculum of the Other Woman*:

But perhaps through this specular surface which sustains discourse is found not the void of nothingness but the dazzle of multi-faceted speleology. A scintillating and incandescent concavity, of language also, that threatens to set fire to fetish-objects and gilded eyes. The recasting of their truth value is already at hand. We need only press on a little further into the depths, into that so-called dark cave which serves as hidden foundation to their speculations. For there where we expect to find the opaque and silent matrix of a logos immutable in the certainty of its light, fires and mirrors are beginning to radiate, sapping the evidence of reason at its base! Not so much by anything stored in the cave—which would still be a claim based on the notion of the closed volume—but again and yet again by their indefinitely rekindled hearths.[35]

A new form of speculation, Irigaray suggests, may replace and explode the old. Instead of being seen and named as object, the woman may begin to take the "speculum" in her own hands, to "press on" into herself, and to find, not the certainty of the named, but the fiery, uncertain, lively, and unlocatable place of the un-named.

The second "object" of *Tender Buttons* suggests Stein's less fiery and more palpable version of such "kindling": "Glazed Glitter." Just as "glazed" creates a picture of a smooth and glossy surface, of paint, ice, sugar, or glass, the name points to its own glossing over, its own covering of our eyes with a film, or perhaps its covering of the object(s) it does not name. What is glossed over, what may need a gloss, is something paradoxically impossible to glaze: "glitter," a kind of sparkling light or lustre. And, in an even more puzzling sense, the object of sight and of representation may be left out entirely. "Glitter" may be a verb, so that "Glazed [———] Glitter" becomes a sentence with an absent subject. To glitter: "To shine with a brilliant but broken and tremulous light; to emit bright fitful flashes of light; to gleam, sparkle" (*OED*).

This glittering involves both the igniting of traditional representation and the lustre of a new, gleaming form of (non)representation. As Stein hints in "Glazed Glitter":

The change has come. There is no search. But there is, there is that hope and that interpretation and sometime, surely any is unwelcome, sometime there is breath and there will be a sinecure and charming very charming is that clean and cleansing. Certainly glittering is handsome and convincing. (*SW*, 461)

"No search" for an object may be precisely what allows for "hope" and "breath." Interpretation can still exist, but in a different form, in a less "searching" form ("search and destroy"). The reader, according to this form, would be, not a searcher for the truth, of which these words form only the semblances, but a participant, engaged in the words and allowing their entity without attempting to press behind them to something else. In one sense, we would "Come eat it," as one voice invites us to do in "Lifting Belly" (*YGS*, 35). This glaze is sweet. It covers its objects, but it allows us even greater delight in our tasting of the words.

These words, then, *as* words, are "handsome and convincing." They seduce us first with the "hope" that an "interpretation" will emerge, and then with a sense of the words' liveliness, as we sing them ("charming" suggests "carmen") and allow them to touch all our senses. In a further sense, the object may be impossible to find, but its (her) "breath," literally her life and inspiration, is "there," wherever the "there" is.[36] Vision has become replaced by a modality of touch.

Although numerous metaphors and half-suggested metaphors invoke this female presence, "she" cannot be found in these figures in any certain way, for metaphor itself becomes humorously undermined.[37] "A Substance in a Cushion," the third titled "object" of "Objects," may evoke, for example, the image of a finger in (or on) a female "cushion" of some sort: "a little groan grinding makes a trimming such a sweet singing trimming and a red thing not a round thing but a white thing, a red thing and a white thing" (*SW*, 462). This intimation of an erotic kind of "trimming," or sewing, is increased by the suggestiveness of the "cushion," which has a "cover," and is "very clean"; even when there is "dirt," the dirt is "clean where there is a volume," a word hinting at the water Stein usually associates with female wetness or orgasm. A rather ambivalent pleasure—one that might involve "groans"—holds an important place in this section: "What is the use of a violent kind of delightfulness if there is no pleasure in not getting tired of it" (*SW*, 462). Yet the indeterminacy—or, as Pamela Hadas has suggested, the overdeterminacy—of these figures is evident. Although the language hints at an erotic situation, it resists any certainty on this account.

The presence possibly marking this "substance in a cushion" becomes more evident in the titles of other sections of "Food" and "Rooms." Traditional metaphors for female sexuality abound, especially in the titles of the different pieces, in ways that make the link possible: "A Box," "A Piece" (of coffee), a "case," a red rose surrounded by a "gate," a "dress," "a bag," "A Purse," "A

Mounted Umbrella," a "cup," "Red Roses," "A shallow hole rose on red," food of all sorts, especially meat ("Roast Beef," "Mutton"), sugar, "Apple," "Tails," "Fish," "Cake," "Custard," "Chicken," and "Cream."

Yet even as *Tender Buttons* entices us with all these potentially erotic objects and foods, it turns us around so that we become radically unsure of these metaphors. The work uses them with a smile, as if to say, "You think you can find me here, where I have always been said to be? Try again." The sense of enticement and invitation remains, but only in spite of the undercutting of our "search." For "a white hunter is nearly crazy" (*SW*, 475). To approach *Tender Buttons* as a hunter—and a "white" one, one who poaches on the foreign territory of other races and less powerful nations—is to be driven "nearly crazy," since the liveliness both of the words and of their possible referents resists capture.

It is not surprising that in this context the "rose" returns, as one of the oldest metaphors for a desired and loved feminine object, and one that Stein clearly finds significant:

NOTHING ELEGANT

A charm a single charm is doubtful. If the red is rose and there is a gate surrounding it, if inside is let in and there places change then certainly something is upright. It is earnest. (*SW*, 464)

At first glance, our hunting eye seizes on the red rose, "surround[ed]" by a gate: an oddly straightforward image, not difficult to picture, especially with the memory of the Lady and the Unicorn tapestries or illustrations for *The Romance of the Rose*. One could argue for the female symbolism implicit in such an image, and for the male symbolism in the addition of the "something" that is "upright" and "earnest."

Yet the metaphor slips from our grasp. "A single" meaning, like a single charm, is "doubtful," with a singleness that links to the uprightness of the phallic object. In fact, where is the metaphor at all? "Rose" may be, not a noun, but an adjective, modifying "red." The title warns us: there is nothing here, no *thing*. The substitutions for nouns seem insistent: "it," "something." And the locations seem vague, even unimaginable: "inside is let in," "there," "places change." How can what is already inside be let in? The logic breaks down in earnest. The "if" insists upon itself, a warning about doubtfulness. As Irigaray might point out, this language mirrors conventional language, just as *Speculum* mirrors Western philosophical thought from Plato to Freud (from Freud to Plato). The rose is red metamorphoses, in this looking glass, into the red is rose. This reversal cuts away the original ground for the logic of metaphor. Instead of the transparency of that windowing verb, "is," we discover the indecipherability but liveliness of being ("is") itself. If language is in some sense the clothing (the cloaking?) we wear, then Stein asks us to look, with her, in the mirror, not the mirror of representation (re-presentation, Irigaray's *mimétisme*), but the speculum which can undo representation. This new red is "read," it is a color, a figure, which finds a locus in the act of reading words on a page, in a "volume," an act which involves no "single charm." For if a charm originally was a song (carmen), and especially "the chanting of a verse having magic power," we chant it too, in an incantation which disrupts—literally, puts a spell on—metaphor as a defining act.

Stein attempts to "re letter" the object(s) protected from a hunter's eye. The last paragraph of "A Centre in a Table," which comes at the end of the middle section, "Food," touches upon the significance of this re-lettering:

Next to me, next to a folder, next to a folder some waiter, next to a foldersome waiter and *re letter* and read her. Read her with her for less. (*SW*, 497, emphasis added)

On the surface, this still life appears to represent a situation in a restaurant, with a "waiter" and a menu (a "folder") being read by someone together with a woman ("Read her with her"); "for less" may represent a piece of their conversation, as they discuss the prices of the food they will choose. Yet, in a larger sense, the entire section of "Food" has been a new kind of restaurant ("A kind . . . and a cousin"), listing titles of foods, in ways that have challenged the link between names ("letters") and their referents. The situation at the heart (at the "centre") of this "table" groaning with "Food" and sitting in the middle of *Tender Buttons* involves an undoing of the form of representation figured by the conventional establishment, wherein restaurant-goers engage in a transaction of paying money for the food they consume. In ordering the food, one knows what one will get, and because of the payment, one "owns" the food that one has eaten. Stein revises this situation by making any straightforward consumption nearly impossible, even as she rouses our senses ("arouse is arouse is arouse is arouse")[38] by the intimation of the near presence of food. If we order "Orange In" (the title of another piece in "Food"), we may receive "pain soup" (bread soup? *SW*, 496); if we order "salad," we may find ourselves confronting "a winning cake" (*SW*, 495); if we order "Pastry," we appear to be transported to a sensual garden: "Cutting shade, cool spades and little last beds, make violet, violet when" (*SW*, 493).

Yet our hunger may be somewhat abated by the gradual understanding of the "secret" of this place, which may "bestow" its gifts upon us indirectly (*SW*, 497). If we accept our position as being "next to" the words we read ("Next to me, next to a folder"), just as these words stand "next to" (but not necessarily contiguous with) desired "objects," and if we "wait" for "her" ("wait-er") rather than order her to come to our table, then perhaps we may "read," not *about* her, but more literally "read *her*." If this female presence is, in a sense, the body of *Tender Buttons* herself, then Stein may be suggesting that in reading *Tender Buttons* we *are* "reading her," reading a protected but felt female presence.[39] To read in this way is to "let her" ("let-ter") into the writing in such a way that she will not be consumed, but treated tenderly. Such a change in our reading habits will mark a "re[d] letter" day.

Stein's project in this sense is a "cousin" to Emily Dickinson's. Arguing subtly for her own redaction of Emerson, Dickinson writes in "Tell all the Truth but tell it slant" that "Success in Circuit lies." "The Truth," a phrase echoing Emerson with quiet irony, is a kind of light "too bright" for our mortal eyes unless it "dazzle[s] gradually."[40] Stein comes to a similar conclusion, although it is even less directly expressed: "Excellent, more excellence in borrowing and slanting is light and secret and a recitation and emigration" ("Rooms," *SW*, 506). Her writing in *Tender Buttons* allows us, perhaps, to "borrow" its gifts (for its words, in a sense, *are* its "Truth"), but not to claim them, and certainly not to claim them immediately and completely. Its illumination, like the dazzle of "Glazed Glitter," is "slanting," just as the objects it renames remain "secret." In being renamed, these objects are re-cited and re-sighted. We leave the familiar country of known objects, ready to order, in our "emigration" to the unfamiliar shores of Stein's geography.

Indirectly, in this new land we glimpse, not a specific woman or any clear representation, but a circuitously imaged idyll involving a "wedding" and a "near[ness]" to "fairy sea," "A peaceful life to arise her, noon and moon and moon" ("A Little Called Pauline," *SW*, 474). Who "she" is, and who "arises her" (arouses her) remains a secret, yet if we come "nearer" to the writing, allowing ourselves to relish the noises of the isle as the day and night succeed each other ("noon and moon and moon"), and to "moon" about, we will be participating in the "wedding" of the real with the words, as the separation between these realms dissolves and becomes un-important—at least across this "fairy sea."

"Lifting Belly"

Lifting belly is so seen.
You mean here.
Not with spy glasses.   (YGS, 16)

The path of things is silent. Will they suffer a speaker to
go with them? A spy they will not suffer; a lover, a
poet, is the transcendency of their own nature, —him
they will suffer.   (Emerson, "The Poet")

Begun in 1915, two years after Stein finished *Tender Buttons*, "Lifting Belly" comes "nearer" to "what shines in the darkness necessarily" through a more complete movement away from sight and toward the other senses. As with most of Stein's writing of the early war period, during and immediately after Stein's and Toklas's year-long stay in Majorca from 1915 to 1916, "Lifting Belly" is a love poem, written largely as a dialogue between unnamed speakers.[41] The autobiographical element becomes more evident than in Stein's works before the war, as references to Stein's living situation begin to enter her writing more boldly and directly, often in the form of conversational fragments. Stein allows the boundary between life and art to become even more permeable and shifting than in her earlier writing.

On the surface, "Lifting Belly" offers a more recognizable mode of representation. Images appear to be clearer and more visible, as our imaginative movement from words to objects or actions be-comes more direct: as section II opens, "Kiss my lips. She did. / Kiss my lips again she did. / Kiss my lips over and over and over again she did" (*YGS*, 19). Because the dialogue of "Lifting Belly" could be interpreted as a conversation between two actual figures, Gertrude Stein and Alice Toklas, the piece encourages our sense that these words refer to real events.[42] By contrast to the opaque surface of *Tender Buttons*, where a female body and presence may be sensed, yet is barely reached by language, "Lifting Belly" and other Majorcan pieces appear to represent in minute detail the daily existence of two women.

Yet this perception of "Lifting Belly" as a poem grounded in the representation of visible forms is not fully accurate. The movement from the writing to "the real" is not as direct as one might be led to expect. What is being represented may be felt but almost never seen. Stein attempts to present, as immediately as possible, a sense of an ongoing intimacy, yet she carefully refuses to make her representations of this intimacy stable or certain. She achieves this resistance to direct representation partly through the absence of one narrative or lyrical voice speaking throughout the poem from a position of authority, able to describe the figures who speak and make love. In place of such a voice, Stein gives us at least two figures, of whose identity we can never be certain, who speak together in ways that imply a felt world, but rarely name it directly.[43]

Although Stein mentions parts of the body like the lips and the "belly," as she renders an intimate situation of asking and responding, she does not allow us to move far enough away from the speakers to *see* who is speaking, who is kissing, who is being kissed. The lines that follow the kissing—"I have feathers. / Gentle fishes" (*YGS*, 20)—gently and comically point this resistance out, for right where we anticipate a more fully described account of this kissing, or this relationship, a language of indirection fends us off (or the promised images fly off, "feathers" and all). In this way, Stein attempts both to call into her writing the female body and love between women more directly than in *Tender Buttons*, and to avoid reproducing the structures of representation in which the female has been constrained.

The opening of "Lifting Belly" creates an expectation of a more traditional narrative, including representations of the natural world. The poetic and narrative "I" appears at first to refer to a single identity, calling out loved names of objects that are loved. According to Stein's definition of poetry in "Poetry and Grammar," this is pure poetry:

I have been heavy and had much selecting. I saw a star which was low. It was so low it twinkled. Breath was in it. Little pieces are stupid.

I want to tell about fire. Fire is that which we have when we have olive. Olive is a wood. We like linen. Linen is ordered. We are going to order linen. (*YGS*, 4)

Stein appears to create a persona here who approaches the world with as little mediation as possible, through the simplest images placed within the simplest syntax: "star," "fire," "olive," "wood," "linen." Yet the progression of this opening is significant, for these images move quickly from the more distant and visible "star," to the "fire," which is both visible and felt, and then to "linen," which may be seen and felt, as fire is, yet more closely still. As the next line suggests—"All belly belly well" (a pun on "All very very well") —we have approached a place less reliant upon seeing (although one can see a "belly") than upon touch. These "bellies," placed next to each other in the line, suggest an intimacy that remains largely unrepresented, although touched upon.

This opening introduces a landscape that may be a "cousin" to Romantic landscapes. Although Stein's "star," together with the ambiguous "breath" (a physical breath and the inspiration of poetry), offers a general suggestiveness that cannot be tied only to one Romantic source, nevertheless a comparison with Keats's sonnet "Bright Star" illuminates the larger dialogue Stein is holding in "Lifting Belly" with Romantic poetry:[44]

> Bright star, would I were stedfast as thou art—
>   Not in lone splendor hung aloft the night
> And watching, with eternal lids apart,
>   Like nature's patient, sleepless Eremite,
> The moving waters at their priestlike task
>   Of pure ablution round earth's human shores,
> Or gazing on the new soft-fallen mask
>   Of snow upon the mountains and the moors—
> No—yet still stedfast, still unchangeable,
>   Pillow'd upon my fair love's ripening breast,
> To feel for ever its soft fall and swell, .
>   Awake for ever in a sweet unrest,
> Still, still to hear her tender-taken breath,
> And so live ever—or else swoon to death.[45]

Keats moves gradually here from the "bright star," "hung aloft the night," to the "human shores" of earth, and thence to the lower and fully human image of two lovers. From the world of light and of the solitary eye, he retreats to the world of touch and feeling. Whereas the star (an image perhaps for Milton) insists upon distance between itself and the speaker, as between its own "watching" or "gazing" and the earth, the speaker desires the intimacy of the human body, the "ripening breast," filled with "breath." The difficulty, however, implicit throughout the poem lies in the fragility and temporality of this less visionary and more sensual placement. The speaker may desire the "stedfast[ness]" of the star, yet such eternal and unchanging grandeur holds a stability that mortals cannot claim. The speaker can only imagine such steadfastness in a form dangerously close to death. "Awake for ever in a sweet unrest," the speaker and his lover would remain in a continual embrace on the verge of a possible "swoon to death."

Stein's "star" occupies a position of less loftiness, just as her speaker moves more quickly and surely to earth and, implicitly, to a domestic interior including a dining table or a bed ("We like linen"). In contrast to the "splendor" of Keats's star, this star simply "twinkles," with a mischievous and possibly human air. The "star" comes so low, in fact, that "*Breath* was *in* it," whereas Keats's speaker must wait to the end of the sonnet to reach his lover's "tender-taken *breath*." The speaker's associative movement toward bed bears no hint of the "swoon to death" with which Keats's poem ends; in fact, these images form the opening of the poem, not the ending. As Stein quietly observes, "Little pieces are stupid." This poem will be one hardly meeting with closure (much less "death") even at its end.

The existence of these named entities outside Stein's prose poem becomes a matter of some doubt. As the "I" changes to "we," the question of representation becomes more complicated:

Sometimes we readily decide upon wind we decide that there will be stars and perhaps thunder and perhaps rain and perhaps no moon. Sometimes we decide that there will be a storm and rain. (*YGS*, 4)

This "decision" suggests that the presence of "wind" or "stars" depends upon the poet(s). Instead of confronting the poet with their prior and unconquerable existence, both as natural elements and as poetic images, these entities await human choice. The poet(s) "select[s]" words rather than weathers. As one voice soon asks, presumably about the phrase "lifting belly," "Is it a name," to be assured by another voice, "Yes it's a name" (*YGS*, 7), with the implication that it is *simply* a name, not a representation, or at least not as clear a representation as one might think.

The "wood" and the "fire," in fact, may become figures for something else:

> Bed of coals made out of wood.
> I think this one may be an expression. We can understand heating and burning composition. Heating with wood. (*YGS*, 4)

The erotic significance of this fire and heat, implied by "bed," leads to a further significance: "composition" itself forms a "heating and burning," a transformation of wood (and of "would," of desire) into fire. A continuum emerges between a bodily intimacy and the "composing" of this work. The composition takes on a bodily and erotic dimension, as the literal touching of belly to belly enters into the writing. "Lifting belly" is an act (or numerous intricate, changeable acts) as well as a "composition." In an even larger sense, "lifting belly" represents the pregnant *matrix* of language. The "I" of the opening (the parturition) may be interpreted as this matrix speaking out of her immensity and "heaviness."

The poem is brought to birth by at least two figures, who participate in "heating and burning composition" through the fire of their intimacy: "Lifting belly together" (*YGS*, 10). In contrast to Keats's (and other Romantic poets') isolated speaker, who only imagines being "Pillow'd upon [his silent and] fair love's ripening breast," Stein offers a more dialogic mode of speech and creation. These unnamed voices, floating in the space of the poem, speak from within the "belly" (the poem) that they are in the process of "lifting." Because they are already within "Lifting Belly," they have no need to define it, or to make its appearance at any moment fully understandable or visible. Instead of positing this "lifting" as a desire, toward which the poem moves, they already have access to their "wishes" ("Gentle fishes"). In place of the structure of the internalized quest romance, whereby the poem exists by virtue of an unfulfilled desire on the part of a yearning masculine speaker-hero for an absent female figure, Stein's poem substitutes at least two figures already together, in the act of fulfilling their desire erotically and poetically.

Yet a different and more antagonistic voice appears in the opening, and reappears at certain moments throughout the work. The sudden mention of war, after the opening idyll of wood and fire, heralds the arrival of this voice. The "boats" that may be "sunk," and the dangers of "rowing" (rowing a boat, but also quarreling), build into the description of a "quarrel" between the "we" and an unnamed male figure—"We quarreled with him then" (*YGS*, 4) —that remains unresolved—"I don't pardon him. I find him objectionable" (*YGS*, 4).[46] The quarrel involves the man's refusal to acknowledge indebtedness—"Do not forget that I showed you the road. We will forget it because he does not oblige himself to thank me" (*YGS*, 4)—yet it encompasses a larger argument about the nature of representation within "Lifting Belly":

> What is it when it's upset. It isn't in the room. Moonlight and darkness. Sleep and not sleep. We sleep every night.
> What was it.
> I said lifting belly.
> You didn't say it.
> I said it I mean lifting belly.
> Don't misunderstand me.
> Do you.   (*YGS*, 5)

The question, "What was it," goes to the heart of the matter. This "it" refers literally to the series of "it"s in the preceding sentence: "What is it when it's upset. It isn't in the room." When the response comes ("I said lifting belly") the quarrelsome voice makes the accusation: "You didn't say it," meaning that saying "it" is not the same as saying "lifting belly." The first voice then makes a distinction between "saying it" and "meaning lifting belly": she *said* "it," but she *meant* "lifting belly."

Two different representational models enter into conflict here. These voices speak at cross-purposes. The accusing voice desires a language of clear reference: one must say what one means, and mean what one says. The other voice offers a more ambiguous language, one that says and means, but not necessarily together. In one sense, the "it" used by this voice is an indexical word, expressing the immediacy and presence of the entity to which it refers. In another sense, however, "it" remains opaque to an outsider who demands names. The latter voice resists the clear reference of naming, yet the nature of the "it" may still be sensed by the words to which it is adjacent: "Moonlight and darkness. Sleep and not sleep." These pairings indirectly suggest a further and unrepresented human pairing, occurring within the dreaming interstices between moonlight and darkness, sleep and not sleep. These distinct entities come together, conjoined by the "and"s, and in fact manifest a profounder bond; for "moonlight" is only light by virtue of its contrast with darkness, just as the absence of sleep can only be understood in terms of sleep's presence. Just to say "moonlight," then, is not enough, for, as this passage suggests, reference is never a simple affair, but moves through difference. The oscillation between sleep and not sleep may represent a Keatsian "sweet unrest" or else a lovers' quarrel.

The frustration of the question, "What was it," and the accusation, "You didn't say it," may be seen as an expression of Stein's own consciousness of the difficulty involved in bringing the "it"— the presence—into her poem. She attempts this feat partly through her use of similar indexes: "Lifting belly is here" (YGS, 19); "Lifting belly is all there" (YGS, 9); "Lifting belly in here" (YGS, 38). In each instance, the very unspecificity of the term ("here," "there") attempts to assert, paradoxically, something so specific and so intimate that it is not seen at a distance great enough to be named. At the same time, such indexes protect the presence of the unnamed entity from being too easily apprehended.

Stein associates seeing in the poem with a nationalistic impulse leading to war. "Lifting Belly" makes scattered references to the Great War throughout the poem, yet the war remains an emphatically peripheral phenomenon, marginal to the love of words and the love touched upon by the words. The "Star-Spangled Banner," the patriotic song celebrating the vision of a national emblem ("Oh say can you see / By the dawn's early light"), enters into the poem in fragments causing us to question its form of seeing: as the poem says at one point, "We used to play star spangled banner" (YGS, 14), implying both that "we used to be unified" and, in a more critical sense, "we used to agree, with the rest of our country, to rely on our vision to assure ourselves of the sign of our unification." The poem appears to promise such signs, yet seeing them becomes a difficult proposition, as in this sequence punning upon "Caesar" / "sees her" / "seize her":

I say lifting belly and then I say lifting belly and Caesars. I say lifting belly gently and Caesars gently. I say lifting belly again and Caesars again.

I say lifting belly and I say Caesars and I say lifting belly Caesars and cow come out. I say lifting belly and Caesars and cow come out.

Can you read my print.

Lifting belly say can you see the Caesars. I can see what I kiss. (*YGS*, 30)

The "her" within "Caesar / sees her" cannot be "seen" directly; conversely, seeing alone does not ensure understanding ("Can you read my print"). While on the surface these "Caesars" appear to reproduce a nationalistic and imperialistic situation, present to Stein in the form of Germany's threat to Europe and specifically to France —"Some when they sigh by accident say poor country she is betrayed" (*YGS*, 12)—Stein reclaims this name for her more pacific vision—"Lifting belly is peacable" (*YGS*, 14). The "Caesars," as fingers who may "seize," replace the economy of seeing with one of touch: "say can you see," as one voice asks, echoing the "Star-Spangled Banner," yet in refusing this vision, we must "seize" the text in another way.

"I can see what I kiss" suggests that seeing, if it occurs at all, should occur at much closer range; we should see only what we may also touch. The imperialistic vision of Rome thus becomes at once parodied and brought into a relatively safe arena, in which "Caesars" lead, not to rape or occupation, but to "cows" (an image both of the pastoral and of female orgasm) and kisses.[47] "Caesar," as the poem observes at another point, "is plural" (*YGS*, 26); in place of the monomaniacal and isolated emperor, such plurality suggests a dialogue between different "Caesars," just as the seeing, if it is mutual and intimate, may lead to authentic intimacy: "Oh yes you see. / What I see. / You see me. / Yes stretches. / Stretches and stretches of happiness" (*YGS*, 26).

Stein's dialogue invites our own participation as sharers (fellow "Caesars") in the act of "lifting belly," the composing of the poem so intricately entwined with the conversation of lovers, for we too may become the "I" or the "you." If we take the claim, "Lifting belly in here," seriously, we may cross the boundary separating us from the writing and immerse ourselves in the dialogue as it shifts from moment to moment. We may greet the poem and its continuous birth together with the voice who says: "How are you. / Lifting belly how are you lifting belly" (*YGS*, 5). We too may "do it," if the "it" encompasses our reading of the poem, as we resist "caring" about one-to-one correspondences—"Do it. What a splendid example of carelessness. / It gives me a great deal of pleasure to say yes" (*YGS*, 5). In this way, "a great many people come together" (*YGS*, 6).

If we agree to this participation, we agree to take off our "spy glasses"—"Lifting belly is so seen. / You mean here. / Not with spy glasses" (*YGS*, 16). Such glasses imply our strangeness to this landscape; it becomes a foreign country whose secrets a spying reader desires to uncover. As spies, caught in the act of spying but forgiven, we may call out impatiently, "Explain it explain it to me," yet the poem only answers, "Lifting belly is cautious. / Of course these words are said" (*YGS*, 16). Words may be said, but with caution, for only friends may be admitted "in here."

This movement away from vision echoes Keats's substitution of hearing and touch for sight in "Ode to a Nightingale," a poem with which the "ode" of "Lifting Belly" may be in dialogue.

> Lifting belly is a miracle.
> I am with her.
> Lifting belly to me.
> Very nicely done.
> Poetry is very nicely done.
> Can you say pleasure.
> I can easily say please me.
> You do.
> Lifting belly is precious.
> Then *you can sing.*
> *We do not encourage a nightingale.*
> *Do you really mean that.*
> *We literally do.*
>
> (*YGS*, 42–43,
> emphasis added)

This passage raises the question of "singing," and specifically of a poetic singing: the relation between a song of natural beauty (the nightingale's) and poetry. Although one voice somewhat archly rejects "a nightingale," this rejection, like many of the statements in "Lifting Belly," meets with contradiction and qualification: as another voice observes, "We literally do," signifying possibly that "we sing *literally*," rather than through the figuration of a bird-singer. In this sense, the dialogue enacts a form of singing "literally": singing with "letters," as they compose words on the page, and singing in a language as close to the "literal" (in "Lifting Belly," to the female body) as possible.

Keats's poem traces the movement of the speaker toward the nightingale, and then back to his "sole self." Opening himself in imagination to "the [tender] night," and to a richly dark landscape whose "sweet[s]" he can only "guess," the speaker reaches the nightingale through imitating the nightingale's song in "the viewless wings of Poesy": "Already with thee!" This nearness to the bird's mystical otherness leads to the speaker's passive "listen[ing]," which in turn leads by association to thoughts of "easeful Death." Although the speaker appears to value the bird's "immortal" song, in a deeper sense he fears the mortality to which her song has led him. For Keats's male poet-figure, the bliss of listening to a bird song that makes it seem "rich to die" is an ambivalent pleasure indeed. To remain with the nightingale, surrounded by a thick and sensual female nature, would, in effect, signify the end of his own poetic voice.

Stein's poem, in contrast, avoids such a movement "away" from the visible (and linguistic) world, toward a wordless and potentially overwhelming female nature. The categories upon which Keats's poem depends have become untenable, especially the constitution of the poetic "I," which, as a male authorial consciousness, flirts with a nature that is other, yet finally must return to the "sole self." As one of the speakers says in the dialogue quoted above: "Lifting belly is a miracle. / *I am with her.*" The boundaries between the "I" and the nightingale, consciousness and unconsciousness, the "me" and the "not-me," poetic subject and poetic object, become in "Lifting Belly" impossible to sustain. The "I" does not need to "fly" anywhere, because she is already "with her," throughout the poem. Together, the (unseen) figures ("we") "produce music," a music unabashedly and exuberantly linked with an ongoing female erotic: "Kissing and singing." The "sweets" about which Keats's speaker "guesses" become present in "Lifting Belly" both as a general poetic "sweetness" and as a promise of bodily sweetness: "Lifting belly is so sweet" (*YGS*, 13); "We are so likely to be sweet" (*YGS*, 33).

Stein transforms Keats's romantic landscape into a new landscape of female "pleasure" marking an alternate form of the "sublime": "Lifting belly sublimely. / We made a fire this evening" (*YGS*, 28). The boundaries important to Stein are no longer the

Romantic boundary between earth and sky, mortality and immortality, or the body and the spirit. The "sublime," for the speakers in "Lifting Belly," inhabits the interchange between different "I"s on both a poetic and an erotic level. While for Keats's speaker, the final difference between the "immortal" bird and the mortal "I" marks the danger of a sublime flight in which the "I" may ultimately die, for Stein's speakers death is not a possibility partly because of the continual kindling of their "fire," the renewal of each one's presence for the other. The invitation to "come to sing and sit" (*YGS*, 32) suggests a mutual "singing" attached to bodily intimacy ("sitting").

The "here" of the poem draws us close if we can learn to accept a "nearness" that is separate from a spectacle, for "Lifting belly is recognised to be the only spectacle present . . . Lifting belly is a language" (*YGS*, 17): the poem's movements, that is, are the "only spectacle," as the world of love encompassed by "Lifting Belly" remains largely invisible. To say that "This is a picture of lifting belly having a cow" (*YGS*, 30) gently pokes fun at the very concept of "pictures," for to take this image literally *as* a visual image is nearly impossible. The intimacy of which the poem is composed and which it seeks is brought into existence in a form of incantation:

> Lifting belly is so near.
> Lifting belly is so dear.
> Lifting belly all around.
> Lifting belly makes a sound.
> (*YGS*, 14)

This "near" to the poem "Lifting Belly," we cannot "see" it, but we are made to feel it—"Feel me. / I feel you. / Then it is fair to me" (*YGS*, 36). It is not separate from us, just as lovers are not completely separate in lovemaking, but surround each other. The poem moves us to a recognition of the value of language as a "sound," "all around" us, rather than as a continually signifying act.

What is significant, then, is the language's moving presence as it recreates ("Lifting belly is remarkably a recreation"), within the poem, the very forms of intimacy to which it indirectly refers. The poem's rousing and celebratory conclusion asserts this presence:

> Lifting belly enormously and with song.
> Can you sing about a cow.

Yes.
And about signs.
Yes.
And also about Aunt Pauline.
Yes.
Can you sing at your work.
Yes.
In the meantime listen to Miss Cheatham.
In the midst of writing.
In the midst of writing there is merriment.
(*YGS*, 54)

Although the poem affirms the possibility of singing "about" the world, this representation remains stubbornly indirect: "a cow," as the poem has taught us, may not simply be the gentle creature of milk grazing in the field, although it may include this creature; "Aunt Pauline" is both the name of Stein's Ford and the name of her actual aunt, yet it remains also a more indeterminate and floating "sign." The poem may sing "about" signs without making much use of them as a means toward representation. What is most celebrated is the act of singing itself, which evokes the "merriment" that occurs "outside" the poem, and in a more important sense attempts to bring this actual and bodily pleasure into the composing of the poem: "In the midst of writing. / In the midst of writing there is merriment." Like Keats's nightingale, but without the danger she offers her poet-lover, "lifting belly," as the *matrix* of language, "enormous" and full, capable of a continuous profusion of "song," represents a language informed by the body and inseparable from it. It is in this sense that "Lifting Belly" is indeed "so able to be praised" and "so necessary" (*YGS*, 12, 11).

: 4 :

Creation as Dialogue

*In the beginning. In the beginning many may be
and may be there.*
        ("Mildred Aldrich Saturday," P&P, 120)

*Select your song she said and it was done and then she
said and it was done with a nod and then she bent her
head in the direction of the falling water. Amiably.*
                ("Advertisement," LCA)

Stein's concept of representation as a dialogue between the writer
and words, and between words and the world, finds a corollary
in her transformative mythos of creation as a dialogic activity. Just
as the forms of representation she develops in the period of *Tender
Buttons* and then of "Lifting Belly" resist the appropriation of words
by the writer, or of objects in the world by words, this revision
of creation challenges the concept of a God-creator (or Goddess),
holding sway over his or her creation. For Stein, this monologic
model, whereby a literary work emanates from one source, evinces
a dangerous alliance with notions of ownership and priority, leading directly to war. Stein offers an alternate and pacifist paradigm
of "creation" as a shared and ongoing creative process, in which the
creative act mingles inextricably with the created writing. In this
chapter, I shall explore the ways in which Stein's thematic concern
with authorship in early works like *Three Lives* becomes, in her later
writings, overtly and self-consciously incorporated into narrative
and linguistic forms.

I have chosen four works from the mid-1920's that enter into
a dialogue with each other as they experiment with different
formal articulations of creativity: the literary portrait "Mildred
Aldrich Saturday" (written in 1924); the birthday book celebrating
Paulo Picasso's birth, *A Birthday Book* (also written in 1924); the
prose poem "Patriarchal Poetry" (written in 1927); and the "Novel
of Romantic Beauty and Nature," *Lucy Church Amiably* (written

in 1929–30).[1] The conventional narrative authority critiqued in
"Mildred Aldrich Saturday" and present only in linguistic traces in
A Birthday Book and "Patriarchal Poetry" undergoes a metamorphosis within *Lucy Church Amiably*, which reclaims a female creative
power, yet one that is now defined as intricately dialogic in its
"amiability."

Resisting Narrative: "Mildred Aldrich Saturday"

The opening of "Mildred Aldrich Saturday" evokes the possibility of a female origination with comical literality: "And eggs or
eggs or or eggs. Mildred Aldrich or interested in birthdays" (*P&P*,
111). As the beginning both of "Mildred Aldrich Saturday" and of
Mildred Aldrich's life story, this opening appears at first to claim
an originary moment located undeniably within the female: "eggs."
The hesitation marked by the surrounding or's, however, intimates
the uncertainty of such a claim. "Eggs" may signify the ova, yet
the repetition of "eggs" stresses the word's materiality. Rather than
a Female Logos, "eggs" may be simply a word. The "conception"
at issue may be this word's triple birth onto the page: "eggs,"
"eggs," and "eggs." The belief in an "inexorable" ("Andeggsor-
able") female origin ("horror!" or "or or") dissolves into laughter,
as we recognize the unanswerable riddle, "Which comes first, the
chicken or the egg?" Stein's riddling language makes the discovery
of "firsts" impossible.

As if the portrait attempts to make a second beginning, one
that will indeed discover a female origin answering the attempt to
locate one "birthday," the second paragraph begins: "When Mildred
Aldrich was born . . ." Although this second beginning sounds like
the beginning of a novel or a story, it leads to no completing sentence, just as the "eggs" float comically in the air, unanchored by
grammar:

When Mildred Aldrich was born it was not noticeable that when the when
there when there was when there was that that when there was that was
it all. That when there was that was it all there there that when there was
that was was it all it was that where was that it was was it all, it was all
was it all it was all was it there. (*P&P*, 111)

That her birth (and the birth of "Mildred Aldrich Saturday") "was not noticeable" suggests either that it could not be noticed or that it was not significant enough to be noticed. As the portrait will soon explain:

> The first time.
> When was the first time.
> As the first time it was of no importance. (P&P, 115)

The "first time" does not need to be "noticeable," because the concept of priority has become discredited. To be "interested in birthdays" does not necessarily involve an interest in priority.

The digression from a narrative line finds formal embodiment in a repetition resisting syntactical resolution: "that when the when there when there was when there was that that when there was that." Although this line manifests a kind of development, as each phrase grows from the one before ("that when the," "when there," "when there was"), this "growth" represents not a narrative but a linguistic movement. The "origin" of the narrative has led to this circling bracelet of words repeated in a hesitating dance. The hesitation marks a half-articulated question about the nature of literary genesis and authority. These circlings form a ring around an authorial center whose very existence comes into question: "that when there was that was it all." And again: "That when there was that / was it all there . . . it was all / was it all / it was all / was it there."

The open-endedness of these questions compels us to become aware of our own expectations. If we have been hoping for a scene of birth, but are given only the "there" of the page, we might very well ask, "was it all," and remain dissatisfied. If we look for an author or narrator, speaking to us through these words and claiming an originary relation to them, then we might ask the same question, meaning "was this text all there was, or was there someone behind it? Was this someone 'there'?"

The answer to these questions remains ambiguous, for an "author" may be glimpsed, yet her status as a creator originating and ruling her story manifests instability from the beginning. At least two storytellers emerge: Mildred Aldrich herself and the narrator, who (in a sense, but not "eggs-actly") retells the story Aldrich originally told. The sudden naming of Mildred Aldrich halfway through the portrait comes as a surprise: "This is the story that Mildred Aldrich told us Saturday" (P&P, 117). Yet the "story" she "told" remains largely absent from "Mildred Aldrich Saturday." Although traces exist, it is almost impossible to distinguish between the elements told by Mildred Aldrich and the elements composing her portrait. As the narrator observes: "It was all included and originally they said and originally she said and originally she said fancifully and not at all merely an obligation" (*P&P*, 116). Such "origins" may be announced, yet they remain absent ("originally she said . . ."). The narration severs Mildred Aldrich's original sayings both from Mildred and from the portrait, which refuses to represent origins in any stable way. Insofar as "obligations" evince a tie to origins, Stein's portrait is not "obliged" to its origins in Mildred Aldrich's narrative conventionality.

Stein's "dialogue" with Aldrich, as this portrait suggests, must have been an intricate one. Although Aldrich was one of her closest friends and supporters, Stein appears to have questioned (at least inwardly) Aldrich's more conventional forms of writing, especially as these forms manifested for Stein a link with the war forming one of Aldrich's central subjects. Well known as a teller of stories, Aldrich sent Stein and Toklas numerous letters from her house on the Marne during the First World War; there she observed the war at perilously close hand. Her letters offer the promise of oral accounts as well, as in this one about the battles: "But I'll tell you all about it later, all the stories of the soldiers, and of the battles, and of me feeding and cleaning, and serving cigarettes to the boys, and in spite of my almost collapsed condition, swearing that I would *not* get *demoralized*."[2] As James Mellow tells us, this letter arrived at the Whiteheads' home in England, where Gertrude and Leo Stein stayed during the first part of the war. The letter acted as a news bulletin from the front, to be "shown and read to all of the Whiteheads' neighbors." Working from numerous letters, sent to various friends, Aldrich composed *A Hilltop on the Marne*, an account of her experiences during the battle. Stein incorporates elements of this account within her portrait: "Then what came next. The war," which went on "for years" (four years?) and involved the "Front" (*P&P*, 119, 120). Stein's and Toklas's knowledge about Aldrich during these years may be suggested by "The next meant we knew. And the next meant and the next meant and as the next and as the next meant and we knew" (*P&P*, 121), where each "next" could represent a letter, leading to new knowledge ("knew" suggests "news").

Stein's portrait, however, represents her resistance to both the historical war Aldrich describes and the narrative forms quietly attached to the war they represent. Stein literally erases the reality and gritty detail central to the war and to Aldrich's journalistic account. In an even more fundamental sense, Stein refuses the plottedness central to Aldrich's storytelling. She suggests a link between narrative plot and the national plots—the making of "history"—leading to war. The nationalistic assertion of power, grounded in a rhetoric of priority and ownership, finds disturbing reflection within the authorial claim to originary power and possession of one's creation.

Through the voice of her portrait's narrator (which may merge at times with Aldrich's voice), Stein reveals an alliance between storytelling and authoritarian discourse. The narrator slips into this mode at moments, appearing to bark out a command like an officer before the troops:

> What happened and makes no mistakes.
> Next. (*P&P*, 114)

This parodied claim to a controlling correctness recurs in one of the portrait's few complete and "correct" sentences: "It is to be distinctly stated that under no circumstances were the changes other than those anticipated" (*P&P*, 111). Syntactical correctness reveals an alliance to the authoritarian claim of absolute control over one's creation. This statement links with a further one, "One can be historically accurate can one not" (*P&P*, 118) to suggest the profound link between authorial intention and subservience to history: "one" "anticipates" both worldly and literary happenings, just as one follows the prior truth of history. The "one" marks the dangerously monologic nature of such a narrative enterprise.

This patriarchal (and patriotic) mode of discourse and belief, as the portrait intimates, may find reproduction within Aldrich's "matriarchal" narrative. The portrait both exposes this reproduction and prevents its continuance through a refusal of further narrative production:

> Begin again.
> Continually.
> A history.
> Not necessarily in the beginning and not necessarily in the beginning,

she was not necessarily from the beginning she did not necessarily intend from the beginning to do as much as she did. (*P&P*, 114)

"Begin again" captures the struggle at the heart of this portrait, for although "begin" suggests a single originary moment, "again" undercuts this claim through its suggestion of repetition. One may begin a "history," yet if writing "begins again continually," thereby entering the continuous present, the narrative arc of history becomes irrelevant. "In the beginning," there was "not necessarily" the Word, even a newly claimed female Word, since "she" (the authorial figure) cannot claim absolute priority, intending "from the beginning to do [to write] as much as she did." As this unmothered writing, "she" foregoes intentionality as she "begins again continually," at each moment giving birth to herself.

This continuous birth of words, free from the claims of an originary and ordering power, involves an emphasis upon language as an unreferential and sensual entity. The separation of words from "intended" significance forms part of Stein's larger aesthetic and political project. "War" itself becomes simply a word, a sound, as Stein suggests by the narrator's blithe song, "Come to the war, oh come to the war come to the war come come to the war" (*P&P*, 121). Although in one sense this invitation imitates in gently parodic fashion Aldrich's enthusiasm for the war, in another sense it represents a lyrical appropriation of "war" as a pure word, emptied of any referential or historical content.

This lyricism attaches to a redeemed mode of storytelling, involving at least two figures in a situation of intimacy. "Come to the war, oh come to the war" may embody, in this sense, a highly different invitation to the very situation of storytelling. Stein's portrait places Mildred Aldrich's story within a larger community of listeners and tellers; it is this context that Stein asserts as valuable. To return to an earlier passage:

A simple settlement of infinite enjoyment and dismay, also included all that was included. It was all included and originally they said and originally she said and originally she said fancifully and not at all merely an obligation. It was as this that we were astounded.

As I was saying she simply said so.

The next and afterwards finally no one knew more than that and as to the authority for the statement can no one feel more suddenly than if they had met with it.

Finally she said I will say it again.
This is the story that Mildred Aldrich told us Saturday. (*P&P*, 116–17)

What emerges here, in fragmented form, is a conversation rather than a story. Conversation replaces traditional narrative, even as the communal situation of oral storytelling remains prominent. Although parts of the conversation may be overheard ("they said," "she said," "not at all merely an obligation," "afterwards finally no one knew more than that"), these fragments become valuable not for their references to an actual story, but for their communication of a situation of gossip and intimate interchange. "I," "she," and "they" claim no reference, so that we cannot know who is speaking at each point. As these boundaries become permeable, figures may merge and overlap.

Stein's effort to foreground the situation of intimacy at the heart of storytelling bears a significant resemblance to Walter Benjamin's concept of storytelling in his essay "The Storyteller" (published in 1936). Benjamin argues that the modern world has lost the ability to tell stories because it lacks an older crafts or folk community bound by shared experiences. Storytelling in its original (and, for Benjamin, its highest) form involves the passing on of experience "from mouth to mouth," without the distancing mediation of print.[3] He images a "community of listeners," present to the storyteller and engaged in "the rhythm" of manual work, such as "weaving and spinning."[4] In opposition to written forms of communication, including the novel and the newspaper, storytelling for Benjamin eschews the conveyance of "information" in favor of a more material and intimate "sink[ing of] the thing into the life of the storyteller, in order to bring it out of him again."[5] The story mingles with the storyteller's life, just as the new telling of the story mingles with the listeners' lives, who in their turn become storytellers, each leaving some personal mark on the story grounded in the situation of their own reception of the story.

Stein's sense of storytelling shares Benjamin's insistence upon the intimate, "mouth to mouth," democratic and bodily nature of oral narration. Her version of this intimacy, however, springs from the marriage of modernist and post-modernist techniques with premodernist "communities," constituted by more private intimacies. The "story," which for Benjamin holds importance as a vessel of folk wisdom, becomes almost absent within Stein's writing, as she attempts to capture, within her writing, the sensation of an intimacy outside of writing. As Benjamin suggests, intimacy leads to a continuous storytelling, in which the story may be handled by successive tellers, yet never possessed or owned exclusively. For Stein, although the handling alone becomes the important element, this activity is as resistant to possession as Benjamin's storytelling. "Many" share in this continual genesis: "In the beginning many may be and may be there" (*P&P*, 120). "Eggs," after all, cannot be reduced to one "egg." There are plenty to go around.

A Birthday Book

In *A Birthday Book* Stein's concern for an alternative vision of literary creation brings her to a different experimental field. Whereas in "Mildred Aldrich Saturday" storytellers find partial representation, *A Birthday Book* presents no storytelling figure at all. This movement away from representation, especially of an authorial figure, marks Stein's attempt to posit language itself as a matrix, and composition as a continuous but unauthored series of births.[6] In this birthday book, the fictive nature of the calendar and of narrative sequence links with the supreme fiction of language. In opposition to a language claiming a nonarbitrary correspondence between word and referent, Stein's language manifests a lively "variability," an openness to rearrangements through which words may be freed from traditional significance. The gendered nature of language, in particular, becomes exposed as a dangerous fiction. As words become untied from their moorings of significance, language metamorphoses into a field of play in which difference exists without hierarchy. "Birth" becomes a figure for language's continuous assertion of freedom from the weight of its cultural inheritance, as well as from an ordering authorial source.

The concept of a birthday book must have fascinated Stein, in terms of both its history and its structure. On the surface, a birthday book appears strongly attached to history, since its structure relies upon the calendar, each page marking one day of the year. This sequence becomes tied to the presence of one author. As with the Longfellow Birthday Book or the Whittier Birthday Book (popular nineteenth-century books that Gertrude Stein knew), these books held one quotation from the author for each day.[7] Within this struc-

ture, a blank space would be left on each page so that the name of a
baby born on a certain day could be recorded.

On the one hand, then, a grounding in coherent sequence is
inevitable. The book must begin on January 1, just as it must end
on December 31. Quite literally, a baby's name becomes placed at
some specific point along a historical line; through the writing of
the name, the baby enters history. From this angle, the baby is
secondary, since the actual births to be recorded come, of necessity,
after the book itself has come to birth. The author—the Longfellow
or the Whittier—whose words mark each page is also prior, both
in the literal sense of living before, and in the sense of the "living
before" of his words, first within another book and then (through
quotation) in this one. Such a text lays claim to a certain authority:
the double authority of history and of authorial originary power.
Although the author does not, of course, create the new baby, his
or her words, already on the page where the baby's name is to be
written, represent an indirect authorial power. The quote for each
day, in its appropriateness, may appear to be a prediction about the
child, or even a determining force.

On the other hand, however, Stein illuminates the possibilities
inherent in this form for a radical antihistoricism and a scattering
of authorial power. The problem of how to read a birthday book
suggests the effect of these subversions. It begins with January 1,
and moves to December 31; but how, precisely, does it move? It
is difficult to determine where to begin such a "book," or whether
to read through it at all. The historical frame of the calendar is
merely useful, its arbitrariness self-evident. In a similar way, the
"author" whose works enter this book through quotation can be
seen as a useful fiction. The quotations remain distinct both from
the "original" work and from the author. Although they bear the
author's signature, they stand alone on each page of this new text.
As a new word (a baby's name) becomes written next to them,
an even newer text comes into existence, composed of the new
relation between a quote and a name. The question of parenthood
subsides into the distance. The baby's "author," like the author of
the quotations, holds secondary importance relative to these words
on the page, these linguistic "babies" standing in relation to each
other.

Stein's *A Birthday Book* makes brilliant use of these possibilities.

The (apparent) beginning marks an entrance into Stein's consideration of the notion and forms of literary birth:

Who was born January first.
Who was born in January first.
Who was born and believe me who was born and believe me, who was born who was born and believe me.
At that rate.
Let us sell the bell. (*YGS*, 73)

The first line asks an apparently innocent question about "who was born" on a particular day. The second line, however, reveals the issue of priority implicit within this innocent question: "Who was born *in* January *first?*" The neutrality of the first question about birth and calendar placement becomes questionable, as the second line brings the ideology of these issues to our attention. The third line raises the further question of whether anybody was indeed born "first": "Who was born," it insists, as if to say, "Does anyone really have priority, except perhaps as a matter of *belief?*" "At that rate," in turn, suggests that an entire value system (rate) has been built around these questions, and the fifth line seems to say, "The hell with it. Let us sell the bell: let us get rid of the symbols or means by which those values announce themselves (ring in the new year). It is too much of a toll."

The new poetics, rung in when we "sell the bell," asserts its presence in the insistence upon the continual and changing birth of sound, words, and phrases that dissolve again into sounds. This poetics is present in the annunciation of a new song ("selling the bell") that replaces the old semantics. Although I have suggested a certain transparency to the language of the opening section, and although many moments in *A Birthday Book* bear traces of story and meaning, the work moves toward an unsignifying play with language.

It would seem that this work, in claiming the gift of self-generation, claims also a transcendence of gender. To this extent, *A Birthday Book* accords with Barthes's sense of writing as "that neutral, composite, oblique space where our subject slips away, the negative where all identity is lost, starting with the very identity of the body writing."[8] If we "lose" the identity of the "author," then clearly we must also lose a sense of the author's gender. Gender, however, resides not in human identity alone, but within language.

Whereas Barthes sees language as impersonal and unidentifiable, Stein understands it as a system marked in many ways, including that of gender. Although Stein critiques an ideology of priority, she still must confront the deeply rooted traces of this ideology within the parameters of language itself. Even though no storyteller dominates *A Birthday Book*, language continually asserts a challenge of domination.

Stein addresses this problem by introducing situations of inequality and dominance marked by gendered terms, as in the sudden use of the rhetorical salute, "yes sir," spoken by one or more anonymous voices: "April the first, yes sir" (*YGS*, 80); "Second of May, second of May yes sir" (*YGS*, 82). The voices saying "yes sir" appear to respond to an unvoiced command, as if to an officer calling a roll. *A Birthday Book*, in this sense, parodies the rigid structure of a calendar sequence forming its frame. The "author" calls out, "April the first?" And the text itself responds, like the good soldier it pretends for this moment to be, "yes sir." Yet such an enactment of a patriarchal situation of command and obedience reveals its fictive nature. April the first, after all, is April Fools' Day. "Just fooling," these words seem to say. The drama itself, of officer and soldier, is foolish, just as we are fools if we believe in it ("believe me") or in the sense of authorship upon which it relies.

Where the writing seems the most "written," it becomes most clearly identified with an authoritarian ideology. As in "Mildred Aldrich Saturday," this language often assumes the form of a sentence, both in the grammatical sense and in the sense of a judgment handed down from a system of patriarchal moral authority: "On March the twenty-first it is our duty to call a halt" (*YGS*, 79).[9] The correctness of the grammar meets with the "correctness" of the statement. In fact, the whole system of law comes into play here. What may be a quarrel ("March the twentieth melodrama") finds figuration as a case before a court of law ("And on March the twenty-third witnesses"), eventuating both in further declarations, whether by witnesses or by a judge ("March the twenty-seventh to declare and is it so"), and in further counterstatements ("March the twenty-eighth ordinarily on March the twenty-eighth ordinarily as added as an objection") (*YGS*, 79). The way in which this language evokes a narrative situation suggests Stein's perception of the alliance between traditional narrative and authoritarian discourse.

Whereas in "Mildred Aldrich Saturday" this commanding and declarative language always remains a narrative possibility, countered but not erased, in *A Birthday Book* this form of language undergoes a more complete dissolution. Never wholly "believed" in or claimed by a storyteller, it remains more fragile than it sounds. We experience little surprise when a familiarly masculine form of expression metamorphoses suddenly into something very different, as in "March twenty-fourth able to be able to be able very able he is very able he is a very able man." We hear the words, "he is very able, he is a very able man," at first as the kind of statement Charles Tansley would make as he walks with Mr. Ramsay on the terrace in *To the Lighthouse*. Woolf parodies such authoritative discourse as strongly as Stein does. Woolf's narrative representation of Tansley's language, as filtered through Mrs. Ramsay's memory of the children's mimicry, resembles Stein's parody despite its clearer referentiality: "They knew what he liked best—to be for ever walking up and down, up and down, with Mr. Ramsay, and saying who had won this, who had won that, who was a 'first-rate man' at Latin verses, who was 'brilliant but I think fundamentally unsound,' who was undoubtedly the '*ablest fellow* in Balliol' " (emphasis added).[10]

With Stein, the words themselves seem to leap into revolt. What seems certain makes a shift through the running together of two words, an effect invited by the repetition: "very" and "able," together, make "variable." "He is a variable man." Where has our solid citizen gone? Is he, we may even begin to wonder, really a "he" at all? Or may he, in his variability, become a woman as well? (Although it is not necessary to an understanding of this passage, it is interesting that Alice Toklas's name is encoded here: "able" contains "a" and "b," and "able to be" or "*to be able*" hints at A.B.T.) The possibilities mark a breaking open of what looked like a closed language. The brilliance of this passage lies in its revelation of a "very able" man as a construct of language. His "veryness" and his "ableness" can be turned into a "variableness" because he is only a product of a gender-based language system, a truth rendering him more vulnerable (because more variable) to the play of language. As socially constructed products, we may be undone as easily as we are made, a fact that becomes a matter of celebration in terms of this articulation of Stein's feminist poetics.

This sudden instability emerges even more openly in the following sequence, as the political significance of Stein's linguistic experiment breaks through the surface:

March the fifth or powder.

March the sixth or giggling.

March the seventh patently, patently see, patently saw, she saw he saw patently see to see. He would be. (*YGS*, 73)

Although "March" may be read throughout the month of March as a command—"March at one march at once march at one march for once" (*YGS*, 78)—and a supremely authoritarian one, the text insistently veers away from a stable realization of such command. The word "or" ("March the fifth *or* powder") suggests choice, an offering of at least two possibilities, just as the words "powder" or "giggling," standing outside any sentence *about* powder or giggling, leave the actual command unspoken, even imaginary. "Powder" could suggest either face powder "or" gun powder or the dust created by the crushing of some substance. Such a substance might be the sentence itself, especially when in the imperative mood; or it might be the authoritative and originary pow-er behind such a sentence. Power turns to powder with the sudden disruptive insertion of the letter "d." Power, then, scattered like powder, dispersed randomly over a surface—the lines of *A Birthday Book*—becomes unable to make a shot. Gun powder, in this sense, turns to a less aggressive powder, but a potent one nonetheless.

Following our exploration of "powder," we come upon a possible response: "March the sixth or giggling." It is as if the text, observing our attempt to find the command, and our discovery of the command's dissolution into powder, responds with laughter, just as it invites us to respond. Although "giggling" is a neutral term, its association with the words "gaggle" and "cackle," sounds linked with geese or hens (*OED*), suggests a bias toward the cultural feminine within the constructs of our language, where the feminine attaches to uncontrollability, lightness, and amusement, as opposed to a stern masculine authority.[11] This authority turns again to powder in the next piece: "March the seventh patently, patently see, patently saw, she saw he saw patently see to see. He would be." Again, a command seems just possible: "patently see." As an adjective, "patent" may signify either the presence of a proprietary claim or an openness to general knowledge or use (*OED*). To see patently, in the latter case, might mean to see as openly as possible, with a large vision. What is seen, in that case, is "patent," both in the sense of clear (even obvious) and in the sense of owned. Such sight may own its objects of vision, just as they may lie open for its proprietary claim. A public and nationalistic ideology quietly inhabits the phrase, "see to see," which echoes the patriotic song "America the Beautiful": "And crown thy good with brotherhood from *sea to* shining *sea*."

Yet this national and imperialistic mode of seeing collapses in Stein's text into giggles, just as gun powder dissolves into face powder/power. "Patently see" leads quickly to "patently saw, she saw he saw," evoking a children's nursery rhyme: "She saw, he saw, we all saw a seesaw." This rhyming makes the distinctions of gender ludicrous, if not impossible. "He" and "she" become, not so much identifying pronouns, as sounds that overlap and rhyme, in an infinite interchange. Gender vanishes in the seesaw. As a seesaw, gender becomes, not a hierarchy of "he" *over* "she," but a juggling (a jiggling? a "giggling"?) of he *with* she *with* we, back and forth, to our grateful confusion. It adds to the "patent" nature of this unstable language—in the sense of its "spreading" and "expanding" nature—that such interchangeability of "he" with "she" can include a playful glance at Hebrew, where "who is he and he is she"; the sound "he" signifies the pronoun "she."[12] "He would be . . ."—*she*? "Would be" . . . if what? Perhaps if we are not desirous of a patent, but pat-i-ent: "patiently, patiently see, patiently saw, she saw he saw patiently see to see. He would be." The "i"—or "I"—thus inserted into "patent" "would be" unidentifiable, a participant in both genders, just as both genders seem to participate in each other. A merely phallic "I" is now simply one possibility, but not a necessary one; it can easily be removed or reinterpreted.

A Birthday Book argues for the happy instability of such divisiveness within gendered language through positing an alternative language of variability, even of confusion, where the possibility of one language and one voice gives way to the possibility of an indeterminate number of instances of writing. Although language remains gender-marked, the marks of the text continually dissolve and confound this division.

"Patriarchal Poetry"

Let her be let her be let her be let her be to be to be
let her be let her try.
To be shy.   *("Patriarchal Poetry," YGS, 120)*

In 1927 Stein returns to the question of creation from a new angle. In the earlier "Mildred Aldrich Saturday" she challenges the concept of a storyteller, whether female or male, a challenge heightened in *A Birthday Book*'s eschewal of story or teller in favor of a mythos of continual and unordered linguistic birth. Although her 1927 prose poem "Patriarchal Poetry" continues this mythos, a new element appears in the annunciation of a writing primarily— although not exclusively—attached to a female presence and landscape. This writing will find its fullest expression in the 1927 novel *Lucy Church Amiably*.

"Patriarchal Poetry" grounds its consideration of literary origination and ownership in manifold allusions to Genesis. In rewriting Genesis, Stein's meditation links monotheistic creation with a monologic and authoritarian literary form allied to historical and narrative linearity. We may enter into her meditation via a surprising riddle occurring halfway through "Patriarchal Poetry":

What is the difference between a fig and an apple. One comes before the other. What is the difference between a fig and an apple one comes before the other what is the difference between a fig and an apple one comes before the other. (*YGS*, 128)

At first glance, the answer ("One comes before the other") appears irrelevant. Although "fig" comes before "apple" in the sentence, this priority evinces a humorous arbitrariness, and indeed undergoes a sudden reversal as a second "fig" follows "apple," to be followed in turn by another "apple." The claim to priority itself—to being "before"—becomes comically impossible to sustain.

Whereas the order of "figs" and "apples" in Genesis holds crucial significance for the conceptual shape of Western Judeo-Christian history, Stein blithely changes the original order in her first sentence. In the account of the Fall the apple "comes before" the fig, in that Eve and then Adam, in eating the apple, cause their own Fall, represented by their attempt to hide their nakedness in fig leaves.[13] This story represents and explains the woman's "difference" in a negative sense. The price of Eve's transgression is the pain of child-birth and, as Stein may have interpreted it, the secondary status of women within patriarchal culture: "In pain shall you bear children. Yet your urge shall be for your husband, And he shall rule over you." [14]

The mention of "figs" and "apples" evokes a situation of Adamic naming grounded in the similarity of Adam to the original Namer. John's interpretation of Genesis in linguistic terms—"In the beginning was the Word, and the Word was with God, and the Word was God"—marks the originary power of God as the Word who, in naming, calls into existence and who continues to govern the world He has named. The story's sequence, from God's Creation to the creation of Adam and then to the creation and transgression of Eve, may be said to form an argument about the importance of priority in the establishment, from the beginning, of hierarchical relationships. Stein reveals the arbitrariness and changeability of such a sequence. Priority becomes a comic and even a useless issue, as the Word metamorphoses into words, composed of letters on a page: "f-i-g," "a-p-p-l-e." The order of letters in each word, although agreed upon by all speakers of the English language, manifests itself within Stein's writing as essentially arbitrary, just as the sequence of "apple" to "fig" exists simply through consensus: and who, Stein might ask, gives a fig for consensus? Eve's transgression against God's Word becomes in Stein's text a "mistake"—"Patriarchal poetry makes no mistake" (*YGS*, 124)—to be reclaimed as Stein's project. By making mistakes—"Patriarchal Poetry makes mistakes" (*YGS*, 132)—Stein turns Genesis on its head. She reenters the "Garden," not of Eden (God's and Adam's garden), but of language itself, a field within which words may be loosened from the old order, the old stories and meanings. Eve's capacity to make "mistakes" (a significantly mild term) forms matter for celebration, as in "Poetry and Grammar," where Stein observes:

[Verbs and adverbs] have one very nice quality and that is that they can be so mistaken. It is wonderful the number of mistakes a verb can make and that is equally true of its adverb. Nouns and adjectives never can make mistakes can never be mistaken but verbs can be so endlessly, both as to what they do and how they agree or disagree with whatever they do. (*LIA*, 211–12)

Once words make "mistakes," leaping away from their traditional significances and contexts, "patriarchal poetry" may be "fastened back." "Patriarchal Poetry" suggests this fastening in its beginning: "As long as it took fasten it back to a place where after all
he would be carried away" (YGS, 106). If "it" signifies "patriarchal
poetry," then Stein suggests that this poetry "took" a long time to
make, just as Stein's "Patriarchal Poetry" embarks upon a lengthy
project of unfastening. This poetic tradition, however, may be kept
"back," in the past, where it cannot harm the present text. As the
patriarchal poet, or the poetic tradition, "he" may be carried away
from the present, just as the pronoun "he" may be loosened from
its freightedness as a signifier of dominance within culture.

Stein's "Patriarchal Poetry" also represents a "fastening back,"
not to an historical point but to an imaginary one. She offers us
the utopian possibility of becoming present "before" words became
ordered by the Word. This place of "beforeness" may be understood as a transformation of the presymbolic relation of intimacy
between mother and child, where words have not yet become participants in the Law of the Father, but present themselves as sounds,
alive, unfastened to objects, and fascinating ("fasten-ating") in their
ceaselessly changing nature. Language in its original and potential form, Stein suggests, transcends all our attempts to "fasten" it
down. In Stein's redeemed version of the mother-infant relation,
no figure claims priority.

Words spill with profusion into the opening of Stein's second
paragraph, in a movement illuminating her assertion that paragraphs are "emotional":[15]

For before let it before to be before spell to be before to be before to have
to be to be for before to be tell to be to having held to be to be for before
to call to be for to be before to till until to be till before to be for before to
be until to be for before to for to be for before will for before to be shall
to be to be for to be for to be before still to be will before to be before for
to be to be. (YGS, 106)

We hear a distorted echo of God's first Word here, his "Let there
be . . ." The "original" "Let there be . . ." becomes dispersed: we
see the words "let" and "be," and even an approximation of the
whole phrase, now "let it be——————," yet their location in a sentence of divine significance has been made impossible. The word
that originally might have meant God's (or the human author's)

priority—"before"—becomes far more unstable, capable of breaking in two and coming together again: "to be for to be before." The Word, transformed into this cornucopia of words, has become a matter of spelling ("spell to be before to be before"), whose original "spell" ("Let there be . . .") may be unspelled by Stein's new incantation.

The beginning of this paragraph, "for before," represents a parody in small of the ideology of priority. "For" literally comes before "before": "For [comes before] before." This assertion attaches to a grander claim, as "for," signifying "because," marks the beginning of an explanation that might read: "Because [I came] before, [I have the right to claim power.]" "Before," in this sense, acts as the familiar agent, guarantor, and source of authority in Western culture. This "before," however, joins no complete sentence, divine or human, but opens onto a tumultuous series of words, "befores" scattered among them.

This deconstructive and demythologizing rewriting of Genesis, however, offers simultaneously a new act of origination, a call into literary and linguistic being. Unordered by sentences or syntax, the words in these paragraphs find a new order. As they jostle each other in a continual movement, coming together in a different form each time we attempt to read through them, rhyming, splitting in two and reuniting, repeating with seemingly infinite variations, these words plunge us into the immediacy and presence of language, where each word, even each sound, each letter, marks a birth—not a birth out of one coherent authorial presence, but a different kind, a sudden and delightful appearance of word after word, letter after letter, onto the whiteness of the page.

This continuous birth of language links with a "story" glimpsed but largely unwritten, one countering Genesis with an account of an utterly democratic creation. The "for" in one sense—"let it *be for*"—suggests a gift, an interpretation borne out further on:

Dedicated to all the way through. Dedicated to all the way through.
Dedicated too all the way through. Dedicated too all the way through.
Apples and fishes day-light and wishes apples and fishes day-light and wishes day-light at seven.
All the way through dedicated to you. (*YGS*, 118)

Another presence becomes felt here, one that may in an immediate sense be "fastened" to Alice Toklas. "Alice" indeed comes in as a name within a few lines of this dedication: "Helen greatly relieves Alice patriarchal poetry come too there must be patriarchal poetry come too" (YGS, 119). "Patriarchal poetry" may be transformed to such an extent that it will "come" to these two women; or it may "come too," it may come along with other poetics, for Stein is establishing a democracy. In this sense, the opening passage ("For before") may represent a form of marriage vow, a statement of dedication: "to have," "to be," "to be for," "to be t[w]o" (an allusion to "Alice B. Toklas") "to having held," "to call to." All these infinitives suggest an infinity, an illimitability, of the love between these "two," as Stein vows that she "will" [love], just as she "shall" [always love], "still," and for the duration of time ("while").

This allusion to Stein's relationship with an actual woman forms part of a larger revision of the concept of genesis, for in Stein's alternative "creation" at least two figures are present: the "we" of the "to be we" passage—"To be we to be to be we to be to be to be we to be we" (YGS, 114).[16] The unnamed "they" referred to throughout the piece may refer simultaneously to "patriarchal poets" and to the two whose "wedding"—"Not a piece of which is why a wedding left" (YGS, 113) [not a piece of wedding cake is left?]—"Patriarchal Poetry" announces, and through whom the "poetry" comes into being. Together, "they have it with it reconsider it with it" (YGS, 108), where the "it" may be both their love and, incongruously, patriarchal poetry, which undergoes reconsideration in relation to ("with") "their" intimate creativity, their creation of intimacy. "They might change it as it can be made to be" (YGS, 112): through their doubled efforts, they have the power to change the very conception of authorship.

This half-articulated intimacy gives birth to an alternative language and literary form allied to the female, although open to an interplay of gender. Toward the middle of "Patriarchal Poetry," the birth of this new form is announced (and prayed for) more openly:

Let her be to be to be to be let her be to be to be to be let her to be let her to be let her be to be when is it that they are shy.
Very well to try.
Let her be that is to be let her be that is to be let her be let her try.
Let her be let her be let her be to be to be to be shy let her be to be let her be to be let her try.
Let her try.

Let her be let her be let her be let her be to be to be let her be let her try.
To be shy. (*YGS*, 120)

This pronoun "her," open in its reference, may include Alice "B."
Toklas ("Let her be" can be read as "letter b"), Stein herself ("Let
her try": let her attempt to recreate patriarchal poetry by renaming
and reclaiming it), and a discourse more democratically inclusive
of the feminine ("her try," or "her[s]t[o]ry," the opposite of an ex-
clusive "his story"), for which the text wishes and prays through
its rhythmic incantation. The word "shy," enfolding within itself
both "she" and "I," emblematizes the doubleness of this writing.
Furthermore, the plea to "let her" constitutes an invocation to
the "letter" ("let her try": letter/herstory: a new form of literature), which, as the element composing written language, may be
"rearranged," just as Stein's "Patriarchal Poetry" rearranges traditional "letters": "Rearrangement is nearly rearrangement" (*YGS*,
119). The letter, as a material sign, comes as close as possible to
the literal, as the traditional place of the female, now drawn into
language.[17]
    In the insistence upon language's materiality, upon its graphic
shapes and designs as well as its presence as sheer and delightful sound, Stein attempts ("Let her try") to attach language to the
body, especially to the realm of lesbian relationship, which becomes her figure for the form of writing she (they) urge(s) into
existence. Soon after the incantation of "Let her try," the sexuality
that has been intimated but only obliquely described bursts into
articulation:

Near near near nearly pink near nearly pink nearly near near nearly pink.
Wet inside and pink outside. Pink outside and wet inside wet inside and
pink outside latterly nearly near near pink near near nearly three three
pink two gentle one strong three pink all medium medium as medium as
medium sized as sized. (*YGS*, 121)

This passage "nearly" describes a lesbian erotics. The suggestive
"wet inside and pink outside," although it is not "fastened" to any
particular part of the body, hints at the female genitals, just as the
numbers "one," "two," and "three" may refer to fingers. Stein's
resistance to naming names here forms an essential part of her dis-
mantling of traditional representations of the female body. Further,
the limitlessness of this sexuality, as Stein evokes it, represents the

basis for a utopian transcendence of history. Origin and priority have no hold here, for this erotics has no beginning and no end; it cannot be understood as a linear narrative, just as its participants, its "authors," cannot be identified. Each may be "before" the other, in the sense of being present to the other, yet no one figure emerges as the primary creator of this ongoing event. In this sense, although the model for such dialogic creativity is that of lesbian love-making, the model opens out to a larger field inclusive of both genders, in which gender itself becomes a questionable category, since the hierarchy upon which it has been based becomes no longer possible.

Lucy Church Amiably

In the opening of *Lucy Church Amiably: A Novel of Romantic Beauty and Nature and which Looks Like an Engraving*, the "shyness" and hesitancy marking the annunciation of an unnamed "she" in "Patriarchal Poetry" flower into a more overt claim. The prayer to "Let her be" metamorphoses into a celebratory announcement (within the novel's "Advertisement") of a dialogic and profoundly "amiable" or loving female creator. This "Advertisement" asks us to turn toward this figure, to mark her advent.

The image of Lucy Church combines the female with the sacred and with Nature. As the Church of Lucey, France, near Stein's summer home in Bilignin, "Lucy Church" lay at the heart of the landscape with which Stein was most intimate. In this sense, Lucy Church might be expected to remain a shining ("Lucy" suggests "light") but mute presence, a woman-cathedral resting like a Madonna in the landscape. This aspect of Lucy Church resembles the traditional Romantic association of the female with Nature as a maternal, sacral, and mute presence to be approached and named within the poem. Stein, however, revises this tradition of mute female Nature:

Select your song she said and it was done and then she said and it was done with a nod and then she bent her head in the direction of the falling water. Amiably. ("Advertisement," *LCA*)

Lucy Church's language here echoes God's in Genesis 1, just as "and it was done" resembles the Biblical "and God saw that it was good," a link suggesting Lucy's presence as a divine creator. She becomes both a figure for an inspiring Nature and a poet-creator, a collapse of distinctions undercutting the male romantic division between female Nature and male poet. Her mode of creativity, however, represents a profound revision of Genesis. Whereas God creates the world through His originary Word, Lucy Church asks only that another's "song" be "select[ed]." Instead of creating a world through language, she invites various poet-singers (including Nature) to choose their own songs. The movement from the performative "Let there be . . ." to "Select" marks a larger movement from a divine monologue to a democratic and shared dialogue. The Fall and the expulsion from Eden following Eve's (and then Adam's) transgression of God's Word find new and celebratory form in "the falling water." If a fall exists at all, it is, like the "mistakes" Stein loves, "amiable." Encompassing Lucy Church, the water, the anonymous poets (selecters of songs), and us, "amiably" suggests the dialogic nature of creativity, which becomes a shared enterprise, a common "song," sung in friendship and love. The absence of punctuation to distinguish Lucy's words suggests that these words may be shared.

In Stein's vision of a dialogic genesis, the creator (or creatrice) cannot be distinguished from the creation. Lucy Church already inhabits the landscape, speaking within this landscape rather than naming it from the outside. Her speech retains an intimate connection with the speech of Nature. Although she uses words, the emphasis upon "song" suggests a form of language composed primarily of music and sound, as Lucy's kinship with Saint Lucy, patron saint of music, confirms.

As a poet, Lucy Church appears at first to contradict this intimacy with nature by performing an Adamic naming of creatures within the world:

Imagine she says. Imagine what I say.

Add cows to oxen goats to sheep and add cows and oxen and goats to sheep. Add oxen and cows and chickens and goats and sheep to fields and she will be satisfied so she says. She will be satisfied. (*LCA*, 49)

"Adding," however, differs from naming. Although in one sense Lucy performs a kind of creation, "adding" creatures to the landscape, in another sense this creation occurs primarily within the imagination as it informs the addition of words to the page. "She" adds the word "cows" to the word "oxen," the word "goats" to the word "sheep," in an addition causing "satisfaction"—"so she says." [18] What satisfies her (and us) is this "amiable" caressing of words as objects in their own right. Stein attempts to "resuscitate" a female and sacral nature—"Lucy Church was amiable and very much resuscitated" (LCA, 51)—through the creation of a poetics allowing this nature presence, paradoxically, through a language that comes "to be a thing in itself" (LIA, 242).

In this sense, Lucy Church Amiably attempts, not to describe a landscape, but to present a (written) landscape. The resemblance of this "Novel" to "an Engraving," rather than to "Nature," suggests Stein's desire to "let [Nature in her actuality] be," to "let her be shy," even as Stein "imagines" the presence of Nature's voice *upon the page*, "engraved" within the marks of print. The visual "images" of Romantic poetry metamorphose into the images of letters and words, added to each other in a written wedding, a marriage of "cows" to "oxen," "she" to "I." As a literary landscape, Lucy Church invokes our own "amiable" presence, as we "add" our "song" to this song of addition.

PART III

Reading as Conversation

: 5 :

Blood on the Dining-Room Floor: The Intimacy of Audience

> *Do you really understand.*   (*Blood, 16*)
>
> *Lizzie do you understand.*
> *Of course she does.*
> *Of course do you.*   (*Blood, 79*)

Written in 1933, just after *The Autobiography of Alice B. Toklas, Blood on the Dining-Room Floor* addresses in complex and illuminating ways the situation at the heart of writing with which Stein always grapples: the communication between an "I" and a "you," between an author (or a work) and a reader. In this murder mystery, as in other writings, Stein posits and works to create a mode of response encompassing more than a distanced, purely cerebral, and traditionally masculine logic.[1] Her writing represents a calling out to our fullest responsiveness. "Understanding," as Stein persuasively suggests, incorporates a response composed of the body as well as of the mind, in which this division between body and mind becomes profoundly challenged and begins to dissolve. To read in an authentically "loving" manner is to become open to the writing's yearning for a reader's presence.

Blood on the Dining-Room Floor is one of Stein's most "tender" and yearning works. In its callings out to "Lizzie," to "Edith," and to an unspecified "you," it articulates the possibilities both for a genuine communion and interchange between audience and text, and for the obstruction of this communion through an audience's reluctance to "understand." The extreme of reluctance, as Stein suggests, may be an active hostility leading to "blood on the floor": to the wounding or murder of the writing itself. Although the mystery invites all readers, both of these possibilities become most significant for

Stein in the arena of a female readership. Stein sees redemptive possibilities in a loving and intimate relationship imagined most directly as one between a woman writer and a woman reader. Yet this idyll manifests vulnerability to forms of hostility reproducing masculine violence toward women. Women too, as Stein implies by her anxious callings out to "Lizzie," may have an ax to grind. These different interpretive stances, as I shall suggest, bear important implications for the realm outside books as well, for Stein's vision of the possibilities of understanding holds a larger significance in both political and ethical terms. Only with understanding can bloodshed be prevented, whether on the dining room floor or in a larger theater.

Invitations to the Audience

What did you say. (Blood, 20)

Blood on the Dining-Room Floor, like many of Stein's writings, invites us eagerly into its imagined world. Our presence as readers, certainly implied in any piece of literature, becomes a matter of devoted concern within the narrative itself. It is as if we discover, as we sit holding the book under the lamplight in peaceful isolation, ready to observe a world separate from ourselves, that we have already been anticipated, that we are in a mysterious sense already "inside" the story we have chosen to read. We are "in" it, in a sense, before we even know it.[2] The imagined world of the story, in fact, has more to do with the "story" of reading than with the murder mystery forming its ostensible story; or rather, the story of reading emerges as the actual murder mystery.

In short, a murder may have occurred: an unnamed "hotel-keeper's wife" falls to her death in the courtyard of the hotel, whether by accident, suicide, or murder. She may, it is hinted, have been killed by one Alexander, who may (rumor has it) have plotted with his sister, a maid in the same hotel, to gain control over this business through the sister's possible marriage to the hotel-keeper himself.[3] Most of the ingredients for a detective novel present themselves here: the corpse, the motive, the suspicious characters surrounding the event of death. Yet Stein, as one might guess, handles such elements cavalierly. If *Blood on the Dining-Room Floor* is a detective novel at all, as Stein claimed to hope that it was (*HWIW,*

148–49), then it is a highly modernist one. For it reminds us of the rituals of this genre, even as it completely transforms the genre itself.

One of the major differences between this mystery story and an ordinary detective novel lies in two linked absences: there is no detective, just as there is no solving of the crime (if, that is, a crime may be said to have been committed at all, since the wife's death may have been accident or suicide). Stein shows little interest in detection as it usually occurs. As she says in *Narration*, where she distinguishes between newspapers and crime stories:

And so in the newspapers you like to know the answer in crime stories in reading crime and in written crime stories knowing the answer spoils it. After all in the written thing the answer is a let down from the interest and that is so every time that is what spoils most crime stories unless another mystery crops up during the crime and that mystery remains. (*Narration*, 40)

Stein shows an "interest" here in mystery itself. This mystery goes beyond the specific crime—who killed Mme. X and why?—to include a realm more diffuse and incalculable. In *Blood on the Dining-Room Floor*, although the specific mystery of the wife's death holds importance, other mysteries become equally important. The story gradually moves away from this "central" plot, which by the end is almost out of sight. Almost every element, in its oddity and evasion of the usual interpretive "detection," remains a mystery.

To begin detective work, whether as a bona fide detective or a critic, one generally needs some kind of handle. So, in opening *Blood on the Dining-Room Floor*, one begins to look for such certainty, for signposts that may begin to mark our progress. The first paragraph announces: "They had a country house. A house in the country is not the same as a country house. This was a country house. They had had one servant, a woman. They had changed to two servants, a man and woman that is to say husband and wife" (*Blood*, 11). Who, one might begin to ask, is "they" (a question never to be answered)? And what, precisely, *is* the difference between "a country house" and "a house in the country"? One may start to answer: a house that is simply "in the country" may be a house lived in all year round, thus a more ordinary house, whereas a "country house" may be in contradistinction to a "city house" and so lived in for a few months of the year. Yet, although the narrator appears to find the distinction worthy of comment within the first paragraph, she or he does not go on to affirm or deny our guess, and indeed moves off the point completely. The tone here is, on the surface, extraordinarily positive and definite, even opinionated; yet this air of complete certainty holds an ironic relation to the uncertainty that we feel as we read. In this sense, the narration mocks traditional narrative claims to authority even as it claims a mysterious authority that we cannot easily penetrate.

Characters too appear and disappear within the narrative with an air of questionable absoluteness. For instance, the story introduces two servants who appear to present keys to an anticipated mystery, but who will in fact have nothing at all to do with the murder plot: "The first husband and wife were Italian. They had a queer way of walking, she had a queer way of walking and she made noodles with spinach which made them green. He in his way of walking stooped and picked up sticks instead of chopping them and he dried the sticks on the stove and the fires did not burn" (*Blood*, 11–12). This is the first and last that we see of this odd couple, for the narrative moves immediately on to a series of servants, who come one after the other, with no apparent connection, each with their mysteries. We are left to wonder, among other things, why the servants had "a queer way of walking." Was he lame? Was she lame? Why didn't the sticks burn even though he dried them? Why, in a larger sense, do these characters come onto the scene at all? As one reads, however, one has no time to dwell on such questions. In any case, one begins to suspect that the answers, if they came, would be of less interest than the surprise one feels as one asks. Stein invokes in the reader a sense of curiosity that remains tantalized but unanswered in any direct way. The narrator resists giving us answers, or connecting the bits of information to a central story, allowing them to remain floating, intriguing, and potentially irrelevant.

In a traditional story, questions occur to a reader; yet ordinarily the story, in creating a believable (if fictive) world, presents one with certain givens that have an air of "reality" and substantiality. Stein attempts the opposite of such an air; the world she presents seems largely "unreal," yet in its very dreamlike unreality takes on a surprising presence of its own.[4]

The title, *Blood on the Dining-Room Floor*, surprises us in another way. By its material details of blood on a floor (and not just any floor, but a dining room floor), it appears to offer us palpable clues for our detective work. Within this story, however, we find no blood and no dining room floor. The one death happens outside, in a cement courtyard. Only once does the phrase occur: before the brief tale of the country house sabotage of telephones and other domestic objects, the narrator abruptly asks, "Why should blood on the floor make anyone mad against automobiles and telephones and desks. Why" (*Blood*, 13). The "anyone" may be the male servant who is fired after being suspected of tampering with the cars and the telephone and the desk. Yet the reference to "blood on the floor" (now any floor) remains completely uncertain.[5] It may signify the uncertainty behind clues, behind—in a larger sense—language itself, which gives us signs yet offers no guarantee of our journey from these signs to any certain reality, even as we sense the presence of this reality. Stein hopes to keep us on this edge of uncertainty and to redefine it as both pleasurable and valuable; for it will be in this border territory of mystery that a different form of "understanding" will emerge, through a more diffuse and open-ended act of reading. As Stein said about *Blood*, "the detecting was general . . . nobody did any detecting *except just conversation*" (emphasis added).[6] Such "general" detection has no particular or verifiable truths to uncover; instead, it asserts the value of interpretation as a mutual "conversation."

We participate, in fact, in such "conversation" with the writing as we read. *Blood* creates a surprisingly intimate bond between the story and the listener through the presence of a narrator who seems dedicated to such a bond. The relationship is a colloquial one. At sudden moments throughout the narrative, the narrator seems to pause and turn to the listener with injunctions and questions. Again and again the listener is urged to "listen": "This is what happened. . . . Listen carefully" (*Blood*, 13). "Listen to all about Alexander" (*Blood*, 53). Or, pressing us beyond simply listening, the narrator interrupts the story to add: "Think of all that. / Just think of all that" (*Blood*, 17). Such moments, in marking a place to the side of the ongoing story, from which it may be viewed, ask for a special attentiveness to certain parts of the telling. In a more important sense, however, these moments call us to this shared place on the side, where the most interesting "story" occurs between ourselves as imagined listeners and the narrator as storyteller.

The narrator appears to guess how baffling the story may be. Pausing in moment after moment, s/he comes out to us again, with variations on the startling question, "Do you understand": "Do you see what I mean" (*Blood*, 15); "Do you really understand" (*Blood*, 16); "Do you hear" (*Blood*, 30)—culminating on the last page with "Do you understand anything" (*Blood*, 81). The tone of these questions is often hard to determine, since the asking is usually so sudden and, in a sense, out of context. Each question appears to occupy a possible field of tones ranging from casual interest to earnestness and familiarity to a more forceful insistence, even (at points) to a near despair. Yet each instance of questioning urges our own activity of reading to come forward. It becomes difficult to feel that our responses may remain entirely private and, by implication, unquestionable. "Listening," to use Stein's word, does not remain an act easily distinguishable from "telling."[7] As we listen, we are urged to tell what we hear, just as the narrator, even within the act of telling a story, pauses again and again to listen for our response.

I have used the word "urged." Yet often this word is too weighty for the questioner's voice, which seems more to tease us, to call out to us on a sudden whim, catching us out as we sit apart in our private chair. Or, rather, our chairs—for suddenly one may become aware of oneself as a member of a hitherto unknown, and still undefined, circle of listeners. A fifth of the way through the story, for instance, the narrator's general attitude of questioning and inviting one's private response becomes suddenly expanded and playfully heightened, as the narrator appears to become concerned that some among us may be confused. Assuming for the moment the voice of a teacher, or of a concerned group leader, the narrator calls out to us:

Has everybody got it straight. So far we have two families and besides a country house.

We have three times crime.

Remember there was a country house where everything happened one day, and other things happened the other days.

Then there was a funeral. (*Blood*, 26)

After a brief pause, as if to give us time to confess shamefacedly to our remaining uncertainty, the narrator says with an invisible but palpable nod of the head, "Read the beginning again."

Such directives, together with these busily educative countings-over ("we have three times crime"), are tongue-in-cheek at least in part, for the narration until this point, as reflected in this small summation of its elements, has clearly not been one where a lucid and "straight" plot line has been of the essence. "Four three five," as the narrator remarks immediately before launching into these questions to "everybody": a series of numbers that, in its unconcern with "straightness," suggests a larger unconcern with linear plot. To "begin again," by this token, would in all likelihood land one back in a similar quandary.

I shall address more fully the problematics of "understanding" later in this chapter. I wish to emphasize here the narrator's method of drawing us (whoever the "us" is) into sudden moments of intimacy, whether playful or more serious, in ways causing us to reimagine our own act of reading. At an astonishing extreme, the listener appears to discover her or his own presence within the text, not simply as a reader but as a character or even as a figure listening somehow directly to the narrator from a place within the text. The narrator, for example, turns to us at one point for help with a curious, improbable, and perhaps irrelevant detail: "Do any of you know a disease that makes complete black rings all around the eyes as if the rings were made with shoe black" (*Blood*, 24).

This narrator holds a position of much greater and more sustained uncertainty than would be usual in other mystery stories. Just as the plot contains no detective-figure, the narrator also omits detective work, whether in a literal or a metaphorical sense. At points, the narrator sounds knowledgeable and even opinionated: "The telephone was not working that was a fact" (*Blood*, 13). She or he certainly implies, delicately and indirectly, how the "facts" could be put together to solve the crime. Yet, in a way that increases as the story continues, the narrator allows us to see gaps in his or her knowledge. "Were they really poor. Ah alas. This nobody can know" (*Blood*, 28). Furthermore, the narrator does not claim to be writing from a position of conventional masculine authority. The narration, while at points it may sound "omniscient," reveals its own uncertain movements: false starts, changes of mind, back and forth motions, self-contradictions, digressions, even irrelevancies —all are allowed to remain uncensored. It is as if we are granted a glimpse behind the stage of narration, to study props, artificial sets, the play in rehearsal. The act of storytelling shows itself as an act inherently uncertain and unauthoritarian, where the appearance of a controlling and omniscient mode of authority may be granted only if we stand far enough away, and where such an appearance detracts from the possibility of our participation in the writing's very process.

At points, we even find that we ourselves appear to have asked a question. "What did you say," the narrator abruptly asks, in the midst of the story. And, as if we have responded in the gap between sentences, the narrator "answers," "Yes they had somebody employed there who certainly did her share" (*Blood*, 20). Our question may be reconstructed; we must have asked, "Didn't the wife of the hotel-keeper have any help?" The narrator playfully assumes that we are not as distant as readers of a book, that we are, in a sense, not reading at all, since reading implies the absence of the one who is read, just as writing implies the absence of the one who reads. This belief appears to be understood within the narrative as more mysterious and magical than "real"; that is, the narrator invites us, not actually to be "in" the world of the story, but to imagine the possibility of such intimacy.

Alice Toklas and Reading as Conversation

Then someone says yes to it, to something you are liking, or doing or making. (MOA, 485)

The possibility for such intimacy for Gertrude Stein was not simply imaginary. Stein found in Alice Toklas a first reader in every sense. From Stein's writing of *The Making of Americans* on, in the first decade of the twentieth century, Alice Toklas quite literally read Stein's work immediately after it was written, and she always brought it into print, first by typing it and then by establishing a private publishing house, the Plain Edition, expressly to publish Stein's work. The importance, from Stein's point of view, of Toklas's constant presence as a reader may be calculated by the smallness of Stein's reading public, especially in the years before the success of *The Autobiography* (published 1932). In a further sense, most of Stein's writing embeds Alice Toklas herself in puns and allusions: as a listener referred to as "be" (for "B.," Alice's middle initial, with the further pun on "being" itself; Alice was valuable in her being, in her being there); as "alas" ("Ah alas. This nobody can know" [*Blood*, 28] where the "this" may also refer to the name of "Alice"/"alas," who can, alas, not be known by us); as "a glass" or any number of puns on her name; and, most importantly, as a speaker herself, whose own words often make their way into Stein's writing.[8] It may have been Alice Toklas herself who asked, in reading over what Stein had just written, "Didn't the wife of the hotel-keeper have any help?" and other questions inaudible to us, but apparently audible to the narrator. In her plays and poems especially, Stein worked by this method, drawing into her own writing the actual words and phrases of those around her, especially—we may speculate—the conversational phrases of Alice Toklas, who was so constantly around her.

The possibility of Alice's actual presence suggests important implications for Stein's narrative callings-out. In actual dialogue, if two people participate, usually neither remains completely silent; both figures respond to each other. Further, such responsiveness is not limited to the words one says, for a bodily dimension almost always forms part of the exchange, whether as "body language," facial expression, tone of voice, or an intricate and contradictory mixture of all of these elements. Stein attempts to evoke the full-bodied nature of this actual dialogue between women through her narrator's mode of familiar and conversational address to the audience.

It is illuminating, in light of this potentially loving relationship between listener and teller, to turn briefly to the beginning of Stein's writing, for it is in *The Making of Americans* (written between 1903 and 1911, but published in 1925) that Stein began to imagine an audience as loving. One of her first invocations to an audience —the first in a life of writing filled with such invocations—comes in this work:

Bear it in your mind my reader, but truly I never feel it that there ever can be for me any such a creature, no it is this scribbled and dirty and lined paper that is really to be to me always my receiver,—but anyhow reader, bear it in your mind—will there be for me ever any such a creature,— what I have said always before to you, that this that I write down a little each day here on my scraps of paper for you is not just an ordinary kind of novel . . . and so my reader arm yourself in every kind of a way to be patient, and to be eager. . . . And so listen while I tell you all about us, and wait while I hasten slowly forwards, and love, please, this history of this decent family's progress. (*MOA*, 33–34)

A reader may not be the loving partner implied by the word "receiver." S/he may, instead, be a "stranger," alien to oneself and for whom one is also alien. Stein acknowledges this possibility early on in her famous quote from *The Making of Americans* (famous perhaps because it articulated a truth too well): "I write for myself and strangers. . . . I want readers so strangers must do it" (*MOA*, 289). Reading then can become almost a violation—"strangers must do it." And what, this narrator seems to wonder, will "strangers" make of it? If a reader is too "strange" to a text, if a text is too "strange" for a reader, then the model of reading changes in an immensely disturbing direction: reading becomes an act of disregard or abuse, even rape or murder, "blood on the floor." Instead of a relationship, there are simply two separate worlds, hidden from each other so completely that the writing may not even be read; or, if it is read, it may suffer in the translation.

Yet a more optimistic possibility finds embodiment here as well. For in spite of the fear of an unloving audience—or perhaps even because of the strength of this fear—the narrative voice here attempts to shape another response entirely: "be patient, and . . . be eager . . . listen . . . and wait . . . and love, please." The imagined reader here becomes the embracing and kind lover, utterly receptive to the gift of the telling, brought so consciously and with such deliberation by this "I." Stein gained in Toklas one genuine reader during the writing of this early novel, for Toklas came to Paris and met Stein in 1907, and within a few months of their intimacy she began to type Stein's manuscripts. Alice Toklas certainly became "some one" who "says yes to it, to something you are liking, or doing or making" (*MOA*, 485).[9] Toklas brought Stein out of the painful isolation in which the first half of the book had been written. For the first time, an audience outside herself could be felt to enter and even join in to the writing as it was being written. This entrance, then, may have taken place for Stein much earlier than she says, when she marks *The Autobiography of Alice B. Toklas* as the first moment of her awareness of an audience "outside."

In entering so intimately into the writing, however—by hearing of it daily, going over it letter by letter—Toklas was, in a sense, no longer "outside" after all. As Alice says in her 1963 autobiography, *What Is Remembered*, she became an active participant in the creation of Stein's writing: "Doing the typing of *The Making of Americans* was a very happy time for me. Gertrude talked over her work of the day, which I typed the following morning. Frequently these were the characters or incidents of the previous day. It was like living history. I hoped it would go on forever" (*WIR*, 60). Alice, one gathers from this account, engaged continually in conversations with Gertrude about the subjects of her writing. As Ulla Dydo observes, "the women had for years habitually used the manuscript notebooks for personal messages." Stein wrote "private notes and poems" for Alice within her manuscripts, "carefully offset[ting them] from the Stein compositions."[10] The circle of conversation to writing and back to conversation is one that suggests the possibility of a kind of writing that is itself structured around the give-and-take, the responsiveness, of letters and dialogue.

For Stein, Alice Toklas's new presence as a listener and a teller offered a welcome substitution for the companion who had been closest to her until then, Leo Stein. As Gertrude Stein's older brother—"two years older and a man" (*EA*, 73), Stein notes humorously, quoting Clarissa Harlowe's uncle—Leo had "led in everything" (*EA*, 76); yet as Gertrude began to write, and to find her writing meet only with hostility from Leo, she began to listen less to his "explanations" of her work. As she writes in *Everybody's Autobiography*, "Then slowly he began explaining not what I was doing but he was explaining, and explaining well explaining might have been an explanation. Now and then I was not listening. This had never happened to me before" (*EA*, 76). To "explain," Stein implies, may have more to do with the one explaining than with the writing being explained; Leo, as she notes, "had gotten to be very hard of hearing" (*EA*, 73).[11] "Explanation," in Stein's description of it here, claims to understand an object thoroughly, with certainty and authority—in this case, a particularly masculine authority.

Stein associates this model of reading-as-explanation with both masculinity and authoritarian regimes. Writing *Everybody's Autobiography* in 1936–37, as Hitler was coming to power, Stein in general pretends that politics, in an international sense, does not exist; as in her other writing, she only rarely mentions the presence of politics (in this sense) or war. Yet her brief glances in this direction suggest a theory about the dangers of "rational" intelligence:

It is like it was during the war the most actively war-like nation the Germans always could convince the pacifists to become pro-German. That is because pacifists were such intelligent beings that they could follow what any one is saying.

If you can follow what any one is saying then if you are a pacifist you are pro-German. That follows if any one understands what any one is saying. Therefore understanding is a very dull occupation. (*EA*, 75)

"Understanding," as simply "following," simply a passive receiving of another's logic, is profoundly dangerous. Even propaganda has its "intelligence," its logic, and its system of discourse, whereby "pacifism" may lead to war.

Stein's resistance to "explanation," then, is deeply political, in the sense that she works to defy forms of logic and reason that lay claim to unquestioned and absolute or essential truth. The danger of such mastery appears when dialogue is no longer possible, when one figure's monologues become, not questioned or responded to or even affirmed, but merely copied or explained. Detectives, in their surveillance and search for truths, become implicated in this authoritarian demand for interpretation that is mere "explanation." For Stein, such detection by narrator or by reader would have been profoundly suspect. She responds to the danger of fascist forms of "detection" by creating the possibility—by allowing us to imagine—that authentic dialogue may exist, in art and, by extension, in the world at large. In the realm of reading, Stein makes it impossible for us to locate a position of dominance, whether in the narrator-speaker or in the reader. The narration eschews certainty, and the dominance of certainty, just as we eschew it in order to continue to read. We must meet on other ground, simultaneously and with a mutual openness and uncertainty. Through her incorporation of conversational elements—whether real or imagined—into her writing, Stein suggests both that a listener is present and that this listener may be responsive in words and in a more inchoate but no less valuable bodily form. Through this intimation of a listener's presence, Stein suggests that the act of creating becomes an act intricately bound up with the act of receiving; the two acts, mysteriously, often appear to occur simultaneously and can no longer be easily distinguished. Listening, that is, becomes telling, and telling becomes listening, where both telling and listening possess a corporeal presence and significance.

This simultaneity inhabits Stein's sense of, in her phrase, "how writing is written." In her 1935 lecture, "The Gradual Making of

The Making of Americans," Stein addresses this mutuality of talking and listening:

> To begin with, I seem always to be doing the talking when I am anywhere but in spite of that I do listen. I always listen. I always have listened. I always have listened to the way everybody has to tell what they have to say. In other words I always have listened in my way of listening until they have told me and told me until I really know it, that is know what they are.
>
> I always as I admit seem to be talking but talking can be a way of listening that is if one has the profound need of hearing and seeing what everyone is telling.
>
> And I began very early in life to talk all the time and to listen all the time. At least that is the way I feel about it. (*LIA*, 135–36)

In this description of simultaneous listening and talking, Stein asserts the presence of an other who is also talking and listening. In a bolder version of this idea, Stein says, "That is what genius is to be always going on doing this thing at one and at the same time listening and telling really listening and really telling" (*Narration*, 34). "Talking" and "telling" become tropes for a presence that may include actual words in conversation, but that also includes an entire way of being in the world. One listens, not only to what others say, but to what others *are*. In its inclusion of sight as well as hearing ("if one has the profound need of hearing *and seeing* what every one is telling"), listening becomes an activity of the eyes as well as the ears, where both hearing and sight suggest a larger attentiveness to the body as a world of intricate signs, in themselves possibly inchoate, but nonetheless communicative. Further, this continuous activity of listening to oneself and others at the same time that one is "telling" and others are "telling" argues for a strong sense of democracy. Stein acknowledges that she appears to be "talking" all the time, just as she assures us that she is that rare thing, a "genius." But this talking, as she suggests, unusual as it may be, holds the potential for a democratic dialogue; it "can be a way of listening." "Talking" then may become a figure for responsiveness, for the inward recording of impressions made upon one's own consciousness by another's being. One does not simply talk while another simply listens; such a hierarchy does not enter into this colloquy. One "tells," but only as others "tell" also; their telling forms an inextricable part of one's own.

This figure of simultaneity offers us insight into reading. As readers, we "listen," yet we also "tell." Our own voices, our responses, our sounds do not really stop. Listening cannot remain a purely objective act, but involves our continuing subjective processes. We may "receive" another's words, yet the intricacy of this situation is such that the reception includes our own inner account of such receiving, an account that involves not simply the significance of certain words, but the whole manner in which words (as sounds, as visual objects) come to us.

Lizzie and Mary and "You"

Can no one gather any one. (Blood, 75)

The model of reading as conversation, however, is difficult to achieve and sustain, a situation addressed with poignant clarity by *Blood on the Dining-Room Floor*. Although *Blood* posits this alternate model, it confronts the possibility of an audience's refusal to engage in such a model and to insist instead upon the gap between the writing and the reading. The reader-figures—identified mysteriously as "Lizzie," "Edith," and "Mary"—inscribed within the narrative of *Blood* answer both to the desire for a democratic reading-as-conversation and to the fear that this idyllic paradigm may give way at any moment to a model of reading as disruption and even murder. Stein's naming of these reader-figures as female suggests an identification of the conversational model as specifically feminine, yet it also acknowledges that the masculine authoritarian model may easily become reproduced by a female audience.

Stein's model of reading as conversation incorporates the concept of the difference between readers and the writing. Each question asked to an unidentified "you" ("What did you say") suggests a new response even as it suggests that the "you" differs from the "I" of the narrative. Stein values conversation as a model because it can encompass precisely this difference. Readers may not be reduced to a uniform sameness, whether in regard to each other or in regard to the narrator. A problematic aspect of this situation emerges, however, in Stein's exploration of the forms this difference might take. Instead of participating in a conversation with the writing, reading may establish a "difference"—a serious quarrel—that refuses to listen.

"Mary" manifests an interest in recording her difference that verges on such a refusal. As a mysterious figure, who abruptly enters the narrative in Chapter Three, and as abruptly "disappears" in Chapter Four, she is a reader, apparently, of the book we ourselves have been reading up to this point—a reader who marks her own difference from the story, the narrator, and (possibly) us. Mary takes up certain earlier statements made by the narrator, almost as asides, and disagrees:

> Do you remember way back in the beginning, when the guests were in the country house, and the servants were there there were dogs and they were said [by the narrator] not to be any bother.
> Mary said that this was not true. It could not be true. Dogs could not be anywhere and not be any bother because something always happened to dogs. And one loved dogs so. (*Blood*, 35)

As the response of one listener, Mary's differences find a voice within the story; they make up part of the story. The narrator, in turn, responds to Mary's response: "This [the fact that if you loved dogs, you "thought of nothing else"] had not been true because a great many had thought of other things particularly then." And, as if we make up an integral part of this community of listeners, the narrator turns to us for our own opinion: "Do you remember particularly then" (*Blood*, 35). In this sense, Mary's difference participates in a dialogue with the narrator and with us that remains largely undisrupted. The narrative creates this pause for response; Mary responds to the invitation.

The play on Mary's name directly addresses the question of "difference":

> There is no Mary M. in this case, but if there were this is what she would do.
> Mary M. does not sound the same as Mary I. or even Mary D. or what is the difference between Mary B. and Mary C.
> The confessions of Mary in this case. (*Blood*, 34)

Mary M., that is, may not "sound" the same in the sense that her name, ending with "M.," sounds different from the same name ending with "I." or "D." In a further sense, she herself sounds different. As a teller who is listening to this story, she makes different sounds, different words; she makes a difference.[12] She is, in other words, a special "case," following the insistent repetition of "in this case." The case is, perhaps, the criminal case of the hotel-keeper's wife's death (an open case), a meaning that would imply Mary's involvement as a witness: "The confessions of Mary in this case." And, in another sense, case signifies instance: Mary offers an instance of reading, or a series of such instances.

A Saussurian model and paradox is at work here, for the Saussurian vision of language as convention (as an arbitrary system of signs) turns on acts of difference. Language works by operations of difference, as Mary *M.* marks her difference from all the other Marys through the difference in letters following each name. But as the name "Mary" itself puns ("marry"), this differentiation may itself be returned to a state of relation by its weddedness to the text, the narrator, and the reader. What Mary M. "confesses" "in this case" involves a reintegration of such difference within a marriage bond:

> I do in this case. Possibly for you in this case. I do in this case. Possibly not only possibly, but they will, possibly be you.
> This is what she said. I will remember everything that she said.
> If you, possibly you, could conclude that I love best. (*Blood*, 35)

The "I do" suggests a marriage ceremony, an acceptance of another. If Mary M. ("Marry M[e]"?) is speaking to the narrator here, it is possible ("possibly") that she is participating in a form of marriage vow with the narrator. In a larger sense, given the uncertainty of the pronoun here, we ourselves may be the "you," to which the narrator addresses a vow, or an action ("I do . . . Mary U."). The insistence upon "possibly," however, suggests the tenuousness of this vow; it is manifestly difficult to come to any "conclusion" about the identity of the lover or the beloved.

The autobiographical context surrounding the writing of *Blood* affords insight into this meditation upon difference and the possibility of union. For Stein's relation to her most intimate and "wedded" reader, Alice Toklas, appears to have become marked just before the writing of *Blood* with a difference felt by Stein as immensely painful, in ways that may have intensified the urgency of her desire for an intimate and participatory audience, one whose "difference" would not become too difficult to bridge. Ulla Dydo argues in "*Stanzas in Meditation*: The Other Autobiography" that Stein's and Toklas's relationship became seriously strained upon Alice's discovery of Stein's early novel *Q.E.D.*, based on Stein's love affair with May Bookstaver in 1901–3: "What aroused Alice Toklas's jealousy was less the love affair itself than the discovery that, when Stein and Toklas had exchanged 'confessions' upon falling in love, Stein had not told about the relationship with May (other names used are Mary, May Mary, M.M.)."[13] "The confessions of Mary in this case" allude to Stein's belated confessions to Toklas about this affair with an actual "May/ Marry," whom Stein "may" have "married."[14] In this sense, Stein herself is the possible criminal on trial in *Blood*; she becomes associated with the hotel-keeper, who was unfaithful to his wife, a betrayal that begins her downward slide. The question of who "loves best" and who has betrayed whom, however, is a difficult one; for the reader-figure Mary's irritation with the writing (and the writer?) links with her refusal to love: "Mary said that she could not, not strangely not certainly not love best" (*Blood*, 35). Alice Toklas's withdrawal as a lover and a loving reader from Stein during this period may have amounted, for Stein, to a kind of murder. *Blood on the Dining-Room Floor* alludes indirectly to the daily wounds and deaths occurring in Stein's and Toklas's own relationship. The dining room, usually a place to come together to share meals, becomes a place of blood-shed.

Although knowledge of this autobiographical dimension is valuable for an understanding of the interrelation between Stein's life and work, it is not essential, since *Blood*, like any significant work of art, transmutes autobiographical elements into a new creation. Her situation with Alice Toklas may have spurred Stein to address the treacherous border between the writer and the reader, just as her sudden success with *The Autobiography of Alice B. Toklas* did, yet the literary result may be explored in its own terms. It is not necessary, then, to see Alice Toklas as the only reader to which Stein calls out, under the names of "Lizzie" and "Mary," although Toklas may have been the first reader Stein had in mind.

The figure of marriage occurs again in Stein's *Narration*:

It is certain that any man that is any human being at no time has the same feeling about anything as any one can have who tell them or to whom they tell anything, any one who is alone is alone but no one can have that thing happen and go on living that is continue to be alone and so any one that is every one is always telling any one anything or something.

That is what mysticism is, that is what the Trinity is, that is what marriage is, the absolute conviction that in spite of knowing anything about everything about how any one is never really feeling what any other one is really feeling that after all after all three are one and two are one. One is not one because one is always two that is one is always coming to a recognition of what the one who is one is writing that is telling. (*Narration*, 57)

Stein proposes a paradox here, another mystery. On the one hand, each person differs profoundly from each other person. Listening to another, one must always recognize one's aloneness. Yet, on the other hand, it is this painful situation that urges all of us ("any one that is every one"), each isolated "one" of us, to continue the attempt to "tell." And, despite the knowledge that this telling finds in its listener only difference, "the absolute conviction" comes upon us that "after all after all three are one and two are one." Mary's assertion of difference may be met, then, by the text's own assurance that "after all" her difference may be incorporated into an interchange of listening and telling.

Another inscribed reader ("Lizzie") inhabiting this story represents a less assimilable and more dangerous form of reading. The narrator calls upon this figure as often as s/he calls to yet another reader, "Edith," or to us (if, that is, the narrator does call to us, for the "you" may always be Lizzie or Mary or Edith, just as we may—mysteriously—always "be" these figures too): "Lizzie do you understand." "Lizzie do you mind." "Of course Lizzie you do understand of course you do." "Do you really understand, Edith and Lizzie do you do you really understand." [15]

"Lizzie" may represent an historical figure who became a defendant in a grisly and well-known mystery case: Lizzie Borden.[16] This association is borne out in Stein's 1935 essay "American Crimes and How They Matter," where Stein mentions Lizzie Borden in connection with unsolved crimes:

Everybody remembers a crime when nobody finds out anything about who did it and particularly where the person mixed up with it goes on living.

I know I was perfectly astonished to know that even the present generation knew the name of Lizzie Borden and that she had gone on living. (*HWIW*, 102–3)

"Lizzie" becomes, in one sense, an ally to the narrator of *Blood*. She may indeed "understand," not necessarily "who done it" (who killed the hotel-keeper's wife), but what mystery is, since her life depended upon a mystery remaining unsolved. As a woman who held to her privacy, who may even have destroyed evidence (her own dress) in her "case," Lizzie becomes a figure for mystery itself.

Solving a mystery, in this sense, becomes a form of murder, since it dissolves mystery into logic and order. To close a "case" may represent only another version of warmongering, not because it actually solves or reveals anything, but because it destroys the mystery of dialogic relation. Lizzie's presence as a reader suggests both Stein's commitment to the insoluble and her acknowledgment of her writing's profound vulnerability in the face of a potentially murderous act of reading, even by an ally. Lizzie faces a penalty of death if her murder is solved, yet she also may be a murderer. Her alleged murder of her stepmother and father represents both mystery's murder of authority and the potential murder of the murder mystery itself.

Yet the possibility for a more fruitful bond between the writing and the reading is sustained throughout these callings out, as well as through the more general invocations to an audience. These invocations surprise us with sudden questions about the nature of our relationship to the narrator: "Shall we be cherished as we think often and often" (Blood, 55), the narrator asks; and, as another anonymous "she" apparently "said," "if I add [more cases] will anybody hover as they do hover from cover to cover" (Blood, 61), where the "hovering" is done by a reader, poring over a book "from cover to cover," and where the book itself is filled with "covers," or disguises. In a more discouraged moment, another question is asked: ending one chapter and following a passage in which a "he," presumably the hotel-keeper but possibly another writer-figure, is "writing beautifully" to "every one," the narrator asks suddenly, "Can no one gather any one" (Blood, 75), meaning possibly, "Can no one person (or reader) understand another (or one's writing)," or "Can no one gather another [into their arms]." In a moment of greater imagined and potentially erotic togetherness, the narrator cries: "Oh call out in your excitement" (Blood, 74). And, in one of the last lines of the work, we are thanked for our presence: "Thank you for anxiously" (Blood, 81), where our "anxiety" suggests our discomfort, but also our concern for the well-being of another or of the story itself.[17]

Stein's Dialogue with William James: Knowledge Versus Understanding

Everybody knows all that. (Blood, 15)

Do you really understand. (Blood, 16)

These callings out to an audience underscore the difficulty—the deepest "mystery"—around which the story hovers: *can* a listener "understand"? And what does "understanding" mean? Stein challenges certain kinds of "knowledge," especially the form of knowledge implying a community of belief, where everyone "knows" what the others know; such knowledge intimates a connection with propaganda. "Everybody knew she looked like him and wore a wig" (*Blood*, 23), just as, in the town, the horticulturist's family comes to be "known":

Once upon a time there was a garden. It was an old garden and everybody who had ever been in it had been religious. In their way they had been religious. Even so there had been families. And this family as a history of the family had been famous. That is to say as the town knew about itself it learned to know about them. Not that in a way they were important. In a kind of way they were of no importance of no importance at all but they had come to be known to be of enough importance that they were important anywhere. (*Blood*, 22)

What can really be "known" about this family, and what do the townspeople claim to "know"? This passage, in fact, tantalizes our own wish, as readers, for certain knowledge, our desire for an interpretation that could uncover truth. This garden, for instance: could it be *the* Garden? Those in it "had been religious": are we, now, in Genesis and in the Old Testament, that "history of the family" that "had been famous"? These hints cannot be verified. If we make the interpretive effort to "detect" a connection between Eden and this garden, we can find certain signs, but they do not form a completely closed case. The passage begins with the fairy-tale formula, "once upon a time," a characteristically Steinian opening that calls into doubt not only the "reality" of the original Garden, but the newer association of this garden with that one. "This," the narrator seems to say, "is a story, just as your attempts to understand it, to 'know' what it means, involve your own creation of a story." To feel that, as interpreters, we can "know" whether our story is true or not is to be in the position of these townspeople who claim to "know" all about this family, yet whose knowledge is clearly built, not on an absolute agreement with "reality," but on their own agreed-upon *sense* of such agreement. The family *may* be of no importance at all; "but they had come to be *known to be* of *enough* importance." Their importance is as sufficient as the townspeople's "knowledge."

Stein enters here into the field of her Harvard mentor William James's pragmatic philosophy. As James argues in his 1907 essay, "Pragmatism's Conception of Truth," "truth is *made*," not found.[18] "Reality" is simply what works for us; it is a social construction, socially encoded. In this sense, reality is a rhetoric persuading us that things are true because the code we employ corresponds with the codes of the larger culture. We assume agreement when we can *"assimilate, validate, corroborate, and verify"*[19] a new "truth" in the context of other "known" truths. James addresses the intricate processes by which such "verification" occurs. He places emphasis, not on "truth" itself, which in his terms is always a concept impossible to explore in any transcendent sense, but on the way we feel that we come to know truths—the plural now signifying the nonessentiality of truth, its manifold possibilities.

In *Blood on the Dining-Room Floor*, as in her other writings, Stein alludes to such discussions of pragmatic philosophy, yet with a significantly different result. If Stein begins from a pragmatist position, she carries its implications further than James himself did. Although James makes the philosophical leap to a concept of "truth" as a product of the mind's processes—a leap Stein certainly took as well—he still finds value and importance in our *perceptions* of something as "true," where truth goes beyond one individual's perceptions. Human attempts at verification lead toward a coherent and reliable sense of the world, no matter how grounded such a sense may be in what is essentially fiction. James's essay on truth presents a useful passage to consider, in terms of the difference between Stein and James:

All human thinking gets discursified; we exchange ideas; we lend and borrow verifications, get them from one another by means of social intercourse. All truth thus gets verbally built out, stored up, and made available for every one. Hence, we must *talk* consistently just as we must *think* consistently: for both in talk and thought we deal with kinds. Names are arbitrary, but once understood they must be kept to. We mustn't now call Abel "Cain" or Cain "Abel." If we do, we ungear ourselves from the whole book of Genesis, and from all its connexions with the universe of speech and fact down to the present time. We throw ourselves out of whatever truth that entire system of speech and fact may embody.[20]

James imagines a kind of community of verification and consensus. "Truth" forms a common and continuously growing store. As human beings, we enter into a tacit contract with each other to be "consistent," to build upon the store already there. James begins to follow out his own implications here: that if such a "building out" of truth were suddenly to cease, if the consensus of language, culture, and literature were to meet with disagreement or revision, then the "systems" of truth upon which our culture rests would become lost to us. James differs, however, from Stein in his interpretation of such "ungearing" as a loss. For Stein, as her parodic allusion to Eden testifies, the deviation from the consensus, or the undermining of consensus itself, becomes a clear gain.

Stein carries the pragmatist concept of truth in a different direction. Her impulse, in *Blood on the Dining-Room Floor* and in her other writings, is toward precisely the inconsistency that James considers profoundly disruptive; in this sense, she is closer to Emerson than to James. *Blood on the Dining-Room Floor* plays humorously upon the idea of a community working to add "knowledge" to an already accepted store. Stein's "everybody" resembles James's "every one," yet in a way that makes the act of truth-building and consistency seem less necessary or even desirable. Stein's "everybody"—who is also often "anybody"—sounds at many points energetically willful and blind to other possibilities: "Everybody knows all that," as the narrator asserts at one point (*Blood*, 15). Yet the very absoluteness of this language suggests other possibilities for knowledge, other ways of knowing.

This "verified" common knowledge of consensus ("Everybody knows . . .") meets with the possibility of its own contradiction far more often, as one might predict, in Stein than in William James. As Stein's narrator asserts, in a philosophical argument-in-small, "Everybody proposes that nobody knows even if everybody knows" (*Blood*, 25). Nobody genuinely knows, even if everybody thinks that they have access to authentic, objective knowledge. William James himself might have said this; yet the formulation, in its contradictory sound—even its "inconsistency"—is Steinian. While James still emphasizes the positive value of a "knowing" that is both subjective and culturally affirmed, Stein's language draws our attention away from the essentially progressive process of knowing to the acknowledgment of uncertainty. The confidence with which the narrator makes the statement in the first place— "Everybody proposes that . . ."—becomes questionable with the second "everybody," who claims to "know," but who apparently does not.

James's theory of truth bears a largely invisible but nonetheless crucial ideological component. Though his account seems commonsensical as an understanding of the workings of cultural consensus, it serves to hide the patriarchal patterns of power built into "common sense." James has no quarrel with the language community in which he finds himself. Stein shares James's sense of the value of "social intercourse," yet she also requires a form of discourse that violates common sense and the consensual. For Stein, one does not need to "know" what "everybody" says that "everybody" knows. Our knowledge may come to us differently— less certainly, less absolutely—yet this very difference is welcome insofar as certainty and absoluteness represent dangerous forms of power over others and over ourselves. Through making such certainty impossible, Stein urges us to consider other forms of relationship to the world and to literature that do not depend upon such "knowledge."

Where does this questioning of knowledge, even as a pragmatist enterprise, bring us, then, as "knowers" of Gertrude Stein's own writing? When the narrator asks us, along with Lizzie or Edith, "Do you understand," and "Do you really understand," what kind of "understanding" is possible, and how do we come to it? It is significant that we are asked about our "understanding," not our "knowing." To say that one understands something, in a certain sense of understanding, may not imply that it is completely "known." In a situation of ordinary conversation, in saying "I understand," what one may be saying is "I *sense* what you mean, even if I cannot claim to *know*, either literally or precisely." Understanding may include an intuitive and emotional response, in addition to an intellective one, and in this sense it may revise the nature of how one "knows."

On the one hand, then, insofar as understanding does involve a clear and evident knowledge, a reader of *Blood on the Dining-Room Floor* could not with certainty respond, "Yes, I really understand." On the other hand, if understanding can suggest a fuller response— a response of the body and the emotions as well as the mind—then one might indeed respond, "Yes." In the most fundamental sense, we may understand the yearning for our own presence, as listeners, that makes itself felt here through Stein's narrative voice. As the narrator urges in the final chapter of *Blood on the Dining-Room Floor*, "You could [understand] if you wanted to," and, as if in answer to our own unwritten and unspoken question ("How?") the narrator adds, "Listen while I tell you all the time" (*Blood*, 79). What we may come to understand is not necessarily or simply the content of what is said, but the importance of the acts of telling and of listening, as these acts come together.

The Dining Room as Scene of (Literary) Consumption

> She would know about clean linen, about peaches and
> little cakes, as few as possible of each, and yet always
> enough. (*Blood*, 17)

> He was unfaithful to her. (*Blood*, 20)

In light of this "understanding" of reading-as-conversation, we may turn back to the title. The "Dining-Room" forms an oblique metaphor for the place where reading and writing occur. The scene of reading may, on the one hand, be a scene of murder; or, on the other, it may become a place of nourishment and communion.

In the first case, if reading is seen not as "conversation," but as a search or a quest for knowledge, the relationship becomes unequal and endangered. The result may be "blood," where the corpse is the writing itself, and the murderer is the reader. The figure who actually becomes a "corpse" in *Blood* is a woman, a fact suggesting an association of the writing with the feminine. In reconceiving the relationship of writer to reader, Stein urges us to understand how destructive a relationship this could be, where the power resides only in the writer or only in the reader. Where such a hierarchy exists, "murder" may occur; one could even say that such hierarchy is itself murderous.

Although a dining room becomes, in this sense, a place of consumption, the concept of consumption can also suggest a more positive possibility. In a dining room, instead of consuming another or being consumed (creating blood on the floor), one may eat food and be nourished by it, just as one finds nourishment in stories and words; further, "one" is not usually one alone, but in company, a community not of James's like-minded believers, content in the patriarchal discourse they confirm, but of Stein's listeners and tellers in mutual and subversive exchange. "Blood," in this revisionary sense, represents a bond more fundamental, more of the "heart," than a narrowly intellectual and abstracted relationship.

The danger of "blood on the [literary] dining-room floor" may have occurred to Stein as an immediate and actual danger in terms of her own writing, in a way that included but went beyond her difficulty with Alice Toklas as a reader. Stein wrote *Blood on the Dining-Room Floor* during a period in her life when she had begun seriously to question her identity as a writer in relation to an outside readership. *The Autobiography of Alice B. Toklas* had just been published (in 1932); it became a best-seller and was proclaimed a tour de force. Such a response certainly gratified Stein; although she had been creating a major body of writing since the first decade of the twentieth century, she had remained largely unread. Yet, in a deeper sense, this sudden and belated acclaim could not seem innocent to her. As she wrote in *Everybody's Autobiography*,

Before one is successful that is before any one is ready to pay money for anything you do then you are certain that every word you have written is an important word to have written and that any word you have written is as important as any other word and you keep everything you have written with great care. And then it happens sometimes sooner and sometimes later that it has a money value I had mine very much later and it is upsetting because when nothing had any commercial value everything was important and when something began having a commercial value it was upsetting, I imagine this is true of any one. (*EA*, 39)

The audience, in "buying" the *Autobiography*, acts the part of consumers in a figurative as well as a literal sense; for in paying money for her words, they come to own her words more than she herself does. They take away her own certainty as to the "importance" of these words. As she articulates it, "The minute you or anybody else knows what you are you are not it, you are what you or anybody else knows you are" (*EA*, 92). One is left with an absence where one's authentic self should be.

Stein's fear of her writing's appropriation took shape in a temporary inability to write. For Stein, such a pass must have seemed astonishing. She was an enormously prolific writer, who had written almost daily for over thirty years. As Stein wrote later,

All this time [during the summer of 1933] I did no writing. I had written and was writing nothing. Nothing inside me needed to be written. Nothing needed any word and there was no word inside me that could not be spoken and so there was no word inside me. And I was not writing. I began to worry about identity. I had always been I because I had words that had to be written inside me and now any word I had inside could be spoken it did not need to be written. I am I because my little dog knows me. But was I I when I had no written word inside me. It was very bothersome. I sometimes thought I would try but to try is to die and so I did not really try. I was not doing any writing. (*EA*, 64–65)

"I am I because my little dog knows me" was one of Stein's "signatures," especially in the 1930's as she addressed the problem of identity. Its allusion to the English folk rhyme "Lawkamercyme" suggests an interesting connection to Stein's situation in 1933. The rhyme tells of "an old woman" who "went to the market her eggs for to sell." This intention to "sell" in the market begins the comical but disturbing story of her metaphorical rape "on the king's highway" by a "pedlar" who "cut her petticoats up to the knees." The last half of the poem bears further connections to Stein, who had also, in a sense, become unrecognizable to herself through the violence she perceived in the public's response to her writing:

When this old woman first did wake,
She began to shiver, and she began to shake;
She began to wonder, and she began to cry—
"Lawkamercyme, this is none of I!"

"But if it be I, as I do hope it be,
I've a little dog at home, and he'll know me;
If it be I, he'll wag his little tail,
And if it be not I, he'll loudly bark and wail."

Home went the little woman, all in the dark;
Up got the little dog, and he began to bark;
He began to bark, so she began to cry—
"Lawkamercyme, this is none of I!"[21]

The dark humor of this rhyme lies in the old woman's reliance on her dog for her own identity. Since he cannot recognize her, she feels that she must not exist. For Stein, this feeling appears to have presented itself as a genuine fear, in relation to her audience. She felt the danger of allowing her identity to rest in the recognition of herself by someone outside, even by a companion as knowledgeable about her "outside" as a household dog can be. The audience, in this sense, is in the position of the "dog"—a position opposite (at least linguistically) to that of a "god."

Stein's language in this passage from *Everybody's Autobiography*— "to try is to die"—bears a resemblance to her language in *Blood*, where the narrator describes the wife of the hotel-keeper. This "wife"—the woman who dies—may represent, in a subtle and indirect way, Stein herself and her writing. Anonymous, replaceable —"He was unfaithful to her" (*Blood*, 20)—this figure is defined only from the outside—in effect, by "strangers." "That is the way to see a thing, see it from the outside," the narrator says (*Blood*, 19). Such "seeing," however, represents a dangerous form of knowledge, in its implied reduction of a human being to a "thing," an object. The narrator participates in this reification to an extent, yet in such a way that it becomes questioned and exposed as a harmful way to read or write.

As the wife and her husband become "richer and richer" (as Stein and Toklas became richer after *The Autobiography*), she begins to lose the rhythm of her usual domestic movement, which has seemed to fill the hotel with a kind of sensual and mutual dance. Stein gives the dance to us through the medium of her own rhythmical language:

He [the hotel-keeper] saw a young girl [the hotel-keeper's wife] who was also small but rather flat of face, who had a smile and who also later on would be stout but she would be stout and charming and be very steadily moving. She would be occupied with every little thing that she ever saw. She would know about clean linen, about peaches and little cakes, as few as possible of each, and yet always enough. She would oversee the maids at work, she would push them gently forward to do what there was to do and there was always all of that to do. For them and for her. All day and every day. She was always very nearly perfect when she stood. (*Blood*, 17)

This is a female world of daily cleanliness and ritual, circling around the bedrooms and the dining room, sleeping and eating, the rhythms of everyday existence. As in "The Good Anna" of *Three Lives*, the wife is said to "oversee" the maids, yet she actually seems less to "see" them—or "over-see" them—than to be always next to them, sharing their movements. The separation of owner and owned, mistress and servants, dissolves through the simultaneity of all of their movements together. The wife's authority is not an authority "over" the others; the very term "over" no longer has meaning.

This steady movement, involving a preoccupation with "every little thing" and suggesting self-containment and sufficiency ("always enough"), ceases, perhaps because the husband "was unfaithful to her." The wife attempts to keep her rhythm going, yet the secret of the rhythm had been its spontaneity, its utter and pleasurable lack of self-consciousness. Stein's word for this attempt is "try," a word that, with its rhyming words, "cry" and "die," echo her articulation of her own difficulty with writing after the success of her autobiography:

She cried when she tried but soon she did not try and so she did not cry. As a day was a day it came to be that way. But it was never only a day, and that a little left it to her still to cry, because it was a day, but it was not only a day. Every day had a day in its way.

In every day there was a day in the way. Do you think she tried. No she did not try because it always happened that way that the day was all day. (*Blood*, 18)

"Days" here are only "in the way." Nothing happens but repetition, which is now felt as empty, yawning open just as the long vowel "a" opens out at the ends of these sentences, to be followed only by periods. "Trying" brings only "crying," and, possibly, dying; this further rhyme is made by the narrator:

He said he did not want another even if she cried. He did not say he did not want another even if she tried and died.

Oh dear. We all cried. When we heard she was dead. Not that anybody minded. But they said. She is dead.

How did she die. Now I will try to tell. How she fell. (*Blood*, 15)

"Trying" apparently leads to "dying," both for the wife and for the writer. Stein makes this connection through the sudden appearance of a "we" who also "cried," in sympathy with the crying wife, and then through the link of the "I" with the words "die" and "try." The task of telling seems onerous here: "Oh dear."

This trinity of words, as I have mentioned, emerges again in *Everybody's Autobiography*. Yet, as Stein notes briefly, "it happened again, differently but it did happen again" (*EA*, 52); that is, somehow her writing did return. And I would speculate that, as she "tried" to write *Blood on the Dining-Room Floor*, afraid to find out that she had "died" to her former self, her writing returned gradually through a profound sense that another was there to listen. Toward the end of this mystery story, a curious dialogue is imagined between ourselves and the narrator:

> Now can I think how I will try.
> You will say to me it has not happened and I will answer yes of course it has not happened and you will dream and I will dream and cream. (*Blood*, 50)

The attempt to "think" about "how I will try" gives way here. In the second paragraph, the "I" is no longer in isolation. A "you" appears, if only in imagination and if only to comment on the "I" not writing. Yet this dialogue seems to occur on other levels as well: "you will dream and I will dream and cream." "Dreaming" is quite different from "thinking"; it emerges from the unconscious mind, the world Stein links with the associative play of language, of rhythm and rhyme, where "dream" naturally may lead to "cream," in a form of unconscious logic. "Cream" suggests a dessert, a reward, and perhaps the fleshly dessert of love-making. The "you" and "I," through their dreamings, seem to come closer, to enter together a realm distinct from conscious "trying," which is the realm of thought. The narrator continues: "It has not happened. She slept and it has not happened. He will have been unhappy and it has not happened. They will be dogs dogs and it has not happened" (*Blood*, 50). In this litany of "it has not happened," we seem to wait, on edge, for "it" to "happen," for the consummation of creaming.

Yet, miraculously, it *is* "happening," as we read. We too, brought into the writing in "our" observation that "it has not happened," form a presence here that is sustained even when the "I" appears to be merely alone: "This where I alone finish finally fairly well, I exchange it has not happened for it has not happened and it gives me peace of mind. Like that" (*Blood*, 50). This "exchange" may be of four words for the same four words—an exchange that does not look like much. Yet, in another sense, this exchange may be a figure for the dialogue that occurs between a listener and a teller.

What is important, in this case, is not the fact that "it has not happened," but the mutual act of an exchange, which is an occurrence of the greatest value. We do not need to have this give-and-take explained to us by more than "like that," for we do, in our own ways, "understand" what "that" has been "like"; we are there too, and through our presence have helped dream and cream the writing into existence.

Ida and Twins

She began to sing about her twin and this is the way she sang.   *(Ida, 11)*

Ida presents us with a rich map of Stein's feminist-modernist land-scape. Written largely in 1940 and published in 1941, toward the end of Stein's life, it asks and complicates questions Stein raises in mani-fold forms throughout her work: about representation, authority and authorship, creativity and identity. *Ida* focuses these questions around the concept of "twins," a new formulation of the dyads fig-ured in earlier works.[1] Stein presents twinship as a model for an in-timacy that resists division into opposing and potentially hierarchi-cal sides. This mode of a deeply democratic doubleness finds form in *Ida* within numerous overlapping literary realms. The concept of "twins" encompasses the twinning (and entwining) of words and things, characters and other characters, the author-narrator and the writing, and the writing and the audience.

As both "a novel" (*Ida, A Novel*) and a character named Ida, *Ida*-Ida's major project is the continuous creation and recovery of a mode of intimacy enabling the achievement of subjecthood, of being itself, not through the absence of another but through re-latedness.[2] Stein posits the possibility of a genuine "marriage" of "others," a mutual interchange rather than a dominance of one over another. To this extent, *Ida* resembles other Steinian creations; yet *Ida* differs in the fullness with which it confronts the difficulty of creating and sustaining such a marriage. These various forms of twinning often become lost within *Ida*, as other modes of nar-rative and representation intervene. As an account of such losses and recoveries, *Ida* remains one of Stein's most openly feminist works. Stein approaches these issues with a deft and playful, even a comedic, air that in itself represents a profound celebration and recovery.

The Birth of *Ida*-Ida

Ida opens with a puzzling birth: "There was a baby born named Ida. Its mother held it with her hands to keep Ida from being born but when the time came Ida came. And as Ida came, with her came her twin, so there she was Ida-Ida" (*Ida*, 7). This opening addresses the question of the relation between creator and created. In one sense, the mother appears as the sole creator. Although the father is mentioned soon after the birth, he holds a secondary position in relation to the mother, merely replicating her: "The mother was sweet and gentle and so was the father" (*Ida*, 7). Yet the mother has an odd relation to this birth. She attempts to resist the baby's arrival, "to keep Ida from being born." Although her resistance remains unexplained, this wording suggests that she may wish "to keep Ida," to hold her inside rather than to allow her to become an autonomous being on the outside, distinct from the mother. The baby/writing emerges from the mother, yet without her help or will; the "creator," in this sense, is not equal to her creation, which "comes" on its own. She is emphatically not a Goddess-author, holding sway over the fleshly and literary being that emerges from her. Ida's later comment about mothering suggests a situation made impossible by *Ida*: "if I was married I'd have children and if I had children then I'd be a mother and if I was a mother I'd tell them what to do" (*Ida*, 43).

Within less than a page, both parents abruptly disappear in a mysterious manner: they "went off on a trip and never came back" (*Ida*, 8). Yet Ida's mother, as a presence close to Ida, may not disappear completely. The double birth of two Idas ("Ida-Ida") suggests a possible transformation of Ida's mother into her "other," her twin. The curious shifts in pronouns hint at this metamorphosis: the baby at first is an "it," while the possessive pronoun "her" is owned by the mother ("her hands"), yet by the end of the opening paragraph the baby too has acquired a female pronoun ("so there *she* was"), as if the mother's female presence becomes incorporated into or added to Ida. As an "other" who is so close to Ida that she appears (from Ida's infant angle of vision) to be a part of Ida, the mother cannot be distinguished from her baby, although two beings exist. Ida "comes" because another (an "other") comes "with her": the two Idas represent, in this sense, self and other, in that an identity comes into existence only through the presence of difference. Rather than a Lacanian loss of a narcissistic and fictive wholeness and unitariness, however, this achievement of identity through difference appears to represent a gain and an addition: Ida *and* Ida.

The unusualness of this account of human and literary origin may be measured by contrast with another modernist account, Joyce's *Portrait of the Artist as a Young Man*, a twentieth-century bildungsroman standing in sharp contrast to Stein's "portrait" of a different kind (and a different gender) of artist. In *Portrait*, the father enters the narrative first, specifically in the form of language. He opens his son's portrait by telling a story about a female creature (a "moocow") and "Baby Tuckoo." The mother tells no story; she appears, within the narrator's earliest memory, to have no language at all, since she sings without words ("Tralala").[3] Stephen Dedalus's task, as an "artist," may be understood as the realization of his claim to the position of the father-storyteller through a successful entrance into language and a concomitant escape not only from the maternal but from femaleness itself, which in *Portrait* remains significantly absent from the realm of language.

Ida represents a birth into language as well, yet with an important difference. *Ida* (and Ida) speak(s) a mother tongue, which foregrounds language's potential as sound and as material for play —for forms of composition relying less on representation than on the sensual and material aspects of words. "Ida-Ida," in this sense, marks a form of baby talk, calling us back to the earlier world of intimacy in which such talk could be profoundly valued both for its expression of a link between self and m/other and for its delight in sound. Stein substitutes this serene presence of language ("so there she was Ida-Ida") for a more conventional language of figuration and representation (representing the "moocow") that distances itself from the objects to which it refers. In a crucial sense, *Ida*-Ida never "grows out" of this prelinguistic language; for Stein recreates this language as a mode of being and of composition remaining present and accessible. *Ida*-Ida's quest is precisely to continue this recreation in the face of its threatened loss.

Stein attempts in *Ida* to create a form of writing that retains access to the "id," and to create a mode of "id-entity" not reliant upon the suppression of the id, as in Freud's statement, "Where id was, there ego shall be."[4] Stein would rephrase this significantly: "Where id was, let identity be." The resemblance of *Ida*'s narrative to fantasy and dreams suggests Stein's recreation within narrative of a state of being in which a Freudian sense of the "id" may indeed mingle with "identity."[5] A sense of illogic and mystery prevails, together with a richness that resists any single or final interpretation, just as dreams may be seen as ultimately impenetrable by the conscious mind, although the conscious mind may enter into dialogue with them.

The movement from mother-creator to daughter-text metamorphoses into a movement *between* others, or between sister and sister, as Ida's later imaginary creation of a "twin" sister attests. The novel *Ida* emerges out of this new coupling, in a potentially erotic form of birth. The opening section of *Ida* offers a compelling articulation and embodiment of the erotic nature of writing and reading, figured as acts occurring between two female figures.[6] The copula (-) between the two Idas ("Ida-Ida") offers a visual mark for the potentially erotic link between two female figures, different yet paradoxically identical, where identification suggests a continual interchange.

Luce Irigaray's revision of the metaphor of mother and daughter in "When Our Lips Speak Together" resonates with Stein's movement at the opening of *Ida* from the mother-daughter relation to the bond between Ida and Ida: "Already, I carry you with me, everywhere. Not as a child, a burden, or a weight, no matter how loved or precious. You are not *within me*. I do not contain you or retain you in my stomach, my arms, or my head. Nor in my memory, my mind, or my language. You are just there, like my skin."[7] As both Stein and Irigaray imply, this relationship (I-you; Ida-Ida) cannot be captured by the figure of a child *in* a mother. Irigaray transforms "in" into "with," suggesting adjacency, the opposite of possession. "You are just there," says Irigaray's speaker; "so there she was Ida-Ida." The "you," the "she," *are*—the verb of being, offering no grammatical object to be caught by the subject. "I *da*!" as Ida seems to say ("I am here! I can be found!"), a statement reminiscent of Freud's study of the child's game "fort-da" in *Beyond the Pleasure Principle*.[8] Like Irigaray's "two lips," refiguring female language and (uninterrupted) sexuality, Stein's Ida manifests doubleness from the beginning, a figure tossing aside the distinction between "I" and "you," "self" and "other," "I" and "I."

Immediately after "Ida-Ida" "comes" into being, Stein presents a further set of twins, whose mingled storytelling suggests in part the duplicity of *Ida*'s own narrative:

The whole family was sweet and gentle except the great-aunt. She was the only exception.

An old woman who was no relation and who had known the great-aunt when she was young was always telling that the great-aunt had had something happen to her oh many years ago, it was a soldier, and then the great-aunt had had little twins born to her and then she had quietly, the twins were dead then, born so, she had buried them under a pear tree and nobody knew.

Nobody believed the old woman perhaps it was true but nobody believed it, but all the family always looked at every pear tree and had a funny feeling. (*Ida*, 7)

The storyteller here, like many figures of the artist in *Ida*, is female, her age implying a certain authority. In one sense, however, this woman, as "no relation," eludes the lineage of mother-author to story. She does not form part of the "whole family," which is "sweet and gentle," yet which has no story within *Ida*. Like the great-aunt, she is also novel in this separateness from family and from a relatedness dependent upon mothers and fathers and children, in a chain of descent and succession. Her unrelatedness, in a family sense, could be said to act as the possibility for her "relation," her storytelling.

The old woman's relation of the story accompanies her "relation" with the great-aunt. This "pair" ("pear"?) generates the story-within-a-story (a double *to* the story *Ida*), just as the story generated focuses upon pairs ("little twins born to her"). Although the old woman tells the story, she herself has presumably been told this story by the great-aunt. The ambiguity of the pronoun "she" ("when she was young") suggests a further mingling of these two figures. We hear a voice, yet whose voice is it? Is it the great-aunt's, as she told the old woman? Or is it the old woman's, as she told her own audience? Or—a third possibility—is it both voices together, as they mingle with ("twin" with) *Ida*'s narrator? As the rings of narration expand, the audience too enters as a "twin," for just as the family listens to the old woman's story, we are "there" too, "with" them, and "with" her. The emphasis on an oral narration creates a sensation of immediacy within the novel's listeners.

This happy mingling of tellers and listeners, however, runs di-

rectly counter to the story about the great-aunt in a manner suggestive of a larger danger to the model of twinship Stein introduces.
The story involves "something" that "happen[ed]" to the great-
aunt, involving "a soldier." Whether this "something" was a chosen
affair or a rape, the result for the great-aunt appears to be the same:
she bears twins, who are (ap-pear-ently) born dead, a fact that she
buries, just as she buries these illegitimate children. This story hints
at violence, in terms both of the possible rape and of a possible
infanticide: the "quietness" surrounding the twins' birth, together
with the awkward sequence of "dead then, born so" (as if the narrator fumbles to reassure us that this death was natural: "born so"),
intimates that the stillbirth may—contrary to asserted fact—have
been a murder. Given that *Ida* has just opened with an account of
another birth of twins (and that Stein originally intended to title
this work *Ida, A Twin*),[9] this burial of "little twins" seems omi-
nous and monitory. The great-aunt may in this sense represent an
Irigarayan form of the "culture-mother," who has become caught
within a heterosexual story, by which she has essentially been raped
and made to bear only dead children, or else children she must
kill or silence. As with gentle Lena, the great-aunt's submission to
this heterosexual economy marks a larger silencing of the female
voice. Ida herself faces this danger as she enters a world in which
her desire to speak intimately becomes threatened by authoritarian
figures (primarily masculine) who would silence her and bury her
creativity, which forms the essence of her twinning.

The old woman's "telling" bears a sinister aspect in the context
of such burials. Although she appears to be the great-aunt's ally
and co-narrator, she also marks her difference from the great-aunt
through her act of storytelling. She tells precisely the story that the
great-aunt wished to bury. Telling becomes telling *on*, as well as
telling *about*; to tell such a tale is at once to risk making the other
woman into an object and to betray her by exposing her secret.
The teller, in this sense, enters into the heterosexual economy of
traditional narration. Ida and *Ida* (like Stein herself) run the risk of
this danger, as all writers and writings do. Yet the careful acknowledgment and exposure of the potential bad faith between a female
creator or creation and her subject (between the old woman and the
great-aunt, *Ida* and Ida, or Ida and her twin) represents in itself an
important movement away from this economy. *Ida* offers an alternative "relation" between twin-figures that allows for mutuality

and intimacy as it challenges the distance traditionally established between subject and object, teller and (mute) listener.

The Quest for a Twin

The ambiguous nature of the old woman's storytelling prepares us for the discovery that Ida actually lacks a twin, even though she was born as "Ida-Ida." The possibility for a twin-relationship, glimpsed in the opening, becomes buried within *Ida*, just as Ida's twin Ida in effect becomes buried after "coming" into *Ida*. This twin makes no further appearance until Ida decides to "make" her, an act attended by the dangers of narration glimpsed in the relation between the old woman and the great-aunt. Before she makes her twin, Ida's primary characteristic is her isolation.

Ida centers around Ida's response to this isolation, her quest for a twin who could aid her in moving out of her singleness and unrelatedness. This untraditional and revisionary "quest" reveals a circular rather than a linear design, since in one sense Ida holds the potential for having her twin from the beginning, if her twin is defined as her "genius" or her gift for creativity (for "novel-ty," creating newly). Ida (like *Ida*) must rediscover this gift constantly. In contrast to the male romantic quest model, where the male quester seeks a continually elusive female object of desire, and where the quest ends once this object is attained (a model entering the twentieth century preeminently in the form of *Ulysses*), Stein offers an alternate model of the female quester who seeks her other self, an alter ego (or alter id, alter id-e-a or spirit) who is always present as soon as she (or he, as in the later marriage between Ida and Andrew) is called upon, and who becomes lost only when her nearness is temporarily forgotten.

Ida's childhood isolation leaves her vulnerable to a dependence upon the distancing effects of sight rather than the intimacies of touch. She enters a specular economy, where subject and object do not mingle but undergo a separation marking only difference, not identification:

She saw the moon and she saw the sun and she saw the grass and she saw the streets.
The first time she saw anything it frightened her. She saw a little boy and when he waved to her she would not look his way. (*Ida*, 8)

Ida's fright about seeing "anything" becomes quickly linked to a specifically phallic "anything," which she may see for the first time as she looks at "a little boy." The boy's "anything" marks his otherness. Even though he "waved to her," making an attempt to cross visually the distance between them, Ida refuses to continue looking. Ida's other childhood and adolescent encounters with male figures clarify the reasons for Ida's fear. Men threaten her physically by jumping out at her from bushes or lolling drunkenly by the side of the road. The threat at other moments becomes refined into language, yet remains frightening. To be seen implies a vulnerability to being overtaken and possibly raped, whether literally or metaphorically:

Once she was lost that is to say a man followed her and that frightened her so that she was crying just as if she had been lost. (*Ida*, 9)

Ida senses a "loss" of herself (her "Ida") attendant upon the man's attempt to follow and perhaps possess her.

The claims of such men upon Ida find legitimation within Ida's world, for those in power reproduce these claims in only slightly more subtle forms, as Ida's mysterious and uneasy encounter with a policeman suggests:

She was out it was towards evening it was time when public parks were closed and Ida was looking in through the railing, and she saw right across the corner that some one else was looking and looking at her. It was a policeman. He was bending down and looking at her. She was not worrying but she did wonder why he was getting down to look at her across the corner. (*Ida*, 15)

Again, looking comes first. Yet Ida's "looking" differs from the policeman's, since she simply looks "in." Her sight has no recorded object. The policeman's insistent "looking and looking," by contrast, claims Ida grammatically and figuratively as an object (he looks "at her"). She becomes the unwilling object of his gaze. As a figure of authority, he holds power within this situation, suggestive of a more general claim to power over female otherness grounded in distance and separation. The image of the closed park, with its "railing," marks this separation. To cross the railing would be to defy a law, to make the transgression for which the policeman seems to "look."

The uneasiness Ida feels in response to this authoritarian gaze continues as she recognizes a second, more obscure figure of "a very old woman," "next to" Ida, who may twin with the old woman storyteller:

And then she saw next to her a very old woman, well was it or was it not a woman, she had so much clothing on and so many things hanging from her and she was carrying so many things she might have been anything.
Ida went away it was time for her to be at home. (*Ida*, 15–16)

Ida's uncertainty about this figure's sex ("well was it or was it not a woman") suggests the monitory aspect of this figure. If she is a woman, her femaleness has become curiously obscured and diffi-cult to read.[10] This unsettling figure may represent the logical and age-old (she was "very old") female response to the male gaze: the obscuring of authentic sex and sexuality, together with the reifi-cation of sex in "things hanging" and "things" being carried. This old woman becomes a form of mother, from a young daughter's point of view, with her obscuring baggage of mystery. Whereas the "twin" may explore her twin's body, she may not see under her mother's skirts. Irigaray's distinction between a new "naked-ness" and the clothing of representation in which women have been immobilized and obscured within culture illuminates Stein's per-ception. Irigaray attempts to "remind you, to remind us, that we can touch each other only when naked. And that to find ourselves and each other, we have a great deal to take off. So many images and appearances separate us, one from another. They decked us out according to their desires for so long, and we adorned ourselves so often to please them, that we forgot the feel of our skin. Removed from our own skin, we remain distant. You and I, divided."[11]

Ida's desire for a twin-figure involves her wish to escape the vul-nerability of being seen and possibly possessed. As Ida implies, the twin *is*, but does not necessarily *look* at her twin, unless looking mingles with a touch that is without invasion. The twin makes pos-sible the pleasure of a dialogue that is both spoken and sung, where singing suggests an extra-linguistic and more immediate composi-tion: Ida "liked to talk and to sing songs and she liked to change places" (*Ida*, 8). This sequence from linguistic "talk" to the melodi-ous and more child-like singing ("sing songs" suggests "sing-song," nursery rhyme), and then to "changing places" traces a continuum between language and the body that is necessary to *Ida* and to Ida in the creation of a new intimacy within narrative form.[12]

Ida's relation with her dog Love provides a model for such dialogue, even though (or perhaps because) Love's response comes in an extra-linguistic form. As a "twin," Love invites Ida's words and songs through a bodily and immediate responsiveness: "Ida called him Love, she liked to call him naturally she [did] and he liked to come even without her calling him" (*Ida*, 10).[13] This "calling," both an act of naming and a calling *to*, represents a Steinian poetics. To return to "Poetry and Grammar": "Anybody knows how anybody calls out the name of anybody one loves. And so that is poetry really loving the name of anything and that is not prose" (*LIA*, 232). Ida, as a poet, names the dog "Love," yet this calling remains distinguishable from Love's own being; he comes without being "called." He represents both a loved word and a loved being, and in a further sense, "love" itself, as the bond between two "twins."

Love, of course, is blind: "nice dogs often are" (*Ida*, 10). The "god" of Love, transmuted into a "dog," emphatically cannot see well enough to shoot arrows, old tropes for the erotic bridge across the distance from a lover to a beloved who is seen but not yet touched. Love does not gaze *at* Ida, as the policeman does; instead, he comes to listen: "Though he was blind naturally she could always talk to him" (*Ida*, 10). His pleasure in listening becomes essential for her telling:

> One day she said. Listen Love, but listen to everything and listen while I tell you something.
>
> Yes Love she said to him, you have always had me and now you are going to have two, I am going to have a twin yes I am Love, I am tired of being just one and when I am a twin one of us can go out and one of us can stay in, yes Love yes I am yes I am going to have a twin. You know Love I am like that when I have to have it I have to have it. And I have to have a twin, yes Love. (*Ida*, 10–11)

Love, like "some one" in "Ada," offers Ida complete listening. He listens to "everything" and to "something." Such listening creates a space within which Ida's new "love" may be born: "yes Love yes I am yes I am going to have a twin." "Love" is present at the inception of the twin, for Ida conceives the idea of the twin (the "id[e]a" of "Ida") through this "dialogue" (this "ida-logue") with Love. Love represents the bond and the muse in one: a silent male animal muse, whose listening inspires the birth of a female twin. Ida, in giving birth to an other, will become a(nother) mother.

The twin, in a sense, represents the poem, or the process of creating the poem, a composition of loved names calling to loved figures. Being "just one" signifies remaining apart from a linguistic and profoundly sensual engagement with words and the world. The sensuality of language emerges in the lyrical rhythms and repetitions, especially of the word "yes." This is a "little language such as lovers use," in Virginia Woolf's phrase: "words of one syllable."[14] Ida's decision to enter into such an engagement is self-affirming ("yes I am yes I am") because the self is no longer in isolation: "I" can exist because "Love" (the other, and the bond to the other) exists. To glance again at Irigaray's articulation of a similar doubleness in "When Our Lips Speak Together": "I know that I live because you duplicate my life. Which doesn't mean that you subordinate your life to mine. *Because you live, I feel alive*, so long as you are neither my reply nor my imitation" (emphasis added).[15] "I" and "Love" both create (an other, a novelty, a poem) and become created through this relationship. This double creation, in *Ida*, occurs within a utopian space of language, where language acts as a bond rather than a means of traditional representation ("imitation").

Although Stein seems to link her Ida here to Joyce's yes-sayer, Molly Bloom, these two figures differ significantly. Molly says "yes," in memory and in the present, to a male figure, or a series of male figures, who people her imagination with profusion. Ida says "yes" to Love itself: to the dog, to the natural side of human or creaturely nature ("she liked to call him naturally"), to herself ("yes I am Love"), and to her female twin ("And I have to have a twin, yes Love"). When Ida loses her Ida, her "yes" begins to resemble Molly's in dangerous ways.

This affirmation of "I" and "you," as Ida intimates, may not last, for "killing" may be a counterpart to "making." After these first lyrical outbursts to Love, Ida strikes a different note:

And then she said Love later on they will call me a suicide blonde because my twin will have dyed her hair. And then they will call me a murderess because there will come the time when I will have killed my twin which I first made come. If you make her can you kill her. Tell me Love my dog tell me and tell her. (*Ida*, 11)

The "dying" of the hair, an act of disguise marking the twin as different from her former self (and from Ida), becomes literalized into murder. The little twins in the opening story seem to reappear here in a haunting way. If twins are born, they can be killed. And if one twin (or one work of art) "makes" another, she may also kill the one she made. The mutual exchange involved in "making" has a fragile edge; whenever the mutuality ceases, one may have power over the other, a situation leading to a shared death and silencing.[16] To slip out of touch, and out of the continuous process of "making" each other (up), is to reproduce the situation of representation in which the other remains distant and objectified.

Ida, as her twin Ida's author, does not "kill" Ida immediately. To the contrary, she becomes primarily preoccupied with writing her letters—love letters. As she writes in her first recorded letter, "here I am all alone and I am thinking of you Ida my dear twin" (*Ida*, 18). The letter acts as the bond between Ida and Ida, the longer, linguistic manifestation of the copula between the two Idas in the book's opening. It represents a calling out, from a position of isolation, to a listening figure, who is also oneself: "Ida often wrote letters to herself that is to say she wrote to her twin" (*Ida*, 18).

Stein writes in *Narration* of letter writing as a form of marriage: "an imitation of marrying of two being one, and yet being two" (*Narration*, 55). In this sense, the letter forms a compelling figure for *Ida*'s narrative project. A personal letter may be familiar, written with affection and love within a private situation of intimacy ("Dear Ida my twin," "from your twin Ida"). It changes hands and tends to be handwritten. The hands of both the writer and the receiver hold the paper, establishing a bodily intimacy with the act of writing and reading. Although Ida writes her letters in isolation, writing transforms her isolation into relatedness ("marriage") by calling the absent one ("Dear Ida") into being, at least imaginatively. Ida is unsure of her twin's appearance and location, yet she happily writes to her anyway, as if the act of writing is enough to create a presence to replace an absence. In writing, Ida assumes the presence of another, whose silence will be transformed into a further letter, a written response, for the idea of letter writing involves answers to one's letters; just as a letter represents a kind of question, the letter of response represents an answer, as well as a new question. The possibility of an exchange of letters suggests the further possibility of a written dialogue.

The linguistic bond formed through a letter to a loved but absent figure has an oral dimension, in that letters incorporate more of the spoken word than other texts. Ida makes use of a speaking voice in her letters to her twin/herself: "Do you know what I think Ida, I think that you could be a queen of beauty"; "Dear Ida oh dear Ida do do be one" (*Ida*, 19). Punctuation is crucial to this speaking mode of writing. Stein's punctuation, which is also Ida's, works with the breath, with actual speech, in a way that invites us to hear the words as they would be grouped together and emphasized in speech. Ida's language moves toward one of pure sound, as she imaginatively (and breathlessly) approaches her Ida/self: the repetitions of word and sound in "Dear Ida oh dear Ida do do be one" suggest this tendency toward a language that is not only oral but musical (the singing of "songs"). The two Idas (the Ida who writes and the Ida who receives the writing) intermingle (entwine), for as Ida observes: "if I had a twin well nobody would know which one I was and which one she was" (*Ida*, 11). Within the imaginative and utopian realm of this "if," Ida's relation to Ida is one of intimacy, equality, and safety from an outside eye.

This possibility, however, meets contradiction in the form of a further and more disturbing possibility. Ida's letters to her twin/ self, oral and intimate as they are, still evidence a writtenness that resists a more bodily bond. Although Ida calls out in writing to Ida, she acknowledges that her writing can exist only at the cost of her twin/self's absence: "but you dear Ida you are not, you are not here, if you were I could not write to you" (*Ida*, 19). The twin's absence makes the absent one vulnerable to the representations even of her twin. Ida begins to represent her twin/self almost as soon as she starts to write (*Ida*, 18–19):

Are you beautiful as beautiful as I am dear twin Ida, are you, and if you are perhaps I am not. . . . Do you know what I think Ida, I think that you could be a queen of beauty, one of the ones they elect when everybody has a vote. They are elected and they go everywhere and everybody looks at them and everybody sees them. Dear Ida oh dear Ida do do be one. Do not let them know you have any name but Ida and I know Ida will win, Ida Ida Ida,

from your twin
Ida

Ida's division of the "I" from the "you" marks her acceptance of a potential hierarchy based on "looking": "if you are [beautiful] perhaps I am not." She increases this distance by setting her twin/self up as "a queen of beauty, one of the ones they elect." As Ida says earlier to Love, "when I am a twin one of us can go out and one of us can stay in" (*Ida*, 10). Yet if "one" remains "in," and "one" remains "out," so that the interchange gives way to a fixed division and separation, the doubleness of twinning vanishes, leaving only two distinct "ones." The twin, as an elected "beauty," comes to represent the visible self, within a public world run by a heterosexual system through which women become divided from each other: only "one" woman can "win" (and be "won").

Once the twin Ida wins the "beauty prize for all the world" (*Ida*, 19–20), her distance from her twin/self increases, marked by the writing Ida's further linguistic representations of the twin.[17] In her second letter, Ida renames Ida Winnie "because you are winning. You have won being a beautiful one the most beautiful one" (*Ida*, 23). Yet, to echo the title of a later Stein work, "the winner loses": "winning" entails loss, both for Ida and Winnie. As Ida writes, remembering the surreal sequence described in Part Two of the First Half: "And one day the day you won, I saw a funny thing, I saw my dog Love belonging to some one. He did not belong to me he did belong to them. That made me feel very funny, but really it is not true he is here he belongs to me and you and now I will call you Winnie" (*Ida*, 23). The sudden and disturbing loss of the dog "Love" to others ("them") figures the further loss of "love," or of a beloved. Ida's twin Ida, through "winning," suddenly "belongs" not to Ida but to those who vote for her, an anonymous audience. Ida herself returns to an isolated "I" held within an economy of looking, where sight's distancing effect becomes a figure for separation and loss of the other self: "you won, I saw" (*Ida*, 23).

"Winnie," as a figure for Ida's own public and visible identity, enters the world as an object of vision: "Winnie Winnie is what they said when they saw her and they were beginning to see her" (*Ida*, 23). Ida, in a sense, pushes Winnie out from the intimate and private space between them, figured through the giving and receiving of letters. This act represents a figurative murder, insofar as Winnie becomes caught and reified within the "knowledge" of others. As the narrator observes, "It is easy to make everybody say Winnie, yes Winnie. Sure I know Winnie. Everybody knows who Winnie is" (*Ida*, 24). This superficial and dangerous "knowledge" begins with a possession of Winnie through sight, and ends with Winnie's complete absence.

Ida suffers the realization of her twin's absence (and concomitantly of her own absence within others' discourse) as she stands in a shoe store, a location suggestive of the measurements and possible uncertainties of identity. "If the shoe fits, wear it," an imperative with an ambiguous message: each foot has its own proper (and unique) shoe, yet many people could "fit" into the same shoe, just as the shoe store is so filled with people that Ida must wait for her turn. "The place was full, nobody looked at Ida. Some of them were talking about Winnie. They said. But really, is Winnie so interesting? They just talked and talked about that" (*Ida*, 25). "Winnie" has become merely a name, a signifier without a signified (a shoe without a foot). In a sense, Ida *is* the signified, yet the discourse about Winnie continues, and in fact depends upon, a suppression of this fact. Ida must observe her own absence within this discourse: "nobody looked at Ida," since her reality is irrelevant and even disruptive of their discussion.[18] Ida makes her final renunciation of Winnie after a man (mistaking her for Winnie) "follows" her home. By implication, he sees only her surface, expecting to "know" it in a physical as well as an ontological sense. "Ida," however, "was not the same as Winnie. Not at all" (*Ida*, 26). Although the man continues to believe that Ida is Winnie ("He did follow Winnie again but he never rang the bell again"), Ida distinguishes herself from this public identity vulnerable to appropriation and following. As this sequence ends, "Ida lived alone" with another dog named Iris (*Ida*, 26).

This loss of "love" (the dog Love seems to have become lost as well) and intimacy through the division between one's inner and outer self finds an unusual and illuminating recovery. Soon after these uncanny incidents marking Winnie's separateness and absence, a parable appears:

One day she was there doing nothing and suddenly she felt very funny. She knew she had lost something. She looked everywhere and she could not find out what it was that she had lost but she knew she had lost something. All of a sudden she felt or rather she heard somebody call to her. She stopped, she really had not been walking but anyway she stopped and she turned and she heard them say, Ida is that you Ida. She saw somebody coming toward her. She had never seen them before. There were three of them, three women. But soon there was only one. That one came right along. It is funny isn't it. She said. Yes said Ida. There, said the woman, I told them I knew it was.

That was all that happened.

> They all three went away.
> Ida did not go on looking for what she had lost, she was too excited.
> (*Ida*, 26–27)

Ida does not continue to "look" for "what she had lost," because the felt "loss" is suddenly irrelevant and perhaps incorrect. She may not have lost anything, or at least anything worth having. The "loss" may be of virginity, a "something" within a heterosexual economy, but a "nothing" when placed outside this light. The dream-like image of the three-in-one female godmother or muse figure calls Ida back to herself, "Ida is that you Ida," in a lyrical circling, a Steinian "ring" of poetry, in which Ida as a loved name and a loved being returns as a presence to her own "novel." In contrast to the men who elect and follow "Winnie," this female trinity offers Ida the unspoken and invisible gift of herself: her id/identity, her creativity, and ultimately her very being.

This restoration of Ida to Ida recurs in a more problematic form later in Part Two of the First Half, as Ida begins to choose "talking to herself" over writing to her twin, a movement that at first seems to mark a greater intimacy with her twin/self that allows for an assertion of her own presence:

> Pretty soon she said to herself Now listen to me, I am here and I know it, if I go away I will not like it because I am so used to my being here. . . .
> Ida decided that she was just going to talk to herself. Anybody could stand around and listen but as for her she was just going to talk to herself.
> She no longer even needed a twin.
> Somebody tried to interrupt her, he was an officer of course but how could he interrupt her if she was not talking to him but just talking to herself. (*Ida*, 43)

Ida comes so close to herself that she does not call herself a twin, but simply "herself." Ida's talk forms a circle of talking and listening, with no divisions. The talker is the listener, the listener the talker, just as talking *is* listening, listening talking. Ida's project, in this sense, resembles Stein's, insofar as the intimacy and simultaneity of these two acts forms a crucial aspect of Stein's mode of composition.

This act of talking to oneself, however, becomes questionable, for if talker and listener collapse completely into one another, the possibility of dialogue vanishes. Ida's sense that she has no further need of a twin suggests a claim of self-sufficiency leading potentially to a narcissistic monologue. Despite her announcement, Ida continues to desire an other with whom she could enter into dialogue. Yet the "others" who appear in her life shape relationships with her in opposition to the interchange of dialogue; they speak monologues with a vengeance. Before she finds her "twin" (her "second half") again, in the Second Half of the book, Ida is indeed "interrupted" through the loss of her self, her own voice and presence, within marital and extra-marital relationships with men. A surprisingly long list of husbands parades through the First Half, in which the husbands tend to *be* "first," and to hold an ideology of priority and hierarchy. Her husbands appear and disappear with an unsettling irregularity, sometimes half-named and sometimes never named at all: Frank Arthur, a man from Montana, Frederick, Andrew Hamilton, and Gerald Seaton. Marriage in the First Half of *Ida* presents itself as a divided landscape, for married couples do not become "twins," as Ida is a twin to Ida. The two sexes occupy two countries, and the commerce between these countries is less than mutual, if it exists at all. The "first" country (or "First Half") often invades and colonizes the "second."

"Officers" and Marriage as Interruption

Ida was not careful about whom she met.   (Ida, 48)

It is significant that the figure who attempts to "interrupt" Ida's "talking to herself" is male. Like most of the male figures in *Ida*, until the elusive figure of Andrew (a new Andrew, apparently, and not Andrew Hamilton), he is *very* male. As the narrator remarks: "Somebody tried to interrupt her, he was an officer of course but how could he interrupt her if she was not talking to him but just talking to herself" (*Ida*, 43). The "of course" signifies that only an "officer" would be an interrupter. The fact that in the First Half of *Ida* Ida primarily meets officers suggests that such interruption forms a masculine trait. Women never interrupt Ida, and in fact remain curiously silent, as if Ida's relation to them inhabits a realm distinct from the arena of language, or at least from a language of "officers." Ida's difficulty lies in her tendency to enter this official and patriarchal linguistic arena, although she achieves again and again a restoration of her immunity and separateness from it, as well as her establishment of an alternate language. She continues to talk to "officers," just as she continues to get married in ways allowing her own loss to herself.

The following dialogue suggests *Ida*-Ida's oscillating movement into and away from linguistic encounters with "officers":

> If I am an officer, said an officer to Ida, and I am an officer. I am an officer and I give orders. Would you, he said looking at Ida. Would you like to see me giving orders. Ida looked at him and did not answer. If I were to give orders and everybody obeyed me and they do, said the officer, would that impress you. Ida looked at him, she looked at him and the officer felt that she must like him, otherwise she would not look at him and so he said to her, you do like me or else you would not look at me. But Ida sighed. She said, yes and no. You see, said Ida, I do look at you but that is not enough. I look at you and you look at me but we neither of us say more than how do you do and very well I thank you, if we do then there is always the question. What is your name. And really, said Ida, if I knew your name I would not be interested in you, no, I would not, and if I do not know your name. I could not be interested, certainly I could not. Good-bye, said Ida, and she went away.
>
> Ida not only said good-bye but she went away to live somewhere else. (*Ida*, 30)

The officer's language assumes the role of display, of a self-advertisement associated implicitly with the display of the phallus. This is a phallic discourse in the sense of its intended assertion of the "I" (the "one") over others. The officer's emphasis on "looking" corresponds to his phallic claim. In Irigaray's terms, he represents the specular economy within which the female has appeared to lack both sexual power and a concomitant linguistic power.

Ida's lack of interest in such visibility, in the signs of such linguistic power, offers a gentle and comical deflation of the officer's mastery. It is the officer, not the woman, who now has the "lack": "I do look at you but that is not enough," a situation of inadequacy contrasting with Ida's continuous possibility (whether or not it is always realized) of plenitude—"She was not unemployed. She just sat and she always had enough" (*Ida*, 40). "Looking" itself is "not enough." Ida wishes for an intimacy that can erase the gap between the subject and the object by erasing this language of command.

Ida's response to the officer's language offers a figure for Stein's response too: "Ida not only said good-bye but she went away to live somewhere else." The "somewhere else" is the place of *Ida* itself, a geography holding out the possibility of a dialogic discourse "interrupted" by "officers" but sustained in spite of the interruptions. As Stein suggests by the adjacent anecdote about the gate—"Once upon a time way back there were always gates," and "By and by there was no gate" (*Ida*, 30)—her own art tosses out the "gate," the fixed boundary between speaker and listener, subject and object. "Talking to herself" forms a trope for the absence of a gate or an interruption.

Ida's marriages and other heterosexual relationships depend upon linguistic and erotic distance:

Ida saw herself come, then she saw a man come, then she saw a man go away, then she saw herself go away.

And all the time well all the time she said something, she said nice little things, she said all right, she said I do. (*Ida*, 34)

As in other moments of distancing, the two figures connect through sight. The seeing subject separates herself from the object of sight. As both seer and seen, subject and object ("Ida saw herself"), Ida becomes a voyeur, distanced from her own love-making. "Love"-making becomes impossible, given the separateness between her "coming" and his "coming," his retreat and her retreat. The language corresponding to this distance is markedly conventional: Ida says "nice little things," the common currency of small talk. Ida's politeness, coming as it does in the midst of this disturbing separation from her authentic self, represents an acquiescence to a whole cultural system of language confining the feminine voice to "littleness" and affirmation of the masculine. Ida's "I do," a form of marriage vow, suggests the culmination of this feminine position by marking the woman's acceptance of her secondary status within language.

This "all right" and "I do" contrast with other moments of affirmation in *Ida*, in which Ida's "yes" signifies an embrace of her own being; for instance, in the Second Half, Ida's "excitement" (which is also the excitement of *Ida*'s sheer movement and being) manifests itself in her continual yes-saying:

This is what Ida said. Ida said yes, and then Ida said oh yes, and then Ida said, I said yes, and then Ida said, Yes.

Once when Ida was excited she said I know what it is I do, I do know that it is, yes.

That is what she said when she was excited. (*Ida*, 132)

Ida's "yes" here is not an acquiescence ("all right") to another's request. Her "yes" represents a celebration in and of itself, just as the writing affirms its moving presence in each new word and sentence. "I do" enters a new context, associated not with a conventional marriage but with a new form of "marriage," of the "I" to herself, and of the talker (or writer) to her speech (or writing). As I shall suggest later in this chapter, Ida's marital "I do" resembles Molly Bloom's yes-saying in *Ulysses* in ways that illuminate both Stein's project and Joyce's.

Ida's marriages never last long, yet she does get "yoked": "How many of those who are yoked together have ever seen oxen. / This is what Ida said and she cried" (*Ida*, 43). Within such a bond, two may merge unhappily into one. The linguistic customs of polite society have already decided the question of *which* one: "Ida was Mrs. Gerald Seaton and Seaton was Gerald Seaton and they both wore their wedding rings" (*Ida*, 82). Ida's fear about marriage comes true, for as a younger woman "she knew that a husband meant marriage and marriage meant changes and changes meant names and after all she had so many changes but she did have just that one name Ida and she liked it to stay with her" (*Ida*, 16). To lose her name is tantamount to losing her self. Her name "stay[s] *with* her," a form of twin. The name "Ida" does not distance her from herself, or bury her identity, as does the patriarchal appropriation of the wife through naming ("Mrs. Gerald Seaton").

In this form of marriage, *one* talks while the other listens. The husbands do all the talking while Ida remains relatively silent. Yet Ida's silence is the silence of the critic, given voice within the narration. Ida's response to her first husband Arthur's talk about kings evinces her unspoken but recorded thought:

He began to talk. He said. All the world is crying crying about it all. They all want a king.

She looked at him and then she did not. Everybody might want a king but anybody did not want a queen. (*Ida*, 39)

Ida's skepticism about such kingship helps us respond with equal skepticism: her "might" works against Arthur's certainty. The word "might" invokes the concept of power; Ida's power here is one of uncertainty, as opposed to her husband's confidence. Such uncertainty represents a refusal to accept his pronouncements ("They all want a king"), even as it leads to new insights about the status of gender within culture ("anybody did not want a queen").

The male figures who succeed Arthur reproduce this kingly discourse, beginning with Arthur's surprisingly immediate replacement, Philip:

> Philip was the kind that said everything out loud.
> I knew her, he said and he said he knew Ida, hell he said, yes I know Ida. He said it to every one, he said it to her. He said he knew her.
> Ida never saw Arthur again.
> She just did not.
> She went somewhere and there she just sat, she did not even have a dog, she did not have a town, she lived alone and just sat. (*Ida*, 40)

"King," with the alteration of one letter, becomes "kind": Philip is just one of a group not distinguishable from each other, just as "kings" come to seem pretty much the same. Arthur simply disappears from the story, to be replaced by another kind/king, who is actually the same, just as a succession of kings replace the legendary King Arthur. The legend becomes dissolved as each replacement occupies one and the same place, in occupying the name of king. The language of kings is a public one claiming to "know" its subjects (or its objects, for this language makes subjects into objects) and to represent them. Ida's name, rather than remaining her loved twin, becomes in Philip's mouth a handle by which he may capture her: "hell he said, yes I know Ida." "Kings" say things "out loud": Stein hints here at a language that is phallically "out," predicated on the separateness of subject and object, "I" and "her." This separation allows for the "I" 's possession of "Ida."

Ida's act, in response to this husband-king, is Stein's also in *Ida*: "Ida never saw Arthur again." In refusing to "see" Arthur, Ida lightly tosses him out of her life (and her *Life*, *Ida*) with an effortless and welcome coup (a "for crying out loud" that must be read between the lines). "Philip" too makes no further appearance after his dogged claims to knowledge of Ida. Two pages later, we return to the alternative language of twinship, where subject and object differ yet mingle, and where an ongoing exchange of dialogue emerges between *two* subjects/sisters:

She began to say to herself Ida dear Ida do you want to have two sisters
or do you want to be one.

There were five sisters once and Ida might have been one.

Anybody likes to know about then and now, Ida was one and it is easy
to have one sister and be a twin too and be a triplet three and be a quartet
and four and be a quintuplet it is easy to have four but that just about does
shut the door. (*Ida*, 42)

Ida's question reinstates her own desire: "Ida dear Ida do you
want . . ." Ida's "I do" metamorphoses into "do you," a question
and an invitation. Uncertainty (Ida's "might") becomes an opening
out to another. The language Stein offers is one of question, not
statement; illogic, not logic; mutuality, not isolation; multiplicity,
not unity. One sister "easily" increases to two, two to three, three
to four, in a kind of exuberant and nonlogical progression; as Stein
writes in *Tender Buttons*, "the difference is spreading." This return
to a possibility of being more than "one" (and of not being "won")
heralds the arrival of a genuine twin for Ida, with whom she may
engage in dialogue.

And Andrew Too

As the First Half approaches the Second Half, a genuine twin
enters Ida's life. From the moment of his first appearance, Andrew
manifests a doubleness echoing Ida's birth as Ida-Ida, as if this original twinning may finally be realized:

Everybody knew that Andrew was one of two. He was so completely
one of two that he was two. Andrew was his name and he was not tall,
not tall at all. . . .

Ida had not known that she would be there when he came in and when
he went out but she was.

Ida was. (*Ida*, 87)

"Andrew" ("*And*-rew") suggests addition and conjunction: he adds
to Ida, as she adds to him.[19] The contiguity of the two "Halves"
("First" and "Second") of *Ida* suggests the further contiguity of
Andrew to Ida, where neither is "first" or "second." Andrew appears in both halves, just as he "is two." His presence echoes the
imagined presence of Ida's twin, who could exchange places with
Ida ("one of us could go out and one of us could stay in"), for she
is "there" "when he came in and when he went out," a potentially

sexual movement suddenly holding for Ida no anxiety. She remains present to herself, throughout his movements, for his coming "in" and going "out" make additions to her life rather than substitutions.

The relation between Ida and Andrew becomes so intimate that the two figures begin quite literally to "change places." Gendered pronouns begin to shift and slide, so that "she" becomes suddenly "he," "he" becomes "she":[20] "Andrew never looked around when Ida called him but she really never called him. She did not see him but *he* was with him and she called Andrew just like that" (*Ida*, 90, emphasis added). "She did not see him but he was with him": who is this "he"? Is it Ida or Andrew? And if it is Ida, how can she be a he?

Toward the beginning of the Second Half, the case becomes even more magnificently complicated:

> For which reason, Andrew's name changed to Ida and eight changed to four and sixteen changed to twenty-five and they all sat down.
>
> For which all day *she* sat down. As I said *she* had that habit the habit of sitting down and only once every day *she* went out walking and *she* always talked about that. That made Ida listen. *She* knew how to listen.
>
> This is what *she* said.
>
> *She* did not say Ida knew how to listen but *she* talked as if *she* knew that Ida knew how to listen.
>
> Every day *she* talked the same way and every day *she* took a walk and every day Ida was there and every day *she* talked about *his* walk, and every day Ida did listen while *she* talked about *his* walk. It can be very pleasant to walk every day and to talk about the walk and every day and it can be very pleasant to listen every day to *him* talk about *his* every-day walk.
>
> You see there was *he* it came to be Andrew again and *it* was Ida. (*Ida*, 94–95, emphasis added)[21]

The "For which reason" that opens this startling passage refers to no reason at all. As in most of *Ida*, it marks a conjunction signaling a non sequitur, a leap of illogic. "Reason" has nothing to do with the kinds of structures and transformations celebrated by *Ida*. Names too are changeable, unfixed, like other symbols. Andrew's name can "change" to Ida just as the symbol "sixteen" can change to the symbol "twenty-five." "He" can change to "she" with the same (il)logic.

The absence of logical and unitary significance here suggests a further possibility: the absence of a coherent representation of gender. If "he" can represent, at the very least, *both* a female and a

male, then our knowledge of precisely which sex is being represented becomes utterly baffled. The opposition and inequality of
the sexes dissolves with the mingling and confusion of each sex
with the other, until we are catapulted to a place beyond gender entirely. This rich confusion of gender replaces the hierarchical male-
female "marriage" with the profoundly democratic model of twins.
Within each "she" and each "he" in the name-changing passage, at
least two figures may exist. Language becomes the place for a coupling as idyllic as the pastoral setting in which these changes occur,
where one goes out and one stays in, where one talks about a walk
and the other listens, and where each of these "ones" may at any
point be "two."

Ida, Molly Bloom, and the Plot of Quest-Romance

> Nobody ever followed Ida. What was the use of
> following Ida.   (Ida, 68)

The model of twins, as Ida knows, leads to the confusion of any
figure who wishes to pin "one" Ida down. Even before Andrew's
arrival as a "twin," Ida is elusive to others and apparently to herself. As she remarks at one point, "I change all the time. I say to
myself, Ida, and that startles me and then I sit still" (Ida, 35). The
relation between the name "Ida" and the "I" as it appears in each
new instance changes incalculably and magically.

This changeability holds significance both for Ida's life and her
"Life" or "history." In one sense, Ida forms a modern bildungsroman, resembling Stein's earlier Three Lives: Ida (as a single, identifiable character) is born, grows older, and becomes married.[22] Stein
handles this marriage plot, however, with a comic insouciance. The
startling appearances and disappearances of Ida's various husbands
transform the traditional movement toward one marriage into an
arbitrary series of marriages. The sense of each husband as replaceable, merely one figure in an unaccountable (and uncountable)
procession of similar figures, deflates the significance of each marriage as part of Ida's plot. Whereas the Gentle Lena acquiesces to
a predetermined narrative line leading to her imprisonment within
one marriage and one plot, Ida continually steps into marriage,
only to step right out again, just as Ida plays upon conventional

narrative structures only to demonstrate how exciting and possible it is to escape.

Ida substitutes for this plottedness a sense of an ongoing, lively, and spontaneous composition, in which the composing (the "making" and giving birth) of *Ida* twins with the creation that *is Ida*. As Ida (and *Ida*) asks at one point, "Is there anything strange in just walking along" (*Ida*, 56). As Ida "just walks along," without any one goal, so *Ida* replaces plot with an emphasis on the incalculable and immediate present. *Ida* makes (her)self up as she goes along. She is a "novel" in the sense that she offers the surprise of novelty at every point. In Stein's revisionary definition, the "novel" is a being who rests, walks, and (in a twinning rhyme) talks; who says, again and again, "How do you do," in a series of greetings and interchanges initiated not only between characters but between the writing and the audience.

Stein's modernist composition depends upon the forms of interchange Ida most loves. The earlier description of Ida's childhood activities forms a paradigm for Stein's narrative strategy in *Ida*: "She liked to talk and to sing songs and she liked to change places. Wherever she was she always liked to change places. Otherwise there was nothing to do all day. Of course she went to bed early but even so she always could say, what shall I do now, now what shall I do" (*Ida*, 8). *Ida* too forms a composition grounded in a "singing" of "songs" and a changing of places. Ida continually eludes the relegation to one "place." Within the utopian "place" of the text, her desire to move from place to place and to exchange places with other figures may find fulfillment. The changing of "places," finally, occurs within language itself, just as the activity Ida chooses involves the "exchange" of one phrase for another: "now what shall I do" offers a new placement of the words "what shall I do now." In contrast to an Eliotic despair (as in *The Waste Land*: "What shall we do now? What shall we ever do?"), Stein offers the Ida-like project of creating a language of continual movement, unfixity, and exchange.

Through the embrace of the present, Ida-*Ida* makes a traditional romantic quest-plot impossible. Although men attempt to "follow" Ida, her doubleness eludes them. Although she finds herself saying "yes" to their designs, she is able to transform this "yes" into an affirmation of her own presence, distinct from and inviolable by theirs. In this sense, *Ida* begins where *Ulysses* ends. It is as if Stein

took Joyce's modernist quest-romance and, cutting out the movements, the mythic journeyings of Leopold Bloom and Stephen
Dedalus, began instead with Molly.[23] Yet even Molly, the female
figure allied with the immediacy and spontaneity of the present
moment, manifests a preoccupation with the telling and retelling
of the various questings—the history—that lead toward herself and
her "yes." Although her narrative occurs in a fluid present, it depends profoundly upon memory. In her narrative recreation, her
memories may be fragmented and confused, yet the fragments fit
together into an historical line of events as precise as Joyce's map
of Dublin. Although the structure of quest-romance has become
both internalized and fragmented in *Ulysses*, it remains central to
Joyce's form, and the woman's status as object of the quest remains
unchallenged. Molly is not silent; but the epic-quest she inhabits
contains and defines her.

Molly acknowledges her confinement within Joyce's epic by the
sudden cry, "O Jamesy let me up out of this poo."[24] Held to nature
and the body, held in fact quite literally to the bed, the floor, and
the chamber pot, she pleads to the higher authority of the author
who has written her into existence. She may plead, but she has
no power of her own—a situation all characters are in, to some
extent, if we allow them the fiction of their actuality, but one which
appears strikingly emphatic in this plea from female character to
male author. Despite Molly's ambivalence toward her life, despite
her frequent statements of hostility about the men who have made
love to her, she must, finally, acquiesce. Her final yeses, ecstatic
as they seem to be, represent also her agreement to a male plot
of desire, structured around the phallic movement into (back to)
the female; as Molly puts it, "theyre all mad to get in there where
they come out of youd think they could never get far enough up."[25]

The endings of *Ulysses* and *Ida* manifest the difference Stein has
made. Molly's interior monologue ends:

yes when I put the rose in my hair like the Andalusian girls used or shall I
wear a red yes and how he kissed me under the Moorish wall and I thought
well as well him as another and then I asked him with my eyes to ask again
yes and then he asked me would I yes to say yes my mountain flower and
first I put my arms around him yes and drew him down to me so he could
feel my breasts all perfume yes and his heart was going like mad and yes I
said yes I will Yes.[26]

This passage resembles Stein's writing in the ecstatic repetitions and incompletions, suggestive of a transcendence of history. Molly's yes has been spoken at different moments, and may be spoken also in the present, as past moments and present moment converge. Her history condenses so thoroughly, its boundaries and chronology become so confused, that history almost erases itself. Yet the story Molly tells, however scattered, remains the narrative of male quest for the Penelope figure: "he," whichever "he" it is, is the asker, she the one to respond, to give a home to his desire. Although Molly's "stream" of consciousness may have no beginning or end, her monologue does have a resounding and wholly conclusive ending, marked by the last "Yes."

Ida ends with the same word: "Yes." Yet the affirmation markedly differs. Whereas Molly's monologue concludes with a double con- summation of male quester(s) with female object of desire, and of past moment with present, *Ida* resists both conclusion and consum- mation in a way similar to Whitman's resistance to closure at the end of "Song of Myself," as he "twins" with his later readers.

> If Ida goes on, does she go on even when she does not go on any more. No and yes.
>
> Ida is resting but not resting enough. She is resting but she is not saying yes. Why should she say yes. There is no reason why she should so there is nothing to say.
>
> She sat and when she sat she did not always rest, not enough.
>
> She did rest.
>
> If she said anything she said yes. More than once nothing was said. She said something. If nothing is said then Ida does not say yes. If she goes out she comes in. If she does not go away she is there and she does not go away. She dresses, well perhaps in black why not, and a hat, why not, and another hat, why not, and another dress, why not, so much why not.
>
> She dresses in another hat and she dresses in another dress and Andrew is in, and they go in and that is where they are. They are there. Thank them.
>
> Yes. (*Ida*, 154)

Stein seems to speak directly to Joyce: "She is resting but she is not saying yes. Why should she say yes. There is no reason why . . ." There is no reason for a conclusion, apart from the convention that separates one piece of writing from subsequent writings, a con- vention met ruefully ("And rue is in . . .") by Stein. The novel, beginning again and again, has just "gone on," intermingling rest with "saying" something. As a revision of Molly's monologue, *Ida*'s ending implies a certain arbitrariness underlying Molly's (and Joyce's) sense of significant choice. Molly's "shall I wear a red" turns into "she dresses, well perhaps in black why not, and a hat, why not." *Ida*'s final "Yes" is double: it revises the female acquiescence embodied in Molly's "Yes," even as it represents a new affirmation of being itself—Ida's and Andrew's being, and the being of the novel, at each moment of its existence.

This passage also evokes an illuminating contrast with another of Stein's contemporaries, Samuel Beckett. For Beckett, inconclusiveness and the difficulty of ending form part of our modern disease; we may wish to die, but we keep on living, just as our literature—which is, in a sense, written with laughter from the grave—keeps going, even as it gradually and disconcertingly dissolves from a *Molloy* to an *Unnamable*. I can't go on, I'll go on, as Beckett puts it, in a near repetition of Stein ("If Ida goes on, does she go on even when she does not go on any more"). Stein, however, steers clear of the region Beckett will inhabit, even when she hints at a modern and essentially tragic notion of arbitrariness and aimlessness ("So much why not"). Stein differs from Beckett in the final affirmation. "They are there," a fact inviting our gratitude: "Thank them."

Instead of concluding, or even ending with an expressed desire to conclude (as Beckett might), *Ida* struggles against any sense of an ending at all. We find ourselves invited, instead, back into the novel we think we are about to leave: "and they go in and that is where they are." A tentative answer to the question, "If Ida goes on, does she go on even when she does not go on any more," seems clear: "No and yes." No, in that the lines on the page must stop somewhere if a book is to "twin" with an audience through publication. Yes, in that the novel's being does not rely upon this closure. As the narrator assures us earlier in the Second Half:

> Her life never began again because it was always there.
> And now it was astonishing that it was always there. Yes it was.
> Ida
> Yes it was. (*Ida*, 118)

Ida does not have to go anywhere, because she is quite simply "there," not as Molly Bloom is there, in a bedroom at the end of another's journey, but as a being separate from any other's quest.

The narrator affirms the sheer wonder of Ida's (and *Ida*'s) being, just as the "always" leaps beyond any temporal, familial, Romantic, or grammatical line: the one word "Ida" remains as free as the yeses surrounding it as it floats outside any sentence *about* Ida. In this sense, *Ida* agrees with Ida's distaste for "doors": "One of the things Ida never liked was a door. / People *should be there* and not come through a door" (*Ida*, 134, emphasis added). Whether as actual objects within the code of the realistic novel, or as a figure for closure, doors imply movement bound within a line.

Ida herself becomes a storyteller whose stories provide a comical resemblance to the story she inhabits. In a lull during the first part of the Second Half, Ida suddenly tells about "her life with dogs," an autobiographical "Life" written by Stein as a separate (and autobiographical) piece and inserted into *Ida*.[27] Just as *Ida* plays upon a realistic narrative framework that it continually disrupts, Ida creates a tale that promises an historical shape even as it transforms this "history" into a comical series of "thens." Although the events Ida tells manifest connectedness insofar as they follow in an historical line, this link of one dog to the next subverts a sense of history as progressive or even significant. Ida's narrative relies on the arbitrary and accidental. For instance, after the sad death of Sandy the Pekinese—"and then one day an automobile went over him, poor Sandy and that was the end of Sandy" (*Ida*, 98–99)—the narrative records an unaccountable "change," representing a larger sense of history's accidental nature: "So one changed to two and two changed to five and the next dog was also not a big one, his name was Lillieman" (*Ida*, 99). Sandy's life (and *Life*) ends abruptly, without rhyme or reason, just as the account of all the dogs shifts from dog to dog with no further logic than a "then" or a "next" can accommodate.

Ida's narrative concludes with a description of two dog games that offer new figures for history and quest. Quest metamorphoses into a series of games in which the two partners ("Never Sleeps" and "Basket") change places continuously: "tag" and "pussy wants a corner." In "tag," one dog attempts to tag another, yet this brief and exciting "quest" becomes immediately reversed upon the dog's success, as tagger becomes the object of the tag, and vice versa. The purpose is not primarily to reach a goal or conclusion, but to continue the play. Linearity dissolves into a spontaneous and incalculable movement, as dog responds immediately to dog: "To play tag," as Ida notes, "you have to be able to run forward and back to run around things and to start one way and to go the other way" (*Ida*, 106). This description of tag could serve as well for *Ida*, whose pages are scattered with "once" and "once upon a time," invoking history, yet whose "history" scatters into a sequence of stories, running forward and back, starting one way and going another. Just as "any dog is new" (*Ida*, 98), any Ida is new; each instance of *Ida*-Ida marks a new beginning in the general running-around.

Elusive as an object of quest, Ida becomes a new kind of quest-figure, within a "game" of continuous questing akin to the innocent and pleasurable games played by dogs. The Second Half opens with a romantic and mysterious moonlit and snowy pastoral landscape in which Ida (whose immediate companion is a dog) appears to decide to seek "her" Andrew, yet this is no ordinary quest: "She said to herself what am I doing, I have my genius and I am looking for my Andrew and she went on looking" (*Ida*, 93). Ida "looks" for Andrew from a position of plenitude, not of loss or emptiness. She has as companion-spirits not only her dog, successor to "Love," but "herself" and her "genius"—her imagination and creativity as she continues to make herself up. She even has Andrew, in the sense that he is already hers ("my Andrew"), a twin who may be called into existence simply by his name. She "went on looking," then, not because she has not found what she is looking for, but because the sense of movement itself, impelled by love and imagination, is pleasurable.

As the First Half has just concluded, "they were both always together" (*Ida*, 90). "Andrew never disappeared, how could he when he was always there and Ida gradually was always there too" (*Ida*, 89). Within a page of Ida's announced search for Andrew, he suddenly appears again, as a figure whose "name changed to Ida," as if he is so close to Ida that he may easily change places with her. In this sense, "Andrew" may already *be* "Ida," or at least be *with* Ida, in the moonlit landscape. He is her "genius," her gift, as well as her muse and composition. To discover the presence of this spirit again and again is seriously pleasurable. The novel creates and sustains this pleasure by allowing Ida's "quest" for her "Andrew" to continue in manifold forms.

The Narrator and the Audience:
Ida-Ida's Twins

Ida never spoke, she just said what she pleased.
Dear Ida.   *(Ida, 130)*

Two further "twins" assert their possible "addition" to *Ida* from the beginning: the narrator-composer and the one(s) who listen(s) to the composition. These twins intermingle and change places as the "song" of *Ida* is sung, just as both positions (teller and listener) twin with the character Ida, as the preeminent teller-listener who "talks to herself." The narration inscribes its own audience in such a way that we become imaginatively an intimate part of the talking to herself that constitutes *Ida*.

Although *Ida*'s narrator appears at first to "follow" Ida along a traditional narrative path, Stein does not allow this "following" to replicate forms of pursuit figured in the male figures' hunting of Ida. The narrator presents Ida, but stops short of explanation or of claims to knowledge akin to the officious "hell he said, yes I know Ida. He said it to everyone, he said it to her" (*Ida*, 40). Instead, the narrator creates a position close to Ida, even intermingling with Ida's voice, yet in a form of intimacy that leaves Ida inviolate, her own words intact, as in this passage:

Ida began talking.
She never began but sometimes she was talking, she did not understand so she said, she did not sit down so she said, she did not stand up so she said, she did not go out or come in, so she said. And it was all true enough.
This was Ida
Dear Ida. (*Ida*, 136)

The "so she said" both presents Ida's words and suggests a refusal to evaluate them. The "truth" of Ida's comings and goings remains uncertain. Although the narrator assures us that "it was all true enough," we receive little sense of what "true enough" signifies apart from a general sense that it was as true as it needed to be. As William James suggests, truth is what works, a necessary fiction. As if to encourage our acceptance of this "truth," the narrator steps back and says, with a smile, "This was Ida / Dear Ida."

The often-repeated "Dear Ida" suggests that the relationship be-

tween the narrator and Ida is one of affection and love. The narration becomes a letter to Ida from *Ida* ("Dear Ida my twin, . . . from
your twin Ida"); the narrator invokes Ida's presence through calling
upon her name, just as the trinity of women calls upon her ("Ida
is that you Ida") and restores her to herself. The "letter" is also,
however, to us. We become "Ida" to the extent that we "come" in
response to the calling. Like Love, blind and mute, we cannot see
Ida and we remain silent, yet the dog Love encourages us to see
our presence as transformative and necessary to the creation of *Ida*.
"Dear Ida," the narrator says; and in reading these words, in twinning with the narrator, whom we "follow" closely throughout *Ida*,
we say them too. The final "Yes" may, in this sense, be shared by
a trinity of Ida, the narrator, and ourselves: "Thank them. / Yes."
Ida-Ida come(s) to us as a gift for whose surprising and continually
new presence we are grateful. "Yes."

Epilogue

Among the questions Susan B. Anthony asks in the haunting finale of Stein's last opera, *The Mother of Us All* (1945–46), is one that urges us to confront the limits and possibilities of dialogue: "Do you know because I tell you so, or do you know, do you know" (*LO&P*, 88).[1] The question could be Stein's as well; ill from cancer, pressed against the limits of her "long life" (*LO&P*, 87–88), this lover of the rich dialogic liveliness possible within the continuous present may have wished to know how fully her "public" had participated in the dialogue to which she had invited them. Had the dialogue been, in reality, merely a "telling" on her part, a monologue, or had her words met with the kind of responsiveness that could create—at least in a Steinian utopia of shared language—the sense of a mutual "knowing"?[2]

This Susan B. Anthony, however, resembles her creator only partially, occupying a position with regard to subjectivity and language that differs from the Steinian poetics of dialogue I have described in this book. Her "I" remains singular throughout the opera. As she observes in her declaration of oneness:

I am not married and the reason why is that I have had to do what I have had to do, I have had to be what I have had to be, I could never be one of two I could never be two in one as married couples do and can, I am but one all one, one and all one, and so I have never been married to any one. (*LO&P*, 75)

Anthony holds to her "I"—her separate selfhood—with determination, often inscribing it into a language of declaration, injunction, and closure that brings her dangerously close to the self-important male figures of the opera, including Daniel Webster and the other two characters known as the "V.I.P.s." Although she responds to the questions of those around her (as Jo notes, "no use to ask the

V.I.P., they never answer me but you Susan B. you answer, answer me," *LO&P*, 69), and although her language is enjoined to the winning of a voice (a vote) for women as for men, its structures remain largely fastened to her assumption of an isolated "I."

Even Susan B.'s private conversation with her intimate acquaintance Anne in the "Interlude" assumes the form of Susan B. Anthony's statements followed by Anne's echoing and deflecting civility: "I am not tired said Susan. No not said Anne. . . . In each place Susan B. said here I am I am here. Well said Anne. Do not let it trouble you said Susan politely" (*LO&P*, 59). Susan B., insisting on her role as the one who, god-like ("I am I am"), is "here" to "tell" others, places not only men but women too into the position of listener. If men "cannot either see or hear unless [Susan B. Anthony] tell[s] them so, poor things" (*LO&P*, 60), Anne occupies the place of listener as well, however willingly. Anne diverges from this position in domestic altercations and in her attempts to urge Susan B. to "speak louder" (*LO&P*, 60) or to go out of the house to speak to the public (*LO&P*, 76). The playful interchange of unidentified voices possible in Stein's more experimental plays and love poems, however, does not occur here. Susan B. remains not only a stubbornly individual "I," but a central "I" as well—a situation emphasized in the actual opera, where Susan B.'s intensely sweet and lyrical soprano melodies help to distinguish her—as the two Saint Theresas become distinguished in *Four Saints in Three Acts*—from the crowd around her. Susan B. is presented as a powerful if reluctant matriarch, revealing a dangerous link to Stein's earlier and less benign maternal author-figures in *Three Lives* and "Ada," while her companion Anne is less her double than a liminal figure between the others and Susan B., her help-mate and familiar.

Susan B. Anthony's insistence on her singularity links with the opera's probing of the difference between art and politics. *The Mother of Us All* raises problematic questions about the efficacy of action within the world (or at least within the democracy of the U.S.A., "Us All") as it is presently constructed: how possible is it to effect deep changes within the political sphere, working along the avenues already available? How possible is it for someone—a woman or a man—to enter this arena without reproducing the authoritarian structures against which one is struggling, even if the struggle is in the name of the people?[3] *The Mother of Us All* reveals the ironies attendant upon the achievement of the vote, first for all men, including black men ("Susan B. Yes it is wonderful as the result of my work for the first time the word male has been written into the constitution of the United States concerning suffrage." *LO&P*, 79–80), and then, after Anthony's death, for women too. To win the vote for women, Anthony observes with bitterness, will "do them no good because having the vote they will become like men, they will be afraid" (*LO&P*, 81).

The nature of this fear affords insight into the difficulty of achieving authentic change. As Susan B. Anthony argues:

[Men] fear women, they fear each other, they fear their neighbor, they fear other countries and then they hearten themselves in their fear by crowding together and following each other, and when they crowd together and follow each other they are brutes, like animals who stampede. (*LO&P*, 80)

What Anthony describes here is a situation in which dialogue is impossible. Even to "say these things out loud," as Anne urges Susan B. to do, becomes futile since "they would not listen" but would "revenge themselves" (*LO&P*, 81). The vote turns into a means of making such absence of dialogue into law and ultimately into legitimated war.

In a further sense, once the vote has been "won" (with its pun on "one," the singular and nondialogic), it seems to make absent precisely what it represents. As Susan B. asks in her finale: "But do I want what we have got, has it not gone, what made it live, has it not gone because now it is had" (*LO&P*, 88). To make the vote literal, to materialize it and so to make it vulnerable to ownership, is paradoxically to allow its participation in a system of representation whereby what is signified becomes absent, its place usurped by the sign itself. "The vote" is won, but what is it that is won? The sign is emptied of precisely "what made it live": this is how we are "had" by the politics of traditional representation.

Despite the ironies attendant upon the achievement of the actual vote through suffrage, the vote remains significant even within *The Mother of Us All* as a figure for the possibility of the dialogic. Susan B. continues to believe in the concept behind the vote, even though she remains cynical about bringing this concept into reality: she decides to "fight for the right, for the right to vote for [women] even though they become like men, become afraid like men, become like men" (*LO&P*, 81). Susan B.'s effort (her "long life of effort and strife," *LO&P*, 87) resembles Stein's; both attempt to find a form—

directly political in one case, political in a literary sense in another
—for the idea of suffrage.

In Stein's 1946 "Transatlantic Interview" (recorded six months
before she died), she describes the idea of equality as the basis for
a compositional method inherited from Cézanne: "After all, to me
one human being is as important as another human being," just as
"each part of a composition [is] as important as the whole." Defining her early experiments in *Three Lives* as the attempt to create
"the evenness of everybody having a vote," she suggests the project
at the heart of all her writing.[4] Voting, in its largest sense, may be
understood as a metaphor for the activity possible, if not within the
world at large, then at least within Stein's utopian linguistic realm,
in which language is attached to the body through an evocative
nonrepresentation. Each word, each sound, each textual moment
has a vote, and each part of the world voiced by (not only represented by) the writing has a vote as well.

The Mother of Us All opens out, however, into the further question: can this poetics of dialogue, grounded as it is in the concept
of equality, be realized only within the utopian discourse a writer
like Stein offers? Does the movement out of a literary realm and
into the world at large—signified by Susan B.'s reluctant sallies out
of her own house and into the public arena—mean a loss of the
dialogic mode possible within language when it remains safely on
the page or in the theater?[5] The opera invites our own response:
do we, after all, "know"—have we entered into a dialogic relationship with this public figure appearing before us on the stage—or
do we know because she "tells us so"? The moments of "Silence"
indicated in the original libretto between the sections of Susan B.'s
final aria leave room for our response, even as this silence assumes
an eerily monitory air.[6] As emissaries from the world outside the
opera, we must listen closely to the answers we make.

Reference Matter

Notes

The dates I give for Stein's writings are those generally accepted for the time of composition, as cited in Bridgman's "Key to the *Yale Catalogue*," Part 4 (in *Gertrude Stein in Pieces*), unless otherwise indicated. Because so many of Stein's writings found their way into print only after many years, the composition date is more useful than the publication date.

INTRODUCTION

1. This attitude toward Stein reflects cultural attitudes toward women writers in general. Most importantly, her life is often considered more interesting than her writing, as Stein herself noted with concern in *Everybody's Autobiography*: "It always did bother me that the American public were more interested in me than in my work. And after all there is no sense in it because if it were not for my work they would not be interested in me so why should they not be more interested in my work than in me" (*EA*, 50). For a good discussion of the shaping of Stein's reputation, see Stimpson, "Gertrude Stein: Humanism."

2. As if to make this situation of reading as self-conscious as possible, Stein interrupts the columns of dialogue with page numbers in Roman numerals. As any reader of Stein knows, it is difficult to define most of her writing in terms of traditional genre categories. "The King or Something" appears in *Geography and Plays* and could be termed a "play," yet the humorous and assertive use of page numbers makes this definition problematic. The term "voice poem" seems to come closest to the composition's intent. Further, many critics might define these voices as Stein's and Toklas's. Although this identification is possible, it is important not to limit the possibilities of such open-ended dialogue to these two figures.

3. Two approaches to dialogue that have provoked, inspired, and influenced my understanding of Stein's poetics of dialogue are those of Patricia Meyer Spacks and Mikhail Bakhtin. The dialogic situation in Stein resembles the mode of gossip defined by Spacks as "serious": "exist[ing] only as a function of intimacy," "it takes place in private, at leisure, in a context of trust, usually among no more than two or three people. . . . The relation-

206 • Notes to Page 3

ship such gossip expresses and sustains matters more than the information it promulgates" (*Gossip*, 5–6). For a modernist as experimental as Stein, this emphasis on relationship rather than on the content of the dialogue, or even on the act of interpretation, becomes intensified almost to the exclusion of a recognizable content that would allow the "enlarge[ment of the participants'] knowledge of one another" or of the world (*Gossip*, 5). One of the most important contributions of Spacks's work on gossip lies in her analysis of "the importance of relationship as an issue of literary interpretation" (*Gossip*, 12). See especially chap. 3 ("How It Feels") and chap. 9 ("Stepping Down from the Platform," on the narrator-reader relationship). Stein's poetics of dialogue also shares certain assumptions with Bakhtin's concept of language as articulated in his "Discourse in the Novel" (*Dialogic Imagination*, 259–422). Bakhtin argues that living language (as opposed to its abstraction within a linguistic system) "is never unitary" (288), but richly multiple and polyphonic, and that the novel as a form embodies this "heteroglossia," this many-voiced and many-tongued discourse. As Yaeger writes in her illuminating essay, " 'Because a Fire Was in My Head,' " bringing Bakhtin's concept of the dialogic into the field of gender, "Disruptive, emotional, nonhegemonic, language, according to Bakhtin, is open to intention and change. Moreover, both spoken and written language are dynamic and plural, and, as such, language resists all attempts to foster a unitary or absolute system of expression within its boundaries" (955). For Bakhtin each linguistic act occurs within a kind of battlefield, among competing styles and ideologies. Although this model works for Stein to a certain extent, her "dialogues" appear to be more pacific than Bakhtin's charged struggle between opposing forces. In this book, I shall be primarily concerned with dialogue as intimate relationship, with a potential both for the "battle" of difference and for a mutual agreement or pleasurable resemblance.

4. Schmitz makes a similar point in *Of Huck and Alice*, where he notes that Stein's style works "to keep Gertrude Stein, as a writer, out of the fixation of a particular identity, *he said she said*, out of the power of the Name, in the present motion of her thinking" (228). Schmitz's concept of "double-talk" bears an interesting connection to the poetics of dialogue I have found in Stein. He locates this "double-talk" in two voices, woven together in Stein's different styles: Alice's signifies "the mother tongue," or speech, "which the writer [Gertrude] humorously appropriates" (202). I agree with this doubling of Stein and Toklas to an extent, yet I would wish not to limit the concept of double-voicedness to these two particular and historical voices.

5. Ruddick discovers within *Tender Buttons* a "central story about loss of the mother, entry into the world of the father, and the imagined recovery of the mother" ("Rosy Charm," 230). Although Ruddick suggests that she

is grounding her interpretation of this "story" in a Lacanian sense of the Symbolic, she does not elaborate on this idea; rather, she maps William James onto object relations theory by linking "the domain of the mother" to "the life of immediate or raw perception" (235). Burke suggests that in the early portrait "Ada," Stein makes use of the "semiotic mode" described by Kristeva ("Gertrude Stein, the Cone Sisters," 560–61 n. 44). DeKoven accepts Kristeva's theory about the antipatriarchal nature of experimental writing, including Stein's. She argues that the experimental project includes, but goes beyond, the "presymbolic foregrounding of the signifier": "Experimental writing is only partly explicitly female, of the mother; it is entirely anti-patriarchal" (*A Different Language*, 22). Stimpson argues that "[Stein] shows how pre- and post-Oedipal mix—how the semiotic and the symbolic play off and against each other" ("Somagrams," 78).

6. Burke, "Gertrude Stein, the Cone Sisters," 560 n. 44.

7. Ruddick, "Rosy Charm," 235.

8. Stimpson addresses this problem through her critique of the reliance upon Kristeva and Derrida in DeKoven's assertion that there are "two languages," which remain utterly separate: the patriarchal and the antipatriarchal, the male and the female, the post-Oedipal and the pre-Oedipal, "the father's dictionary" and "the mother's body" ("Somagrams," 77). Stimpson also questions the "picture of childhood that transforms children into boys and girls whose primary schooling in language is first with the mother's body and then with the father's rule" (78).

9. Stanton, "Language and Revolution," 73.

10. See Patricia Yaeger's important contribution to the ongoing debate about women's relation to patriarchal discourse in *Honey-Mad Women*. Yaeger works to "define an alternate mythology of feminine speech," not focusing on "the ways in which the woman writer is terrorized by the texts of others," but rather on the woman writer's "ecstatic espionage, her expropriation of the language she needs, her own invention of a 'terrorist text'" (*Honey-Mad Women*, 3).

11. Stanton, "Language and Revolution," 75. Although Kristeva does not define this "semiotic" mode as female or feminine, its source within the nonsignifying early language between mother and child seems to place it implicitly on the side of the female.

12. For good overviews of French feminist thought, see Marks, "Women and Literature," and Burke, "Report from Paris." Two of the most important texts experimenting with the concept of *écriture féminine* are Irigaray, "When Our Lips Speak Together," and Cixous, "The Laugh of the Medusa." The critique of this strain of thought in French feminism is well known. Stanton, for example, notes the "danger . . . in the recurring identification of the female in *écriture féminine* with madness, antireason, primitive darkness" ("Language and Revolution," 86 n. 39).

13. This question of Stein's relationship to French feminist writing has recently begun to be explored, although much more work is needed. See, for example, Gibbs, "Hélène Cixous and Gertrude Stein."

14. See, for example, "Pink Melon Joy" (*G&P*), "If You Had Three Husbands" (*G&P*), "All Sunday" (*A&B*), and "Lifting Belly" (*YGS*).

15. See DeKoven, *A Different Language* (especially xviii–xix) for a different approach to this question of a female language in Stein. DeKoven argues that "we all, except in experimental writing, speak and write patriarchal language" (xix). She emphasizes that her terms, "patriarchal" and "anti-patriarchal" or "experimental," are not attached to "male" or "female" languages. Yet, as Stimpson notes in "Reading Gertrude Stein" (269–70), DeKoven's "genderizing" of language still involves fairly rigid assumptions about what is "masculine," what "feminine." Further, this equation of the experimental with the antipatriarchal makes a dubious swerve around the evident presence of patriarchal elements in much experimental writing.

16. Secor suggests that "Stein's most serious contribution may be in her challenge to gender as a significant category in human experience" ("Gertrude Stein: The Complex Force," 30).

17. Both Fifer ("'Is Flesh Advisable?'") and Stimpson ("Gertrice/Altrude") explore the "interior theater" (Fifer's term) within which Stein played with various roles, especially masculine ones. I would like to extend this vision of role-playing from its specific anchoring in the actual relationship of Stein and Toklas to the larger field of Stein's language-play with regard to gender.

18. See, however, Secor's different interpretation of this statement. As she suggests ("Gertrude Stein: The Complex Force," 30), Stein shows here "that gender is meaningless," not that the issue of gender is without value.

19. See, for example, Cook: "Heterosexist society is little threatened by a relationship that appeared so culturally determined. Stein wrote and slept while Toklas cooked, embroidered, and typed. Few feminist principles are evident there to challenge the ruling scheme of things" ("'Women Alone Stir My Imagination,'" 730). See also Benstock (*Women of the Left Bank*, 18–19), who presents a similar version of this relationship. Stimpson offers a psychologically more complex picture of the Stein/Toklas ménage in "Gertrice/Altrude."

20. Stimpson, "The Mind, the Body," 490. See also Blankley, "Beyond the 'Talent of Knowing,'" for a good discussion of Stein's changing responses in the 1890's and the early years of the twentieth century to the model of the "New Woman." Blankley reads *The Making of Americans* and *Fernhurst* as enabling Stein to "discover her power as an artist by letting her confront her own internalized images of female powerlessness that may have prevented her from writing all her later experimental work" (202).

21. Stimpson, "The Mind, the Body," 135–36.

22. DeKoven, *A Different Language*, 36, 134–37.

23. Burke, "Gertrude Stein, the Cone Sisters," 558.

24. Valuable interpretations of Stein that suggest either her concern with women and women's relationships or with the situation of women (and the cultural feminine) within patriarchal culture include those by DeKoven, Doane, Fifer, Ruddick, Schmitz, Secor, Simon, and Stimpson. Bridgman, in *Gertrude Stein in Pieces*, opened up many of the issues of sexual and gender identity that have since undergone further exploration, although he does not perceive Stein as "feminist" per se.

25. DeKoven claims that Stein's writing is "anti-patriarchal," but not intentionally so (*A Different Language*, xvi–xvii), a position that seems to me difficult to verify: how can we know what Stein's intentions were? Schmitz compares Stein's project with Mary Daly's in *Gyn/Ecology* in terms of the "deconstruct[ion of] an entire system of patriarchal identification," adding that "her writing is never polemical, or programmatic. The deconstructive energy of her style does not involve a rhetoric of contradiction, which substitutes a new identity for an old identity, but rather does away entirely with the concept of identity" (*Of Huck and Alice*, 189). Doane (*Silence and Narrative*) traces the first decade of Stein's writing as a movement from the Logos to "illegitimacy." See Stimpson's argument, however, that "even as [Stein's] poetry moves against some patriarchal habits, it reconstitutes others." Stimpson argues that Stein often "transposes gender" merely by "rearranging" its "orders, codes, and poses," not by destroying them ("Gertrude Stein and the Transposition of Gender," 2).

26. Gass, "Gertrude Stein: Her Escape," 87.

27. Stein appears to argue against this concept of her art in the lecture she delivered at Oxford and Cambridge in 1936, "What Are Masterpieces," where she argues that creation is not in the realm of "identity" or "human nature," but is instead in the realm of the "human mind," constructing its "master-pieces" in pure isolation from an audience. Yet I think that this late essay must be placed in the context of Stein's own difficulty with the fact of her sudden success from *The Autobiography of Alice B. Toklas*, which was written precisely from a position of "identity." Stein's defensiveness about the relatively small audience held by her more experimental texts seems to infuse this account of how unimportant audience has been to her. Her writings present evidence to the contrary.

28. Fifer recognizes this call to a reader-as-lover in her essay "Guardians and Witnesses," although she limits this concept, in a more literal sense, to Stein's erotic writings. I would like to emphasize that, just as the "unreconstructed" reader may be either biologically female or male (since there is nothing inherent in femaleness that would make a female reader ipso facto a Steinian reader), the newly constructed Steinian reader may be either male or female. To become a reader who participates in the

writing intimately and as an equal, one sheds (at least for the duration of the reading) a mode of structure and response reliant upon the hierarchy of masculine over feminine. Therefore, although a reader may be literally male, he may accept Stein's invitation to leap beyond the constructions of masculine and feminine, and to enter into dialogic forms in which the old hierarchy has no place.

29. Iser, in "The Reading Process," *Implied Reader*, 275, 278–79, 280. DeKoven also notes that Iser "insists on the centrality of constructing coherent patterns of meaning" (*A Different Language*, 8), yet she does not mention the sexual politics inherent in his metaphors.

30. Barthes, *Pleasure of the Text*, 3.

31. Ibid., 37.

32. Ibid., 16. Barthes argues here indirectly against Bakhtin's sense of the text as a "rivalry of ideolects."

33. DeKoven finds in Stein's writing "limitless, dense semantic plenitude, and what Roland Barthes calls '*la jouissance de la texte*': writing as erotic celebration" (*A Different Language*, 16), although she does not question the sexual politics of this model for reading.

34. Dydo, "Must Horses Drink," 273.

35. Kostelanetz, "Introduction," xxi.

36. Gass, "Gertrude Stein: Her Escape," 92, 95. This insistence on the "word" has a long tradition in Stein criticism. Sherwood Anderson, one of Stein's earliest and most enthusiastic critics, described Stein's project as "laying word against word, relating sound to sound, feeling for the taste, the smell, the rhythm of the individual word" ("Four American Impressions," 171). Sutherland too, although he made numerous connections between Stein's work and nineteenth- and twentieth-century philosophy and art, perceived Stein's writing as essentially pure of meaning. He argues that twentieth-century art "usually does exist in disconnection from any reference or extrinsic meaning, by the beauty or intensity or character of its immediate properties" (*Gertrude Stein*, 150). Hoffman explores this aesthetic in *Development of Abstractionism*, in which he understands Stein's writing as moving toward nonrepresentationalism, through a progressive "leaving-out" of conventional elements (28).

37. DeKoven, *A Different Language*, xiii–xiv.

38. Ibid., 5.

39. Ibid., 74.

40. Ibid., 81–82.

41. Ibid., 10, 11. Stimpson suggests that DeKoven is "implicitly . . . imposing patriarchal standards, limits, on writing that allegedly exists to remind us of the standardless, the limitless" ("Reading Gertrude Stein," 270).

42. Steiner, *Exact Resemblance*, 4. For another perspective on this issue

of referentiality, see Dubnick, *Structure of Obscurity*. Dubnick argues for the presence of two "obscure" styles in Stein, illuminated by Jakobson's descriptions of metaphor and metonymy. Dubnick warns against "under-reading Stein—seeing too little meaning in her work and regarding it as empty words—or . . . overreading—insisting on finding discursive meaning where none exists" (*Structure of Obscurity*, xv). Dubnick attempts to avoid these mistakes by focusing primarily on Stein's language as it moves toward "obscurity."

43. Ibid., 54. It is intriguing that Stein's most difficult writings of the 1920's cause two critics with approaches as different as DeKoven and Steiner to term them, finally, unreadable. Although DeKoven values Stein's "anarchic" and "open-ended" play of language, she discovers a limit to the value once it seems to leave its readers too far outside, a limit that Steiner discovers from the different angle of valuing the "indexical" function of Stein's portraiture.

44. It is important to note, however, that very few critics have explored Stein's writing between 1920 and 1932. Dydo is an exception; she is now completing a chronological study of Stein's writing from 1923 to 1932, which makes careful and thorough use of Stein's manuscripts during this period.

45. Walker, *Making of a Modernist*, xi.

46. See, for example, Dydo's recent essay "*Stanzas in Meditation*."

47. Perloff, "Poetry as Word-System," 75. Schmitz shares Perloff's perspective to a great extent, in his use of Derrida as the proponent of an interpretation that "affirms freeplay"; see *Of Huck and Alice*, 190. As Schmitz argues, "The discursive site of *Tender Buttons* is already cleared, already decentered, free of all the tricks of incarnation" (190). See also Stimpson's discussion of "the guerilla war against certainty" ("Gertrude Stein and the Transposition of Gender," 10) and Doane's discussion of Stein's creation of meaning "in a new way" (*Silence and Narrative*, xx–xxi).

48. Perloff, "Poetry as Word-System," 76.

49. See Gass, "Gertrude Stein and the Geography"; Hadas, "Spreading the Difference"; and Schmitz, "The Gaiety of Gertrude Stein," in *Of Huck and Alice*. It is intriguing that all three of these essays focus on interpretations of *Tender Buttons*.

50. Hadas, "Spreading the Difference," 59.

CHAPTER I

1. This scene of birth bears an interesting connection to Stein's experiences as a medical student at Johns Hopkins: she disliked obstetrics and was disturbed by the births she witnessed.

2. Although I will not focus in this chapter on the racism evident in

the descriptions of characters in "Melanctha," I think that it is necessary to acknowledge this disturbing element. I would link the racist definitions in this story with Stein's interest in achieving an authoritative narrative voice. Such a voice, although it is countered by the impulse toward a democratic sharing of the narrative space, allows her the opportunity to define otherness in a constricting and brutal way.

3. Gilbert and Gubar, *Madwoman*, 4–5.

4. See Homans's account, in *Bearing the Word*, of nineteenth-century women writers' complex and often revisionary literary responses to the cultural placement of women on the side of nature and the literal, rather than on the side of culture and the word.

5. In their recent study of modernism and the woman writer, *No Man's Land*, Gilbert and Gubar describe modernism as a "product" of the late nineteenth- and early twentieth-century "battle of the sexes" (xii). They discuss the recurring theme of "male impotence and female potency" in canonical texts by male modernists (35–36). For many men, the literary field became "a no man's land because it debilitated masculinity," while for many women the no man's land became "if only fleetingly . . . a 'Herland' " (66). See especially chap. 3, "Tradition and the Female Talent: Modernism and Masculinism."

6. Gilbert and Gubar, *Madwoman*, 97.

7. Ibid., 101.

8. Stein is involved in a project similar to that of other women modernists studied by DuPlessis in *Writing Beyond the Ending*. DuPlessis "interprets the project of twentieth-century women writers as the examination and delegitimation of cultural conventions about male and female, romance and quest, hero and heroine, public and private, individual and collective, but especially conventions of romance as a trope for the sex-gender system" (ix). For a very different approach to Stein's resistance to plot, see Caserio, *Plot, Story, and the Novel*, which argues that Stein abjures plot out of her desire to capture reality: "plot depends upon a sense of history, of time, and temporal experience that Stein thinks no longer writeable because no longer liveable" (11). For Caserio, the unplottedness of *Three Lives* represents a radical stasis that undermines the possibility for moral, emotional, or intellectual action in narrative as in the world. I would argue here, in agreement with DuPlessis, that plots and the authority behind them are not innocent for Stein, or for other women writers. Stein struggles in *Three Lives* against her own desire to bind her women characters into traditional plots.

9. Later in this chapter I shall discuss the narrative irony present here, by which the narrator, instead of sharing the narration with Anna, marks his or her difference from and superiority over Anna. Anna, in this sense, is not as strong a speaker as she appears to be.

10. "Verbs and adverbs are more interesting [than nouns and adjectives]. In the first place they have one very nice quality and that is that they can be so mistaken. It is wonderful the number of mistakes a verb can make." (*LIA*, 211)

11. Wilson, *Axel's Castle*, 237–38.

12. I am indebted to Henry Louis Gates Jr. for his work on Zora Neale Hurston's *Their Eyes Were Watching God*, where he defines the use of *discours indirect libre* in terms of a sharing of the power of narration. The (female) narrator gives up absolute control of the storytelling, thereby making room for Janie as a conarrator. Talk at Yale University, spring 1985.

13. For a different approach to the narrator in *Three Lives*, see DeKoven's chapter on *Three Lives* in *A Different Language*, especially p. 29, where DeKoven makes the point that "the narration is 'omniscient third,' yet nonetheless obtuse: there is a discrepancy, sometimes to the point of contradiction, between the tone of the narrative voice and the content of the narrative. . . . The discrepancy is so extreme that the narrator seems at times entirely blind to the import of what she narrates." This appearance of blindness, as I have suggested, springs partly from free indirect discourse; that is, the characters who "share" the narration have their own blindnesses. Yet surely this "blindness" is not complete; as I argue here, the use of characters' voices occurs in a framework of irony. DeKoven treats the narrative voice as a single, consistent voice, "straightforward, factual, reassuring; it is also childish, whimsical, consciously naive" (30), yet this "consciousness" of naïveté clearly contains the opposite of naïveté. In a similar sense, DeKoven suggests that Stein herself was "unconscious" of her use of "narrative tone and temporal structure as a defense against her own anger and despair" (32). If one reads the narrative tone as partly ironic, however, such unconsciousness on Stein's part disappears, and a new set of problems emerges with regard to narrative authority and control.

14. For a good discussion of Stein's debt to Flaubert, especially in "The Good Anna," see Walker, *Making of a Modernist*, 19–23. Walker sees a greater difference between the style of the narrator and the style of the characters in "The Good Anna" than in the later two stories, in which she finds an "assertive, evenly textured verbal surface . . . analogous to the surfaces of Cezanne's canvases" and grounded in Flaubertian techniques of free indirect discourse (23). Although Walker makes the important point that *Three Lives* exposes "language as an instrument of culture, enforcing the dominant values of a community" (26), she does not address the issue of the narrator's superiority or specific implication in this structure of dominance.

15. For a different interpretation of these endings, see DeKoven, *A Different Language*, 32–33. DeKoven argues that these deaths mark the "linear causality" (33) leading to the final "defeat" of the three heroines "by domi-

nant personality traits which are culturally defined as female" (32). I am suggesting that the narration itself represents at least as much of a danger as the culturally shaped characters of these female figures.

16. Mrs. Haydon reproduces the erasure of female difference tradition-ally enacted by Western metaphysics, as described by Irigaray, especially in *Speculum.* According to Irigaray, since masculinity is the standard and the norm, the female has become a mirror, reflecting back the phallic "same-ness."

17. DeKoven states that "Melanctha is defeated by what is emerging as the fatal flaw *par excellence* of heroines in women's fiction: a divided self" (*A Different Language*, 31). I would add both that this "flaw" is culturally inscribed and that in Melanctha's case the narrative's subtle use of irony teaches us how to become less divided than Melanctha, by learning the actual value inherent in the apparent "trouble" that Melanctha "finds."

18. "Wisdom" may be a euphemism for a specifically sexual knowl-edge, although I think it is important not to limit its significance to sexu-ality alone. Bridgman observes that Stein made much use of euphemism in *Three Lives* (*Gertrude Stein in Pieces*, 56–57). As DeKoven notes, however, Bridgman tends to interpret Stein's writing in terms of "pathology rather than intention, seeing guilty evasiveness about lesbian sexuality, not con-certed innovation, as the crucial origin of the opacity and indeterminacy of her experimental writing" (*A Different Language*, xxiii). For a different approach to the issue of Melanctha's wanderings, see Ruddick's valuable essay, " 'Melanctha' and the Psychology of William James," in which she argues for a connection between James's theory of children's (and some adults') greater openness to sense-data, and especially to stimuli of "a directly exciting quality" (547). Ruddick sees Melanctha as open precisely to such sense-data, not as a means to an end, but in themselves, in all their plenitude.

19. DeKoven, *A Different Language*, 29.

20. As many critics have noted, the relationship between Jeff Campbell and Melanctha resembles Stein's early attachment to May Bookstaver. The relationship between Jane Harden and Melanctha surely has a similar re-semblance, although Melanctha occupies the Jeff Campbell–Gertrude Stein position, while Jane Harden occupies the later Melanctha–May Bookstaver position. See Katz's valuable introduction to *Fernhurst, Q.E.D., and Other Early Writings*, i–xxxiv.

21. Doane makes a similar point, arguing that Stein embeds a "new possibility," countering the novelistic conventions so damaging to women, in her style of repetition, which "breaks the linear progress of the plot and offers the possibility of a new style" (*Silence and Narrative*, 80–81).

22. This movement into the continuous present, grounded in the "for-getting" of the past, does not come in this early story without a sense of

guilt, perhaps even on Stein's part. Jane Harden could be said to represent an influential "teacher"/author whom both Melanctha and Stein have absorbed or devoured, in order to move on into the twentieth century and the "continuous present."

23. This creativity is not exclusively female or feminine, however, as evidenced by the fact that Jeff Campbell begins slowly to participate in it, as he and Melanctha engage more and more in dialogue with one another.

24. Both Perloff and Walker discuss this bafflement of the desire for certainty in other contexts. Perloff argues that Stein's repetitions make "peculiar gap[s] in the text. . . . Gertrude Stein can . . . tell us what her characters say and do but not what that speech or action *means*. What engages our attention as readers, then, is that, like Jeff Campbell, we are made to feel that the truth is just about to be disclosed only to learn—in the course of 'beginning again and again'—that such 'truth' can never be accessible" ("Poetry as Word-System," 97). Walker argues that, especially in "Melanctha," rational discourse is Stein's primary target: "the characters' distance from mainstream American culture is used to motivate a systematic stylistic demonstration of the limits of rational discourse as a medium for interpersonal communication" (*Making of a Modernist*, 31).

25. As is evident, I have attempted to avoid using a pronoun for the narrator, because it is impossible to tell whether the narrator is intended to have a gender. Yet evidence points most strongly in the direction of the female, both because so many of the author-narrator-figures in *Three Lives* are female, and because of the narrator's use of an ungrammatical and oral style, similar to that of the main female characters. The gender of the narrator, however, is not made clear by Stein, especially since the narrator is never explicitly a character in the stories.

26. DeKoven makes a similar point in *A Different Language*, 44.

27. Ibid., 42.

CHAPTER 2

1. As many critics have noted, this scene in "Melanctha" revises a similar one in Stein's earlier novel *Q.E.D.*, in which Helen kisses Adele; see *QED*, 66.

2. Chodorow, *Reproduction*, 63; see also 65. Chodorow may be exaggerating the absoluteness of the Freudian baby's isolation.

3. Ibid., 64.

4. This formulation differs markedly from Lacan's theory about the creation of a subject's identity. According to Lacan, "one" (much less "two") does not exist before the mirror stage. It is only when the infant sees the "Ideal I" in the mirror that an "I" is constituted. The gap between the subject and the mirrored subject is irreducible, and lies at the heart of an

alienation irresolvable except by a Romantic yearning to return to the state of preconsciousness where one is not a "One" at all, since one has not yet confronted the other "One" of the mirror. It is striking how little any concept of dialogue plays a part in Lacan's theory. The focus remains on the "I" as an inherently fictive creation, profoundly isolated and alienated. See Lacan, "The Mirror Stage" and "The Signification of the Phallus," in *Ecrits*, 1–7, 281–91. For Irigaray's feminist critique of this insistence upon "oneness," in which "the other [particularly the female] is the image of the one, but an image only," see "When Our Lips Speak Together," especially 71, as well as other essays in *This Sex*.

5. Winnicott, "The Theory of the Parent-Infant Relationship," in *Maturational Processes*, 39.

6. Schmitz explores doubleness in Stein's writing from a different angle. Focusing on Stein's changing forms of "double-talk," he finds the central motive of her writing to be the escape from "the fixation of a particular identity, . . . the power of the Name" (*Of Huck and Alice*, 228). He locates this double-talk in the mingled discourses of Stein and Toklas. Toklas, as he suggests, "is also an amanuensis, another self, a participant in the very process of Gertrude Stein's writing. So her voice is in the dialectic of the style, affirming its humor" (171). Although I agree that this actual relationship finds significant form in Stein, I shall argue that the literary and linguistic doublings of Stein's writing go far beyond any grounding in one particular relationship.

7. Chodorow, *Reproduction*, 67–68.

8. Ibid., 93, 96.

9. Carol Gilligan, in a talk at Yale University, May 2, 1985.

10. See Chodorow's argument about this situation, in her Introduction, *Reproduction*, 8–10.

11. In Homans, *Bearing the Word*. See especially the Introduction, 1–39.

12. Ibid., 12.

13. Ibid., 13–14. It is important to emphasize, as Homans does, the mythic dimension of this "story" about female and male development. To take this myth literally would be dangerous, especially for any poetics that hopes to challenge gender lines and even to transcend gender. Further, it is clear that modernist forms in particular, whether created by male or female writers, make strong use of both "symbolic" and "presymbolic" language.

14. Ibid., 20.

15. Ibid.

16. Stimpson, in considering recent works of lesbian fiction, suggests that "lesbianism is more than a matter of mother/daughter affairs, but the new texts suggest that one of its satisfactions is a return to primal origins, to primal loves, when female/female, not male/female, relationships structured the world" ("Zero Degree," 377). As Stimpson has argued in many of

her essays on Stein, however, the question of "female" and "male" becomes
an intricate one in Stein's writing, in that Stein often assumed a masculine persona (see "The Mind, the Body," and "Gertrice/Altrude"). I would
emphasize here that, although the most important bond for Stein may be
the one between two female figures, her writing suggests an openness and
flexibility in terms of gender. The "others" could often be imagined as two
women, two men, or a woman and a man.

17. Irigaray, "And the One Doesn't Stir," 66.

18. Ibid., 61.

19. Irigaray's fullest challenge both to psychoanalysis and to Western
metaphysics comes in *Speculum of the Other Woman*, originally published in
French as *Speculum de l'autre femme* in 1974.

20. Stein critics have always been attentive to the importance of these
fields, especially of philosophy, in Stein's work, although one of Stein's
most important contributions to both fields, *A Geographical History of America*, remains largely uninterpreted. Sutherland's early and valuable *Gertrude
Stein* uncovered many of Stein's philosophical thematics, as did Stewart's
Gertrude Stein and the Present. More recently, Stimpson has opened up the
question of the central metaphysical split between the mind and body,
as Stein addresses this split in her writing ("The Mind, the Body"), and
Ruddick has explored connections between William James and Stein in
" 'Melanctha' and the Psychology of William James," "Rosy Charm," and
"William James and the Modernism of Gertrude Stein."

21. Schmitz interprets the photograph in this way: Alice Toklas is the
muse and model, while Gertrude Stein is the writer and artist. He sees
Alice's position within the photograph—"Alice looking in upon the scene
of writing, Alice at the door" (*Of Huck and Alice*, 206)—as representative
of Alice's "place" in *The Autobiography*. From Alice's perspective, Stein
occupies "that closed male world where glory is" (209), and it is Alice's
desire to recognize and give voice both to Stein's genius and to the way
in which Stein has been "wronged as a writer because she is a woman,
and thought queer" (208). For Schmitz, the relation between "muse" and
"writer" is a benevolent one. I suggest a more uneasy relation between the
ghostly Alice figure and the substantial, writing Stein.

22. This question of voice has been addressed by many critics. Sutherland observed that Toklas's conversational style resembled Stein's quite
closely, and that Stein "re-created" in Toklas "a figure of herself, established an identity, a twin" (*Gertrude Stein*, 148–49). Although Bridgman
argues that *The Autobiography* "was written by Gertrude Stein alone, with
few hesitations or changes," he suggests that Toklas acted as "some kind
of monitor" for this autobiography, even to the extent, "on at least a few
occasions," that "Gertrude Stein invited Alice Toklas's active participation
in the act of creation" (*Gertrude Stein in Pieces*, 212–13). Bloom represents

another side to this question, in her discussion of this autobiography as a "pseudo-dialogue" ("Gertrude Is Alice Is Everybody," 86), in which the character of Alice acts the different roles of reporter, intermediary, reinforcer, and interpreter for Stein's central and egotistical presence.

23. Stimpson, in her pioneering essay on Stein's lesbian aesthetics, "Gertrice/Altrude," makes a similar point about punctuation. The absence of quotation marks suggests the permeability of boundaries between female lovers. Yet see Stimpson's later essay "Gertrude Stein and the Transposition of Gender," in which she suggests the further possibility of a less "charitable" interpretation of unpunctuated dialogues like "All Sunday": "the poem is a covert dramatic monologue. The author has simply sponged up the wife's voice" (6). I would argue that it is difficult to tell, in *The Autobiography* as in other compositions, whose voice is whose at any one point. Again, it seems unfair to such writings to ground them too specifically in Stein's actual relationship with Toklas.

24. It is not impossible, in fact, that both women helped to create "Ada." In the extant manuscript of "Ada," leaves 1–7 and 11 are in the hand of Alice Toklas. As Bridgman suggests, "Ada" may be "a collaborative effort" (*Gertrude Stein in Pieces*, 210), although this is difficult to prove.

25. Stein adds a twist here to the modernist tendency to self-reference, then, for from the beginning the "self" is never easily locatable and therefore cannot be a reliable point of reference. Although her challenge to the unitary subject has a post-modernist dimension, I do not think that she does away with subjecthood entirely. Instead, she makes the subject always at least plural.

26. His name echoes Jane Harden's, in "Melanctha," a fact that may suggest the masculine aspect of her use of "power." I am grateful to John Elder for pointing out this connection to me.

27. Irigaray, "When Our Lips Speak Together," 72.

28. Burke's excellent essay, "Gertrude Stein, the Cone Sisters," addresses "Ada" from a similar angle, although Burke suggests that the later love relationship represents a straightforward substitution for the earlier mother-daughter relation. Using Abel's definitions of the literary uses of female friendship ("(E)Merging Identities"), Burke explores how "Ada" represents a "female couple's mutual fulfillment" (545): "[Ada's] identity is fulfilled in becoming one with another like herself. . . . Paradoxically, to merge with the other is to discover the self" (554). I am less concerned in this chapter with the "discovery of the self" than with the ways in which two figures—in this case, two female figures—establish a transitional place of in-betweenness, in which to "play" erotically and linguistically. The "product," then, is not two distinct and developed selves, but instead an ongoing process that involves a more Irigarayan exchange.

29. Walker also notes the disappearance of linear narrative within the

final paragraph. See *Making of a Modernist*, 75–77, for an interesting comparison of "Ada" with *The Making of Americans*.

30. Stein addresses her forms of repetition in her essay, "Portraits and Repetition," in *Lectures in America*, 165–206. "Insistence," as Stein says, must be distinguished from repetition, for "insistence . . . in its emphasis can never be repeating, because insistence is always alive and if it is alive it is never saying anything in the same way because emphasis can never be the same not even when it is most the same that is when it has been taught" (*LIA*, 171).

31. See Lynen, *Design of the Present*, and Bercovitch, *American Jeremiad*.

32. This "je/tu" suggests not only the division (by the slash) which has been artificially constructed within language and culture, but also the connection that is there, the mutuality and interchangeability. This double subject is fluid, and can easily dissolve into the "nous," the "notre," within the same sentence or the same paragraph.

33. Irigaray attempts a similar emphasis on the mingling of the bodily and the linguistic. Her two "lips" are both of the mouth and of the vulva, shaping speech and shaping a specifically female erotic (a project that is problematic in its potential reproduction of essentialism). Irigaray's critique of the "specular" (the privileging of the visible, the phallic) leads her in this piece to erase tropes of vision and to substitute tropes of touch and sound, in which the "other" cannot become distanced through reification.

34. Schmitz makes a persuasive argument for Toklas's presence within Stein's texts as a voice representative of an oral discourse and of "chatter," which Schmitz terms "the mother tongue"; see, for instance, *Of Huck and Alice*, 202. I shall explore Toklas's relation to Stein more fully in Chapter 5.

35. Kristeva, "From One Identity to an Other," in *Desire in Language*, 133. DeKoven and Burke make a similar connection between Stein and Kristeva. See Burke, "Gertrude Stein, the Cone Sisters," 560 n. 44, and DeKoven, *A Different Language*, 19–24.

36. Kristeva, *Desire in Language*, 136.

37. Ibid., 142.

38. Ibid., 138. Homans makes a similar point in *Bearing the Word*, 18–19. Homans points out, further, the implications of Kristeva's adherence to a Lacanian system, in which the son's return to the maternal is inherently dangerous, for "too great a prolongation of the mother-child dyad leads to psychosis" (19). Indeed, "the general picture of the mother-child relation, and of such traces of it as carry over into adulthood, is of a situation that must be fled as being dangerous to adult sanity" (19).

39. On the map of development, Winnicott identifies a region lying between mergence with the mother and recognition of one's separateness from the mother. Within this region, a child is free to experiment with identity, always within the nurturing context of the trusted and reliable

maternal presence. Winnicott locates art and religion within this "potential" space, as modes of serious human "play" offering "relief" from the "task of reality acceptance." The "strain of relating inner and outer reality" finds solace in a continual return to the space where such relationship may be imagined into existence. See "Transitional Objects and Transitional Phenomena," in *Playing and Reality*, esp. 13.

40. I shall offer a more extensive interpretation of "Patriarchal Poetry" in Chapter 4.

41. Stein's "to be," however, appears to occur "before" Hamlet's addition of the negative.

42. The "once," interrupting this sequence again and again, suggests an ideology of return, possibly to one origin, that Stein is resisting. By its association with an irrecoverable past, "once" evokes the masculine romantic quest ("once" may pun upon "wants") for what is both absent and past, a quest Stein rejects in favor of a myth of presence based on the immediacy and fullness of the linguistic matrix.

43. This aspect of modernist painting was well documented in the exhibition at the Museum of Modern Art in New York, Sept. 27, 1984 to Jan. 15, 1985, " 'Primitivism' in Twentieth-Century Art: Affinity of the Tribal and the Modern."

44. I hope to suggest by the word "matrix" both the possible association of this playful sense of language with the early maternal-infant bond, and the more general concept of a generative source. Although "matrix" retains the significance of "womb," I do not wish to tie this metaphor wholly to the female. I am indebted to Pamela Hadas for her use of this term in relation to Stein (in conversation).

CHAPTER 3

1. Steiner explores this claim in *Exact Resemblance*, in terms of Steinian portraiture. As Steiner observes, Stein attempts a mimetic portraiture faithful to "the very degree and intensity of movement that its subject has," without being descriptive or transparently referential (45); see especially the chapter on "The Steinian Portrait." In *Making of a Modernist*, Walker also addresses how Stein, during her first decade of writing, experimented with forms adequate to the reality she wished to express. Walker offers one of the best accounts of Stein's development toward the forms of representation marking the *Tender Buttons* period.

2. In her 1935 essay, "What is English Literature," Stein mentions the attempt of "the lake poets" to resist the "nineteenth century" obsession with "explaining," a mode of discourse attached to British imperialism: "The lake poets had other ideas, they felt that it was wrong to live by parts of a whole and they tried and they tried they wanted to serve god not

mammon, but they too inevitably as they wrote longer and longer live by parts of the whole, because after all mammon and god were interchangeable" (*LIA*, 44–45). Stein also mentions two of her American Romantic precursors, Emerson and Whitman, at various points in the same essay (*LIA*, 51). Although Stein thinks of Whitman as her major poetic precursor, as she makes clear in "Poetry and Grammar," her allusions to and near-quotings of Emerson in that essay suggest that she knew Emerson well and found his approach to language and poetry useful.

3. For excellent accounts of this gendered poetics, see Homans, *Women Writers* and her more recent *Bearing the Word*. Homans explores the relation within Romantic poetry between a figurative poetic discourse defined as masculine and a literal, silent, and absent feminine landscape.

4. I should make clear that, although Stein is most interested in representing the female (especially the female body and a female erotic) within works like *Tender Buttons* and "Lifting Belly," she does not accede to a general Romantic concept of "nature" as constitutively female in any essentialist sense. The problem she confronts is how to represent the female body without reducing it to its traditional "place" within the scheme of representation.

5. The line appears in "Sacred Emily," written in 1913 and published in *G&P*, 187. Stein brought the line into other writings too. It recurs in "Lifting Belly," written 1915–17 and published in *A&B*; and in the later children's book, *The World Is Round*, illustrated by a Rose (Sir Francis) and about an actual Rose (the daughter of Stein's neighbors, the d'Aiguys, in Bilignin), who becomes a character, Rose, who finds "Rose is a rose is a rose" carved into a tree—an intricate knot of naming, testing with extravagant persistence the boundary between names and their referents.

6. Stein often changes the exact phrasing of this line about roses: sometimes there are three roses, sometimes four; sometimes the line begins with an article and sometimes simply with "Rose."

7. In "The Poet," Emerson speaks of the poet as "representative": "He stands among partial men for the complete man, and apprises us not of his wealth, but of the common wealth" (*Selected Writings*, 223). Stein democratizes Emerson's already fairly democratic sense of the "representative man" by her genderless and all-inclusive "anybody." Whereas Emerson believes in a line of "genius," Stein often sees genius as a general and shared phenomenon, although her tendency to name herself one of the few geniuses of the twentieth century suggests a less democratic concept. See, for example, *ABT*, 5.

8. Gass speaks of this dimension of Stein's writing as an "escape from protective language," from a kind of language that "names" but never "renders," "replaces events with speech," and "says" rather than "shows." Stein, he suggests, gives "to her words the feelings that arise from things"; she

creates "from her words real objects, valuable for themselves, capable of an independent existence, as physical as statuary" ("Gertrude Stein: Her Escape," 89, 90).

9. Emerson, "The Poet," *Selected Writings*, 224.

10. Stein's wording here echoes Emerson's in "The Poet": "Too feeble fall the impressions of nature on us to make us artists. Every touch should thrill" (*Selected Writings*, 223).

11. Ibid., 229, 231. 12. Ibid., 229, 225.

13. Ibid., 231. 14. Ibid., 157.

15. Ibid., 44. 16. Ibid., 45.

17. Homans, *Bearing the Word*, 4.

18. Emerson, *Selected Writings*, 47–48.

19. "A Transatlantic Interview," in Haas, *Primer*, 25. Steiner places *Tender Buttons* towards the beginning of Stein's "second phase" of portraiture, a phase unified by "the discovery of visuality" (*Exact Resemblance*, 89).

20. Steiner, *Exact Resemblance*, 45.

21. A few critics have begun to approach *Tender Buttons* from a similar perspective. Ruddick sees a "code," comprised of "pieces of the female body." *TB*, in her view, undoes what William James called "selective attention," a pragmatic faculty of the mind by which certain objects and realms of existence become selected for notice, while others become suppressed. The female body, and with it the "pre-Oedipal form of life" ("Rosy Charm," 235), are allowed to emerge in *TB* in a new way, constituting a defense of the devalued female body. While I find this approach both fascinating and useful, I would question the tendency to settle on one-to-one correspondences (e.g., the "rosy charm" signifies menstrual blood) between Stein's images and determinate "pieces" of the body. While Ruddick states that *TB* gives us new "glasses" or "spectacles," in order to see the female body in a better light (226), I suggest instead that spectacles themselves become impossible to use here, as Stein moves into a modality of touch and sound. Schmitz also interprets *TB* as making present a female world, although he does not tie this femaleness to the body. He argues particularly for Alice's presence within the text (*Of Huck and Alice*, e.g., 163–64) and for the "double-talk" and "love-talk" her speaking presence makes possible. Gass, in a brilliant and dense reading, interprets *TB* in part as an encoding of lesbian images ("Gertrude Stein and the Geography"). See Stimpson's argument against interpreting the world of *TB* as female, however ("Gertrude Stein and the Transposition of Gender," 14).

22. Hadas, "Spreading the Difference," 61.

23. Ibid., 66.

24. Ibid., 73 n. 15.

25. See Schmitz, "The Gaiety of Gertrude Stein," in *Of Huck and Alice*. Ruddick sees a similar desire for a loved female presence, although she

defines this presence as "the mother," who becomes associated with "the life of immediate or raw perception, the pre-Oedipal form of life" ("Rosy Charm," 235).

26. The insistence on the medium of art, of course, is a modernist strategy in general. Stein's method has often been compared to that of the Cubists, in particular. In "Gertrude Stein and Modern Painting," DeKoven argues that this analogy has serious limitations, in that words remain signs in a language-system, unlike bits of paint. In *Making of a Modernist*, Walker provides a superb account of how Stein's development parallels Picasso's, in terms of a movement from a radically metonymic aesthetics to a radically metaphoric one; see her last chapter, on *Tender Buttons*, 127–49.

27. Haas, *Primer*, 18.

28. Sutherland makes this argument in Haas, *Primer*, especially 145–46. Walker goes into a more in-depth analysis of Stein's relationship to Cézanne; see *Making of a Modernist*, esp. chap. 1, "The 'Reality' of Cézanne and Caliban," 1–18.

29. Haas, *Primer*, 18.

30. The richness of *TB* may be judged by the immense variety of different interpretations that have been offered of the opening two or three "poems"/fragments: "A Carafe," "Glazed Glitter," and "A Substance in a Cushion." I make no claims to the definitiveness of the following reading; as I shall suggest, part of the point of this opening is that "definitiveness" itself is no longer a possibility or even a valuable goal. Instead, "the difference is spreading," as Stein means it to.

31. It is possible that Stein's word, "spectacle," echoes Emerson's use of this word, as in "Nature," where he discusses "the difference between the observer and the spectacle—between man and nature. Hence arises a pleasure mixed with awe; I may say, a low degree of the sublime is felt, from the fact, probably, that man is hereby apprized that whilst the world is a spectacle, something in himself is stable" (*Selected Writings*, 44). "Spectacle" in this sense suggests something unstable and possibly illusory. Emerson is making an argument for the primacy of consciousness over nature. Stein appears at first to be making a similar argument, although as I shall argue, she is concerned with the world less as a "spectacle" than as something that may be felt and therefore brought closer; her project is, in this way, counter to Emerson's.

32. Ruddick makes a similar point ("Rosy Charm," 230). It is valuable to read *Tender Buttons* in the context of Stein's more openly lesbian works, especially since the language of *Tender Buttons* echoes the language of many Steinian works of the decade following 1910. To anticipate my reading of "Lifting Belly" briefly, we hear the repeated "lifting belly is so kind," and the delight in "making a spectacle" (*YGS*, 29), even though in both cases this is a "spectacle" that remains unseen by the readers; we hear

"lifting belly is so strange" (*YGS*, 20); and we think of another kind of "spreading," a kind and tender one, the "stretching" of "Lifting Belly": "Oh yes you see. / What I see. / You see me. / Yes stretches. / Stretches and stretches of happiness" (*YGS*, 26). Or: "Lifting belly is perfect. / Do you stretch farther. / Come eat it" (*YGS*, 35).

33. Emerson, *Selected Writings*, 26, 230.

34. Ibid., 269, 257, 269.

35. Irigaray, *Speculum*, 143–44.

36. See Schmitz's excellent discussion of the indefinite pronoun "that" (*Of Huck and Alice*, 162–63). Schmitz argues that this pronoun is "curiously 'free,' without feature or gender, always naming and never the name" (162). It is "the purest sign of Gertrude Stein's escape from the fix of definition" (162).

37. Many critics, of course, have found this uncertainty to be profoundly irritating and even unliterary. Lodge, for example, argues that the writing of *TB* is almost wholly opaque: "This is clearly a type of metaphorical writing based on radical substitution (or replacement) of referential nouns. But the perception of similarity on which metaphor depends is in this case private and idiosyncratic to a degree that creates almost insuperable obstacles to understanding" ("Gertrude Stein," 153). I am arguing that, although each image cannot be definitely fixed or understood, the language is rich enough to suggest at any one point a myriad of meanings.

38. Stein herself makes this pun in her essay "Regular Regularly in Narrative," in *How To Write*: "It is natural to suppose that a rose is a rose is a rose is a rose. . . . It is also as natural to suppose that they might be inattentive when they had *aroused* what was why and when it could be lost" (*HTW*, 219, emphasis added).

39. This presentation of the poem as a kind of body suggests a strong resemblance to Whitman's poetic strategies, for example in "Song of Myself," where the "I" of the poetic voice merges with the "body" of the text.

40. Dickinson, 506–7.

41. Other works of the Majorcan period include: "Pink Melon Joy," "Possessive Case," "No," "Farragut or A Husband's Recompense," "If You Had Three Husbands," "This One Is Serious," and "He Said It. Monologue."

42. This is, in fact, the usual interpretation of the works of this period. Bridgman, for example, treats them as completely autobiographical and appears disturbed by the explicitness of the subject matter; quoting Virgil Thomson's description of "Lifting Belly" as being concerned with "the domestic affections," Bridgman agrees, "and so it is, luridly so." His reading of "Lifting Belly" assumes that Stein and Toklas are the two speakers,

with Toklas making the statements of "cool and even sardonic response" (*Gertrude Stein in Pieces*, 149).

43. Schmitz interprets "Lifting Belly" as a "duet," with Stein and Toklas as the two speakers, distinguishable from each other (*Of Huck and Alice*, 228).

44. I wish to emphasize that I do not intend to limit the poetic influence behind this poem—or any other of Stein's compositions—to Keats. Many other influences may be felt here, from Homer to Whitman. The relationship between Whitman's and Stein's poetry, especially, invites further study.

45. Keats, *Poetical Works*, 372.

46. Thomson notes that this man was an American painter named Cook (*BTV*, 63). I do not think that it is necessary to make this autobiographical connection, however; the poem has its own inner logic and integrity.

47. The figure of a "cow," as many commentators have pointed out, represents for Stein the female sexual organs, as well as orgasm. See Fifer's full account of the term, " 'Is Flesh Advisable?' " 480–81.

CHAPTER 4

1. Maubrey-Rose argues for dating *LCA*'s composition as 1929–30, rather than 1927 (*The Anti-Representational Response*, 17). It should be clear that I am not attempting an analysis of the issue of creativity as it shifts and finds new form throughout Stein's oeuvre. I would suggest that, from at least the *Tender Buttons* period on, Stein thought of creativity as a dialogic act, although this concept found different formulations at different points in her writing career. I hope in this chapter to be suggestive rather than exhaustive and to open a door into this important area.

2. Quoted in Mellow, *Charmed Circle*, 214.

3. Benjamin, *Illuminations*, 84. It is interesting to consider the fact that both Benjamin and Stein were of German-Jewish origin, writing during and after the First World War, when the situation of Jews in Europe (especially in Germany) was becoming more and more urgent. Although Stein seldom writes about her Jewish identity, and although she seems to have remained remarkably resistant to knowledge about the Jews' situation, it is possible to speculate that her utopian vision, as I define it in this book, links with a perception of political danger. Gloria Orenstein, at the University of Southern California, is working at present on Jewish and Yiddish themes in Gertrude Stein.

4. Ibid., 91.

5. Ibid., 91–92.

6. Stein originally intended *A Birthday Book* to come out *as* a book, replete with illustrations by Picasso, whose son's birth the book celebrates. See Donald Gallup's introduction to *A&B*, xiv–xvi. Gallup regards the book as largely "decorative," little more than "an exercise in words."

7. Ibid., xv.

8. Barthes, "The Death of the Author," in *Image*, 142.

9. Pamela White Hadas (in conversation) suggests a more referential meaning here: that March 21 is the equinox; on this day we "call a halt" to winter. The following sequence may be read in this way also, for the "melodrama" of March involves the battle between "lion" and "lamb," just as we all become "witnesses" to each sign of Spring as it comes: "is it so?" we ask, as each day verges upon the new season.

10. Woolf, *To the Lighthouse*, 15.

11. I wish to emphasize that Stein is not suggesting a "female" language here, or an *écriture féminine*. This "giggling" marks itself as "feminine" within the system of language itself, and as such it is not the literal domain of one sex only.

12. I have not yet been able to discover how much Hebrew Stein knew. She certainly knew Yiddish, since she uses puns based on Yiddish (for example, "Yet Dish," reprinted in *YGS*, 55–62). I would guess that she had a working knowledge of Hebrew; this confusion of the sounds of basic pronouns in Hebrew and in English in all likelihood was familiar to her. Again, these questions should find clarification in the work of Gloria Orenstein.

13. The fruit of the tree of knowledge remains unnamed in some translations of Genesis, but tradition has named it the apple; Milton, for example, names it this in *Paradise Lost*.

14. Genesis 3:16 in *The Torah*, 7.

15. Stein discusses this idea in various places, among them "Poetry and Grammar," *LIA*, 223.

16. See my discussion of this "To be we" passage in Chapter 3.

17. See Homans, *Bearing the Word*, x–xx. For a similar reading of this passage, see Stimpson, "Gertrude Stein and the Transposition of Gender," 13. Stimpson suggests that this passage shows how Stein "advances the rights of women as authors": "She repeats the imperative sentence, 'Let her be,' and the substantive, 'letter be,' until the two collapse; until autonomous female being and language (especially Alice's middle initial) become one."

18. For another approach to such addition of natural elements, see Maubrey-Rose's discussion of *LCA* as a metonymic text. She defines *LCA* as "an extreme example of the metonymic novel, which intends the breakup of the metaphoric process into its metonymic parts and creates a 'narrative' which frustrates representation" (*The Anti-Representational Response*, 38). Although I think that she exaggerates the frustration of repre-

sentation in this unusually imagistic landscape novel, her understanding of the novel's structure as metonymic is useful.

CHAPTER 5

1. John Herbert Gill adds the subtitle *A Murder Mystery* to his 1982 edition of *Blood*. Although Stein did not herself name *Blood* a murder mystery, I think this is a useful category, more descriptive of her project than the category of the detective story, which she claimed for the work.

2. Stein is of course playing on the convention of the address to the reader. But, whereas in most nineteenth-century narratives this address serves to invite the reader to participate in the story as a listener, as if the narrator occupies a position halfway between the story being told and the audience, in Stein's mystery the address is more unsettling in that the audience's position is more uncertain; we are plunged into the world of the story itself, a world unnerving in its mysteriousness.

3. It is known that Stein modeled this woman on an actual acquaintance in Bilignin, Mme. Pernollet, the wife of a hotel-keeper there, who was indeed found dead in the courtyard of her husband's hotel in the summer of 1933. This event, together with others, some of which make their way into *Blood* (for example, the odd succession of servants for the Stein-Toklas residence in Bilignin; the apparent sabotage of the house phone and of Janet Scudder's and Stein's cars by one of these servants; and the mysterious death of an Englishwoman who had been a "companion" to a wealthy woman in the country), seems to have disturbed Stein greatly. She wrote about the summer of 1933, as she says in *Everybody's Autobiography*, "once more and yet again": not only in *Everybody's Autobiography*, but in two shorter pieces, "A Water-fall and a Piano" (1936) and "Is Dead" (1936), both reprinted in *HWIW*.

4. To dispel some of the enchantment of these mysteries, one could turn to *Everybody's Autobiography*, where Stein tells the story of this strange summer in more realistic and fuller terms (see chap. 2, especially 51–83). Yet such a move, while it appears to fill in many (although certainly not all) holes of the story, actually obstructs our experience of the mystery story itself, as a separate creation. To "know" that "the owner of the [sabotaged] car," for example, was an actual person named Gertrude Stein diminishes our pleasurable sense of curiosity as to who this owner might be. Such "knowledge" would perhaps protect us from what is unfamiliar; but it is the unfamiliar that Stein is after.

5. If one turns to *Everybody's Autobiography* for clarification, this phrase about blood becomes, if anything, more of a mystery. It occurs suddenly in the narrative twice, first with regard to Janet Scudder's arrival in Bilignin and then as part of a dialogue between Gertrude Stein and the servant's

wife. "It is not a very long drive and still they had better not have come in one. Blood on the dining room floor and they had better not have come in one" (*EA*, 60). Then: "The Polish woman was there and I said well and she said yes and she said Jean [her husband] is always like that when anything like that can happen. What I said. Blood on the dining room floor she said. Well I said I will go out and telephone" (*EA*, 61).

6. Stein, "Why I Like Detective Stories," *HWIW*, 148–49.

7. See Stein's discussion of listening and telling as simultaneous in her own existence, for example at the opening of "The Gradual Making of *The Making of Americans*" (*LIA*, 135–36). I shall look more closely at this passage below.

8. Toklas's relationship to Stein's life and work has become a central concern for many critics. Bridgman was the first critic to suggest that Stein's writing method involved Toklas's presence as a reader and as a companion-lover. One of the most imaginative approaches to this issue is Schmitz's, in *Of Huck and Alice*, where he argues for Toklas's presence as a mode of discourse (which he terms "chatter" or "the mother tongue") within Stein's writing. See also Stimpson, "Gertrice/Altrude."

9. Dydo makes a similar point in her essay "*Stanzas in Meditation*," where she discusses Stein's reliance upon Toklas as a loving reader who could allow Stein "to hear her own voice, to affirm the reality of what she was trying to do with words, and to know who she was. . . . Alice was Stein's *alter ego*, allowing her life and work" (14). Alice met Gertrude on September 8, 1907, and by winter Alice was reading *MOA* and making Sunday dinners at 27, rue de Fleurus. Their relationship may have been consummated in the spring of 1908; as Toklas puts it rather cryptically in *WIR*: "The winter commenced gaily. Gertrude during this winter diagnosed me as an old maid mermaid which I resented, the old maid was bad enough but the mermaid was quite unbearable. I cannot remember how this wore thin and finally blew away entirely. But by the time the buttercups were in bloom, the old maid mermaid had gone into oblivion and I had been gathering wild violets" (*WIR*, 48). Stein's marriage proposal to Toklas came the following summer, as they vacationed in Fiesole, Italy. Upon their return to Paris in September, Alice began the typewriting of *MOA*. As Alice says in her autobiography, "I got a Gertrude Stein technique, like playing Bach. My fingers were adapted only to Gertrude's work" (*WIR*, 59).

10. Dydo, "*Stanzas in Meditation*," 13. This habit of Stein's, as Dydo implies, has a significant bearing upon the printing of Stein's works, especially the printing done posthumously.

11. Gertrude's relations with Leo began to disintegrate as she began to write. The gap between them widened when Alice and Gertrude began to become intimate, and once Alice moved into 27, rue de Fleurus, in 1909,

to live with Gertrude, the situation became uncomfortable on all sides. Leo left the household in February of 1913.

12. Stein may also have been thinking of the rhyme Virginia Woolf alludes to in *A Room of One's Own*: "Here then was I (call me Mary Beton, Mary Seton, Mary Carmichael or by any name you please)" (*A Room of One's Own*, 5). The Child ballad to which Woolf refers carries a further significance, for Mary Hamilton, the woman who is imagined as singing the ballad, was hanged in consequence of bearing a child to the king. The word "Mary" becomes overhung with an aura of danger: it makes no difference what one's patronym is, for all "Marys" are alike in the danger they experience within patriarchy. By aligning her own persona in *A Room of One's Own* with these Marys, Woolf extends the danger to the situation of writing itself.

13. Dydo, "*Stanzas in Meditation*," 12.

14. Dydo implies that Stein's relationship with May Bookstaver continued with a certain intensity well after its early beginnings. After May married, she continued to write to Stein, and "it is likely that the two women met in Paris when the Knoblauchs [May and her husband] traveled. It was Mrs. Knoblauch who had placed the portraits of Picasso and Matisse with Alfred Stieglitz, who published them in *Camera Work*. She had also had in safe-keeping for many years copies of most of Stein's pieces and made efforts to place them with publishers" (ibid.). As Dydo goes on to observe, Stein played with the "half-rhyme *Mary/marry* and with puns like *may marry*," as well as with the name "Mabel" (who was the "third young woman in the triangle love affair") in many pieces in the 1920's.

15. Gill suggests that this Edith represents Edith Sitwell, "whose girlhood, indeed whose entire life had been made a hell of physical and psychological torment by a father whose cruelty bordered on insanity" (Gill, "Afterword," 98). Sitwell was a good friend of Stein's and helped to promote Stein's reputation in England. In this sense, "Edith" may represent a friendly listener, one who might attempt to avoid the violence of which she had been a victim.

16. Gill makes this suggestion in his "Afterword" to *Blood*, 88–89.

17. As I have mentioned, these expressive appeals may originally have been intended by Stein to be directed to Toklas, yet they move well beyond this attachment to a specific person. We may base our interpretation on the text itself, which does not attempt to anchor or delimit the "yous" invoked by the narrator.

18. James, *Essays in Pragmatism*, 168.

19. Ibid., 160.

20. Ibid., 166.

21. Jacobs, *More English Fairy Tales*, 65–66.

CHAPTER 6

1. Stein had always been preoccupied with pairings and with triangles, and in many of her works of the 1930's she created twins; see, for example, Stein's children's book, *The World Is Round* (1938) and "Lucretia Borgia. A Play" (1938).

2. Secor is one of the few critics who writes of *Ida* in feminist terms, seeing Stein's lesbian perspective in *Ida* as crucial to its form and meaning. Secor writes of Ida as "a woman, every woman, an American woman, a woman not defined by her relation to woman or man, but to herself. Ida is herself. She is in quest of herself, though quest is much too self-conscious a term for her travels" ("*Ida*," 97). In this chapter, I shall argue that the "self" cannot be understood or gained except through some form of dialogue with another.

3. Joyce, *Portrait*, 7.

4. Freud, *New Introductory Lectures*, 80.

5. Secor notes Stein's definition of the novel, through the novel *Ida*, as "a dream" ("*Ida*," 103).

6. In the novel's Second Half, this female-female relationship becomes replaced by a female-male relationship between Ida and "Andrew," a substitution suggesting the flexibility of this dyadic model of similarity and difference. As I shall argue later in this chapter, the gender of both Andrew and Ida becomes a matter of uncertainty, as Stein moves the whole novel out of the realm of sharply defined and hierarchized genders.

7. Luce Irigaray, "When Our Lips Speak Together," 77.

8. Freud, *Beyond the Pleasure Principle*, 14–17. Although Stein appears not to have been interested directly in Freud (unlike Leo, who began reading Freud in 1909 and later underwent analysis), her concern for the formation of identity and for the workings of the unconscious, as manifested in literature and in dreams, during the last fifteen years of her writing career suggests her awareness of Freudian ideas in the air. This field of relationship between Stein and Freud invites a fuller exploration.

9. On the front cover-page of the first copybook for Stein's draft of *Ida*, Stein has written "Ida, a twin," but has crossed out "a twin" and substituted "A Novel" (YCAL).

10. This form of obscurity with regard to gender differs from the more celebratory unsettling of gender categories in the Second Half of *Ida*.

11. Irigaray, "When Our Lips Speak Together," 78–79.

12. It is interesting to note that this could be a description of Stein herself, for she loved each of these activities as much as Ida does. In addition to her enjoyment of music and singing, as well as of travel (a literal changing of place), she "changed places" figuratively with Alice in *The Autobiography of Alice B. Toklas*. *Ida* could, in fact, be read as a veiled autobiography.

Many of the events were based on real occurrences in Stein's early life as well as in the Stein-Toklas ménage, including the incident in the church where she "felt something" (apparently this occurred in Baltimore, when Stein actually was with her "little aunts") and the sudden discovery of an Arab by the side of the road (which happened to Stein in Bilignin). Ida, like Stein, makes her living by "talking to herself," and both figures resemble Stein's concept of "saints," who "never do anything" (see *EA*, 109), just as "geniuses" "have to sit around so much doing nothing, really doing nothing" (*EA*, 70). Both Secor (in "*Ida*," 105) and Schmitz (in *Of Huck and Alice*, 231–32) note that *Ida* contains autobiographical elements.

13. The manuscript includes the word "did," as bracketed here, which clarifies the sentence, even though it loses the ambiguity of "she and he liked to come." I would speculate that the omission of this word in the printed form was accidental.

14. See Stein's short piece, "Identity a story," published in an appendix in Steiner, *Exact Resemblance*, 208. It includes this passage: "I wish words of one sylable [*sic*] were as bold as told./Anybody can like words of one sylable here and there but I like them anywhere. / I will tell in words of one sylable anything there is to tell not very well but just well."

15. Irigaray, "When Our Lips Speak Together," 77.

16. Stein herself made pieces of writing and "buried" them, in the sense that they did not find publication in her lifetime, "and nobody ever knew," just as the great-aunt buried her twins (although Stein buried only one of these book-children on purpose: Q.E.D., her early story of a triangular lesbian situation). Further, as Pamela Hadas has suggested (in conversation), *The Making of Americans* is a kind of attempt to finish off "the Americans" by categorizing them to death; Stein may have seen this effect as she came to the end of this work (a book that she had hoped would "make her" in return an important writer).

17. For Stein, this situation of a beauty contest may be a figure for her own sudden popularity following *The Autobiography of Alice B. Toklas*, a book that she wrote quickly and never regarded as her authentic writing, but rather as "audience writing." She "won," yet in a way that disturbed her, for in *ABT* she had assumed the voice of her "twin," Alice Toklas. The situation, recorded in Ida's second letter to her twin, of the man congratulating Love on being "the most beautiful one," resembles Stein's sense of confusion and uncertainty about her success: was the audience of *ABT* responding to Gertrude Stein or to her "Love"? Dogs for Stein represent human nature and identity, as opposed to essence or "entity"; it is possible, in this sense, that Stein felt the success she gained was granted only to her surface self, the most accessible and "visible" self, rather than to her true being. See my discussion of "Am I I if my little dog knows me," in Chapter 5.

18. This incident, like many in *Ida*, has an autobiographical ring to it. Stein was disturbed by her sudden accession to a place of enormous visibility, where her authentic self and writing remained largely unknown. People came to "know" her ("Sure I know Gertrude Stein") without knowing her writings (apart from *ABT*) at all.

19. Andrew may also be a covert figure for Alice, just as the "almost" marriage of Ida to Andrew may be a figure for Stein's untraditional marriage to Toklas. Toklas is Stein's "second half," her "twin," in the vocabulary of *Ida*. Secor makes a similar point ("*Ida*," 105–6).

20. This situation becomes even more complicated in the manuscripts of *Ida*, where Stein originally made Andrew a female figure named Lillian (YCAL).

21. Stein herself "walked every day," especially in Bilignin. Again, this picture of Andrew and Ida's marriage may in part form a portrait of Stein's daily existence with Toklas.

22. Secor makes a similar point about *Ida* as a bildungsroman ("*Ida*," 97–98).

23. Secor argues that Joyce's Molly is simply "an earth mother and a cunt. Her 'yes' is a male fantasy. Within Joyce's tradition women do not exist as active figures, as embodiments of the Godhead, as definers of reality; they are vessels, handmaidens, and at their most exciting temptresses of gods and men" ("*Ida*," 99).

24. Joyce, *Ulysses*, 633.

25. Ibid., 626.

26. Ibid., 643–44.

27. *Ida* ms., YCAL.

EPILOGUE

1. *The Mother of Us All* was first performed on May 7, 1947, at Columbia University, following Stein's death from cancer on July 27, 1946. A recording of this first production, which was broadcast simultaneously on radio, can be found in the Historical Sound Recording Room at Yale University's Sterling Library. In Stein's original version of the libretto, printed posthumously in *Last Operas and Plays*, Susan B. Anthony sings in the entire last scene (II.viii.) from behind a statue of herself "and her comrades in the suffrage fight" (*LO&P*, 83). For the actual productions of the opera, scored by Virgil Thomson and with a scenario prepared by Maurice Grosser, Anthony crosses the stage at two different moments, before finally assuming her place on the pedestal, thereby becoming the statue as well as a kind of worshipped saint or martyr. Her "unveiling" and final song become reminiscent of the conclusion of *A Winter's Tale*, when Hermione descends from her pedestal, revealing herself to be alive and no longer a statue.

2. "Knowing" takes two possible forms here: first, the knowing of

certain facts or a body of information that can be "told," and second, the kind of knowing that is more akin to mutual and bodily "understanding" ("or do you know, do you know"), as I have developed this concept in Chapter 5.

3. These questions emerge also in *Brewsie and Willie*, a fictional dialogue written in the same year in which *The Mother of Us All* was begun (1945). In creating the character of Brewsie, Stein addresses a difficulty similar to Susan B.'s: how to conceive of a mode of leadership that does not "lead you where you dont want to go" (*B&W*, 21). As a central male speaker, admired by the male and female characters around him, Brewsie has an authority that would be impossible in earlier Stein texts and that remains problematic in this one. This authority, however, is as open to dialogue as authority can be; as Willie notes, "Brewsie is so earnest, and he is so careful of what he says, and besides you dont have to listen" (*B&W*, 32). And again: "Ah you're no leader, Brewsie, you just talk" (*B&W*, 24).

4. Haas, *Primer*, 15–17.

5. I am aware that "the world" may also be thought of as a text. The distinction between text and world is still a useful one, however, as a way of articulating the problems addressed by *The Mother of Us All*.

6. In the actual opera, the pauses within her final aria are much briefer than the "long silences" Stein indicates in her original libretto, and these pauses become filled with music, which makes a soothing bridge from one fragment to another (Anthony ends many of these parts with the word "but"). Stein's own text is more disturbing, partly because the silence she marks is such a real silence, inscribed as it is into a written text by nature "silent."

Works Cited

Abel, Elizabeth. "(E)Merging Identities: The Dynamics of Female Friendship in Contemporary Fiction by Women." *Signs* 6, 3 (Spring 1981): 413–35.

Anderson, Sherwood. "Four American Impressions." *New Republic* 32 (Oct. 11, 1922): 171.

———. *The Letters of Sherwood Anderson*. Ed. Howard Mumford Jones with Walter B. Rideout. Boston, 1953.

Bakhtin, Mikhail M. *The Dialogic Imagination: Four Essays*. Ed. Michael Holquist. Trans. Caryl Emerson and Michael Holquist. Austin, Tex., 1981.

Barthes, Roland. *Image, Music, Text*. Trans. Stephen Heath. New York, 1977.

———. *The Pleasure of the Text*. Trans. Richard Miller. New York, 1975.

Benjamin, Walter. *Illuminations*. Trans. Harry Zohn. New York, 1969.

Benstock, Shari. *Women of the Left Bank: Paris, 1900–1940*. Austin, Tex., 1986.

Bercovitch, Sacvan. *The American Jeremiad*. Madison, Wis., 1978.

Blankley, Elyse. "Beyond the 'Talent of Knowing': Gertrude Stein and the New Woman." In Hoffman, ed., *Critical Essays*, 196–209.

Bloom, Lynn Z. "Gertrude Is Alice Is Everybody: Innovation and Point of View in Gertrude Stein's Autobiographies." *Twentieth Century Literature* 24, 1 (Spring 1978): 81–93.

Bridgman, Richard. *Gertrude Stein in Pieces*. New York, 1970.

Brodhead, Richard. *Hawthorne, Melville, and the Novel*. Chicago, 1976.

Burke, Carolyn. "Gertrude Stein, the Cone Sisters, and the Puzzle of Female Friendship." *Critical Inquiry* 8, 3 (Spring 1982): 543–64.

———. Introduction to Luce Irigaray's "When Our Lips Speak Together." *Signs* 6, 1 (Autumn 1980): 66–68.

———. "Report from Paris: Women's Writing and the Women's Movement." *Signs* 3, 4 (Summer 1978): 843–55.

Caserio, Robert. *Plot, Story, and the Novel: From Dickens and Poe to the Modern Period*. Princeton, N.J., 1979.

Chodorow, Nancy. *The Reproduction of Mothering: Psychoanalysis and the Sociology of Gender.* Berkeley, Calif., 1978.

Cixous, Hélène. "The Laugh of the Medusa." Trans. Keith Cohen and Paula Cohen. *Signs* 1, 4 (Summer 1976): 875–93.

Cook, Blanche Wiesen. " 'Women Alone Stir My Imagination': Lesbianism and the Cultural Tradition." *Signs* 4, 4 (Summer 1979): 718–39.

DeKoven, Marianne. *A Different Language: Gertrude Stein's Experimental Writing.* Madison, Wis., 1983.

———. "Gertrude Stein and Modern Painting: Beyond Literary Cubism." *Contemporary Literature* 22, 1 (Winter 1981): 81–95.

Dickinson, Emily. *The Complete Poems of Emily Dickinson.* Ed. Thomas H. Johnson. Boston, 1960.

Doane, Janice Louise. *Silence and Narrative: The Early Novels of Gertrude Stein.* Westport, Conn., 1986.

Dubnick, Randa. *The Structure of Obscurity: Gertrude Stein, Language, and Cubism.* Chicago, 1984.

DuPlessis, Rachel Blau. *Writing Beyond the Ending: Narrative Strategies of Twentieth-Century Women Writers.* Bloomington, Ind., 1985.

Dydo, Ulla. "Must Horses Drink. or, 'Any Language is Funny If You Don't Understand It.' " *Tulsa Studies in Women's Literature* 4, 2 (Fall 1985): 272–80.

———. "*Stanzas in Meditation*: The Other Autobiography." *Chicago Review* 35, 2 (Winter 1985): 4–20.

Emerson, Ralph Waldo. *Selected Writings of Ralph Waldo Emerson.* Ed. Stephen Whicher. Boston, 1960.

Fifer, Elizabeth. "Guardians and Witnesses: Narrative Technique in Gertrude Stein's *Useful Knowledge.*" *Journal of Narrative Technique* 10 (Spring 1980): 115–27.

———. " 'Is Flesh Advisable?' The Interior Theater of Gertrude Stein." *Signs* 4, 3 (Spring 1979): 472–83.

Freud, Sigmund. *Beyond the Pleasure Principle, Group Psychology, and Other Works.* Trans. James Strachey. London, 1955.

———. *New Introductory Lectures on Psychoanalysis and Other Works.* Trans. James Strachey. London, 1964.

Gass, William H. "Gertrude Stein and the Geography of the Sentence." In Gass, *The World Within the Word.* New York, 1978, 63–123.

———. "Gertrude Stein: Her Escape from Protective Language." In Gass, *Fiction and the Figures of Life.* New York, 1970, 79–96.

Gibbs, Anna. "Hélène Cixous and Gertrude Stein: New Directions in Feminist Criticism." *Meanjin* 38 (1979): 281–93.

Gilbert, Sandra M., and Susan Gubar. *The Madwoman in the Attic: The Woman Writer and the Nineteenth-Century Literary Imagination.* New Haven, Conn., 1979.

————. *No Man's Land: The Place of the Woman Writer in the Twentieth Century. Volume 1: The War of the Words.* New Haven, Conn., 1987.

Gill, John Herbert. "Afterword." In Stein, *Blood on the Dining-Room Floor.* Berkeley, Calif., 1982.

Haas, Robert B., ed. *A Primer for the Gradual Understanding of Gertrude Stein.* Santa Barbara, Calif., 1971.

Hadas, Pamela. "Spreading the Difference: One Way to Read Gertrude Stein's *Tender Buttons.*" *Twentieth Century Literature* 24, 1 (Spring 1978): 57–75.

Hoffman, Michael J. *The Development of Abstractionism in the Writings of Gertrude Stein.* Philadelphia, 1965.

————, ed. *Critical Essays on Gertrude Stein.* Boston, 1986.

Homans, Margaret. *Bearing the Word: Language and Female Experience in Nineteenth-Century Women's Writing.* Chicago, 1986.

————. *Women Writers and Poetic Identity.* Princeton, N.J., 1980.

Irigaray, Luce. "And the One Doesn't Stir Without the Other." Trans. Hélène Vivienne Wenzel. *Signs* 7, 1 (Autumn 1981): 60–67.

————. *Speculum of the Other Woman.* Trans. Gillian C. Gill. Ithaca, N.Y., 1985.

————. *This Sex Which Is Not One.* Trans. Catherine Porter with Carolyn Burke. Ithaca, N.Y., 1985.

————. "When Our Lips Speak Together." Trans. Carolyn Burke. *Signs* 6, 1 (Autumn 1980): 69–79.

Iser, Wolfgang. *The Implied Reader: Patterns of Communication in Prose Fiction from Bunyan to Beckett.* Baltimore, Md., 1974.

Jacobs, Joseph. *More English Fairy Tales.* London, 1894.

James, William. *Essays in Pragmatism.* Ed. Alburey Castell. New York, 1948.

Joyce, James. *A Portrait of the Artist as a Young Man.* New York, 1964.

————. *Ulysses: The Corrected Text.* Ed. Hans Walter Gabler, with Wolfhard Steppe and Claus Melchior. New York, 1986.

Katz, Leon. "Introduction." *Fernhurst, Q.E.D., and Other Early Writings.* London, 1972, i–xxxiv.

Keats, John. *Keats: Poetical Works.* Ed. H. W. Garrod. London, 1956.

Kiely, Robert, ed. *Modernism Reconsidered.* Cambridge, Mass., 1983.

Kostelanetz, Richard. "Introduction." *The Yale Gertrude Stein.* New Haven, Conn., 1980, xiii–xxxi.

Kristeva, Julia. *Desire in Language: A Semiotic Approach to Literature and Art.* Ed. Leon S. Roudiez. Trans. Thomas Gora, Alice Jardine, and Leon S. Roudiez. New York, 1980.

Lacan, Jacques. *Ecrits: A Selection.* Trans. Alan Sheridan. New York, 1977.

Lodge, David. "Gertrude Stein." In Lodge, *The Modes of Modern Writing: Metaphor, Metonymy, and the Typology of Modern Language.* Ithaca, N.Y., 1977, 144–55.

Lynen, John. *The Design of the Present: Essays on Time and Form in American Literature*. New Haven, Conn., 1969.

Marks, Elaine. "Women and Literature in France." *Signs* 3, 4 (Summer 1978): 832–42.

Maubrey-Rose, Victoria. *The Anti-Representational Response: Gertrude Stein's Lucy Church Amiably*. Stockholm, 1985.

Mellow, James. *Charmed Circle: Gertrude Stein & Company*. London, 1974.

Perloff, Marjorie. "Poetry as Word-System: The Art of Gertrude Stein." In Perloff, *The Poetics of Indeterminacy: Rimbaud to Cage*. Princeton, N.J., 1981, 67–108.

Ruddick, Lisa. " 'Melanctha' and the Psychology of William James." *Modern Fiction Studies* 28, 4 (Winter 1982–83): 545–56.

———. "A Rosy Charm: Gertrude Stein and the Repressed Feminine." In Hoffman, ed., *Critical Essays*, 225–40.

———. "William James and the Modernism of Gertrude Stein." In Kiely, ed., *Modernism Reconsidered*, 47–64.

Said, Edward. *Beginnings: Intentions and Method*. Baltimore, Md., 1975.

Schmitz, Neil. *Of Huck and Alice: Humorous Writing in American Literature*. Minneapolis, 1983.

Secor, Cynthia. "Gertrude Stein: The Complex Force of Her Femininity." In Kenneth W. Wheeler and Virginia Lee Lussier, eds., *Women, the Arts, and the 1920s in Paris and New York*. New Brunswick, N.J., 1982, 96–107.

———. "*Ida*, A Great American Novel." *Twentieth Century Literature* 24, 1 (Spring 1978): 96–107.

———. "The Question of Gertrude Stein." In Fritz Fleischmann, ed., *American Novelists Revisited: Essays in Feminist Criticism*. Boston, 1982, 299–310.

Simon, Linda. *The Biography of Alice B. Toklas*. New York, 1977.

Spacks, Patricia Meyer. *Gossip*. New York, 1985.

Stanton, Domna C. "Language and Revolution: The Franco-American Dis-Connection." In Hester Eisenstein and Alice Jardine, eds., *The Future of Difference*. Boston, 1980, 73–87.

Steiner, Wendy. *Exact Resemblance to Exact Resemblance*. New Haven, Conn., 1978.

Stewart, Allegra. *Gertrude Stein and the Present*. Cambridge, Mass., 1967.

Stimpson, Catharine R. "Gertrice/Altrude: Stein, Toklas, and the Paradox of the Happy Marriage." In Ruth Perry and Martine Watson Brownley, eds., *Mothering the Mind: Twelve Studies of Writers and Their Silent Partners*. New York, 1984, 123–39.

———. "Gertrude Stein: Humanism and Its Freaks." *boundary 2* 22, 3/23, 1.

———. "Gertrude Stein and the Transposition of Gender." In Nancy K. Miller, ed., *The Poetics of Gender*. New York, 1986, 1–18.

————. "The Mind, the Body, and Gertrude Stein." *Critical Inquiry* 3, 3 (Spring 1977): 489–506.

————. "Reading Gertrude Stein." *Tulsa Studies in Women's Literature* 4, 2 (Fall 1985): 265–71.

————. "The Somagrams of Gertrude Stein." *Poetics Today* 6, 1–2 (1985): 67–80.

————. "Zero Degree Deviancy: The Lesbian Novel in English." *Critical Inquiry* 8, 2 (Winter 1981): 363–79.

Sutherland, Donald. *Gertrude Stein: A Biography of Her Work*. New Haven, Conn., 1951.

The Torah: The Five Books of Moses: A New Translation of the Holy Scriptures According to the Masoretic Text. Philadelphia, 1962.

Walker, Jayne L. *The Making of a Modernist: Gertrude Stein from 'Three Lives' to 'Tender Buttons.'* Amherst, Mass., 1984.

Wilson, Edmund. *Axel's Castle: A Study in the Imaginative Literature of 1870– 1930*. New York, 1931.

Winnicott, D. W. *The Maturational Processes and the Facilitating Environment: Studies in the Theory of Emotional Development*. New York, 1974.

————. *Playing and Reality*. New York, 1971.

Woolf, Virginia. *A Room of One's Own*. New York, 1929.

————. *To the Lighthouse*. New York, 1927.

Yaeger, Patricia S. "'Because a Fire Was in My Head': Eudora Welty and the Dialogic Imagination." *PMLA* 99, 5 (Oct. 1984): 955–73.

————. *Honey-Mad Women: Emancipatory Strategies in Women's Writing*. New York, 1988.

Index

French feminism, *see* Feminism
Freud, Sigmund, 55f, 58, 93, 98,
169f, 182, 230

Gallup, Donald, 226
Gass, William, 6, 8, 10, 12, 221–22
Gates, Henry Louis, Jr., 213
Gender, 76, 187, 211, 230; and
subversion of hierarchy, 3f, 125,
132, 190, 230; and language,
4, 6f, 8, 119, 121–22, 123, 189,
208f; and creativity, 9, 78–80,
215f, 226; and hierarchy, 13,
22–23, 57, 120, 187, 211. *See also*
Feminine, Masculine
Genius, 7, 149, 173, 196, 217, 221
Genre, 205
Geographical History of America, 7,
217
Geography and Plays, 63, 205
German language, 22–24, 37
Gilbert, Sandra, 20, 212
Gill, John Herbert, 227, 229
Gilligan, Carol, 57
Gilman, Charlotte Perkins, 212
God/goddess-figures, 20f, 32, 94,
112, 168, 200, 232
"The Gradual Making of *The
Making of Americans*," 148–49,
228
Greek language, 83
Grosser, Maurice, 232
Gubar, Susan, 20, 212

H. D., 21, 58
Hass, Robert Bartlett, 88, 90f,
202
Hadas, Pamela, 12–13, 89, 90, 96,
220, 226, 231
Hawthorne, Nathaniel, 69
Hebrew language, 83, 125, 226
Hemingway, Ernest, 63
"He Said It. Monologue," 224
Heterosexism, 7, 208f
Heterosexuality, 7, 41f, 48, 67,
172, 180, 182f, 185
Hierarchy, 20f, 25, 35, 37, 86, 90,

167; and language, 10, 44, 76,
160. *See also under* Gender
Hitler, Adolph, 147
Hoffman, Michael J., 210, 219, 221
Homans, Margaret, 57–58, 86, 212,
216, 219, 221
Homer, 83, 225
Homosexuality, 7–8. *See also*
Lesbianism
How Writing Is Written, 148, 227
Human mind, 7, 209
Human nature, 7, 209, 231
Hurston, Zora Neale, 213

Ida: A Novel, 3, 6, 14, 19, 35, 42,
167–98, 230–32 *passim*
Identity: and Stein, 7–8, 61–62,
68f, 101, 121, 162f, 206, 217ff,
225; and women, 43f, 46f; and
relationships, 59f, 152, 168ff,
186; in *Ida*, 167, 168ff, 180ff,
186; theory of, 209, 215, 231.
See also Naming
"Identity a story," 231
"If You Had Three Husbands,"
208, 224
Imperialism, 8, 22, 25f, 28, 86,
107, 125, 183, 220
Indeterminacy, 10, 12, 111
Irigaray, Luce, 13, 64, 172, 175,
214, 218f; *Speculum of the Other
Woman*, 5, 94f, 97–98, 184,
217; "When Our Lips Speak
Together," 6, 60, 68ff, 73,
170, 177, 207, 216; "And the
One Doesn't Stir Without the
Other," 59–60
"Is Dead," 227
Iser, Wolfgang, 9, 210

Jakobson, Roman, 211
James, Henry, 42
James, William, 60, 156–61 *passim*,
197, 207, 214, 217, 222
Joyce, James, 71; *Portrait of the Artist
as a Young Man*, 169; *Ulysses* 171,
173, 186, 191ff, 233

Library of Congress Cataloging-in-Publication Data

Chessman, Harriet Scott.
     The public is invited to dance : representation, the body,
and dialogue in Gertrude Stein / Harriet Scott Chessman.
          p. cm.
     Bibliography: p.
     Includes index.
     ISBN 0-8047-1484-3 (alk. paper)
     I. Stein, Gertrude, 1874–1946—Criticism and interpreta-
tion.   I. Title.
PS3537.T323Z578 1989
818'.5209—dc19   88-20178
                                                          CIP